To Stan
Wishing you a very
Happy Birthday
love John x

£3.00

Carmarthen Pals

Carmarthen Pals

A History of the 15th (Service) Battalion
The Welsh Regiment, 1914 - 1919

Steven John

Pen & Sword
MILITARY

First published in Great Britain in 2009 by
PEN & SWORD MILITARY
an imprint of
Pen & Sword Books Limited
47 Church Street
Barnsley
South Yorkshire
S70 2AS

ISBN 978184 884 0775

The right of Steven John as Author of this Work has been asserted
by him in accordance
with the Copyright, Designs and Patents Act 1988.

A CIP catalogue record for this book is
available from the British Library.

Set in Plantin 10 on 12pt
Printed and bound in England by CPI

Pen & Sword Books Ltd incorporates the imprints of
Pen & Sword Aviation, Pen & Sword Maritime,
Pen & Sword Military, Wharncliffe Local History
Pen & Sword Select, Pen & Sword Military Classics
and Leo Cooper

For a complete list of Pen & Sword titles please contact:
PEN & SWORD BOOKS LIMITED
47 Church Street, Barnsley, South Yorkshire, S70 2AS, England.
E-mail: enquiries@pen-and-sword.co.uk
Website: www.pen-and-sword.co.uk

Contents

Dedication   6

Carmarthen Town   7

Chapter 1   **Raising the Battalion**   17

Chapter 2   **Western Front: The Nursery Sector**   37

Chapter 3   **Somme: Mametz Wood**   69

Chapter 4   **Withdrawal from Mametz and the move North**   91

Chapter 5   **First Large Scale Trench Raid**   107

Chapter 6   **Passchendaele: The Build up**   115

Chapter 7   **Passchendaele: The Pilckem Ridge**   119

Chapter 8   **Passchendaele: Langemarck**   129

Chapter 9   **Return to French Flanders**   135

Chapter 10   **Return to the Somme**   149

Chapter 11   **The Great Advance: The Battle of Albert**   163

Chapter 12   **The Great Advance: The Battle of Bapaume**   175

Chapter 13   **Advance to Victory**   179

Appendix I   Casualties of the 15th Welsh   209

Appendix II   Roll of Honour   212

Appendix III   Awards to the Battalion   223

Appendix IV   Nominal Roll of Officers   237

Appendix V   Battle Honours   267

Appendix VI   Order of Battle, 38th (Welsh) Division   267

Appendix VII   Summary   269

Acknowledgements and Bibliography   271

Dedication

This book is written in honour of the memory of the men of the 15th Welsh, who fought and died during the Great War, especially to my great uncle, Private Harry Montague Allen of Whitland. Harry enlisted at Llanelli into the 15th Welsh. He was shot through the chest by a sniper within Mametz Wood, and was evacuated to the Casualty Clearing Station at Heilly Station, where he died later that day, on 11 July 1916. His story is told within the pages of this book. It is also dedicated to the memory of my other military ancestors:

David Thomas John 4th Battalion AIF.

Lance Corporal David Thomas John, of Laugharne, was one of the first men to enlist into the 4th Battalion, Australian Imperial Force on 18 August 1914, being allotted the service number 244. He landed on Gallipoli on 25 April 1915 and survived the horrific fighting during the landings, and also the Battle of Lone Pine, before the Anzacs were evacuated to Egypt in 1916. David was killed during the Battle of the Somme, whilst leading a patrol prior to an assault on Mouquet Farm on 18 August 1916.

His younger brother Private John James John had enlisted into the Pembroke Yeomanry at the outbreak of war, and was with them in Egypt when they were merged with the Glamorgan Yeomanry to form the 24th Battalion of the Welsh Regiment. He fought during the campaign in Palestine, and was present at the capture of Jerusalem, but was killed at the Battle of Epehy on 18 September 1918.

John James John 24th Battalion Welsh Regiment.

Introduction

As a son of the ancient Township of Laugharne, I undertook to research the Laugharne War Memorial several years ago. This interest blossomed, and resulted in my self-publishing a book on the memorial; 'A Township in Mourning'. This work has since expanded to cover the memorials of some of the neighbouring memorials of St. Clears, Llanddowror and Whitland, as well as memorial websites for the county of Carmarthenshire, and the neighbouring county of Pembrokeshire.

This small part of Wales has had the privilege of being the birth place of several great British Army units over the years, most notably during the Great War of 1914-1918, as supplying the Pembroke Yeomanry, which later transformed into the 24th Battalion of the Welsh Regiment; the 4th Battalion of the Welsh Regiment, which was the local Territorial Army Battalion throughout both World Wars, and also for the 15th (Service) Battalion of the Welsh Regiment, known during the time of the Great War as the 'Carmarthen Pals'.

Although gaining a proud reputation for itself during its three years on the Western Front during the Great War, the Carmarthen Pals have no written record of their achievements. This volume aims to correct this anomaly from the history books, and also aims to commemorate the deeds of the brave men of the battalion.

The mother regiment, the Welsh Regiment, was originally raised from the merging of two of the old regiments of foot; the 41st and the 69th. The 41st Regiment of Foot was raised on 1 March 1719. This first regiment was raised by Colonel Edmund Fielding, and consisted of a core nucleus of Chelsea Pensioners, which later moved to Portsmouth as Garrison Troops. This led to the early regimental nickname of the 'Invalids', a somewhat unfortunate name which proved hard to shake off.

On 11 December 1787 the 41st Foot became a line regiment of the British Army. It saw active service for some years throughout the Americas, and also against the French at Quebec. In 1815 the regiment moved to France, seeing service in the campaign against Napoleon under the Duke of Wellington, and through the remainder of the nineteenth century fought in wars throughout the Empire; at Burma, Afghanistan, India and the Crimean Wars. In 1857 the regiment moved to Jamaica on garrison duties, and after a three year spell there returned to Britain.

The regiment was renamed in 1881 after the Cardwell Reforms, and became the Welch Regiment. Two Battalions were formed; the 1st Battalion from the 41st Foot and the 2nd Battalion from the 69th Foot.

This 69th Regiment of Foot had originally been raised on 20 September 1756 as a 2nd Battalion of the 24th Foot. It spent the formulative years of its life on maritime service with the Royal Navy, and during the next 123 years of their history served throughout the British Empire, until being turned into the 2nd Battalion of the Welch Regiment under the Cardwell Reforms.

Thus the 1st Battalion of the Welch Regiment began the next stage of its life in South Africa where it saw service against the Zulus, before moving to Egypt in 1886. After seeing action at Egypt, the regiment spent time on garrison duty back in Britain before embarking again for South Africa, where it fought throughout both of the Anglo-Boer Wars. In July 1904 it returned home to Britain, but was back on the borders of the Empire at the outbreak of the Great War, stationed at Chakrata, India.

The 2nd Battalion of the Welch Regiment in the meantime had spent most of its time on garrison duty in Britain. From 1892 to 1906 it was in India, before moving to South Africa and then to Pembroke Dock.

At the outbreak of the Great War the 2nd Welsh was sent to France as part of the 1st Division of the British Expeditionary Force, and remained on the Western Front for the remainder of the war, gaining for Wales its first Victoria Cross winner of the war, Lance Corporal William Fuller of Laugharne. William was fighting alongside Captain Mark Haggard at the Battle of Chivy-sur-Aisne, when Haggard fell, mortally wounded, due to heavy German machine-gun fire. William, at great danger to himself, rescued Haggard from the battlefield, and carried him to a barn where medics tried in vain to save him.

In the meantime the British Army was rapidly expanding, and gearing up for war. Territorial Battalions were called up, and the first of the Territorial Welsh Battalions, the 1/6th Welsh, arrived on the Western Front by October 1914.

The Welsh Regiment therefore grew throughout August 1914. The 2nd Battalion was in France, the 1st Welsh was on its way back from India, and the Territorial Battalions, the 1/4th (Carmarthenshire), the 1/5th (Glamorgan), the 1/6th (Glamorgan), the 1/7th (Cyclists) and the Pembroke and Glamorgan Yeomanry Battalions (which were later to become affiliated to the Welsh Regiment) were ready for war.

As well as these regular and territorial battalions, 'Service', or war-time only, battalions of the Welsh Regiment were raised throughout the recruiting grounds of south and west Wales during the coming months;

These battalions were; the 8th (Pioneers), 9th (Service), 10th (1st

Rhondda), 11th (Cardiff City), 12th (Reserve), 13th (2nd Rhondda), 14th (Swansea City), 15th (Carmarthenshire), 16th (Cardiff City), 17th (Glamorgan), 18th (2nd Glamorgan), 19th (Glamorgan Pioneers), 20th (3rd Rhondda), 21st (Reserve), 22nd (Reserve), and 23rd (Reserve) Battalions.

The territorial battalions often had reserve battalions attached; for example the front-line unit of the 4th Welsh was numbered the 1st/4th Welsh. The reserve battalion was the 2nd/4th Welsh. These battalions were designed to recruit, train and keep up the flow of reinforcements to the front line units. The reserve battalion for the newly formed service battalions was the 21st Battalion, which was based at Kinmel. On 1 September 1916 the battalion was re-designated as the 61st Training Reserve Battalion, and kept up a constant supply of reinforcements to the 14th, 15th, 16th and 19th battalions during the course of the war.

This book however is concerned with just one of these magnificent battalions of the Welsh Regiment; the 15th (Service) Battalion, the Welsh Regiment: The Carmarthen Pals.

A Grea War era silk of the Welsh Regiment

The medieval Towy Bridge at Carmarthen.

A general view of Carmarthen.

Preface

Carmarthen Town

CARMARTHEN IS THE COUNTY TOWN of the ancient county of Carmarthenshire; a rural county sat on the southern Atlantic coast in south-west Wales. Known in Welsh as Caerfyrddin, Carmarthen is the legendary home to the wizard Merlin of the Arthurian legends. Sat on a commanding position on the main crossing of the River Towy, Carmarthen nowadays has a population of just over 13,000 inhabitants.

The origins of the town stem at least as far back as Roman times, when it was the capital of the Demetae tribe, and was known as Maridunum (Latin for sea fort). Carmarthen is possibly the oldest town in Wales and was recorded both by Ptolemy and in the *Antonine Itinerary*. The Roman fort is believed to date from AD75-77, and near the fort is one of the seven surviving Roman amphitheatres in Britain. It was excavated in 1968, and the arena itself is forty-six by twenty-seven meters, with the circumference of the seating area ninety-two by sixty-seven meters.

The name of the town later became Carmarthen. The strategic importance of Carmarthen was such that the Norman William fitz Baldwin built a castle around the year 1094. The existing castle site is known to have been used since 1105, but was destroyed by Llewellyn the Great in 1215. In 1223 the castle was rebuilt and permission was received to crenelate the town. Carmarthen was thus probably the first medieval walled town in Wales. In 1405 the town was taken and the castle was sacked by Owain Glyndŵr.

Following the Acts of Union, Carmarthen became the judicial headquarters of the Court of Great Sessions for south-west Wales. During the sixteenth and seventeenth centuries the dominant business of Carmarthen was still agriculture, and related trades included the manufacture of woollen goods. Carmarthen was made a county corporate by the charter of James I in 1604. The charter decreed that Carmarthen should be known as the 'Town of the County of Carmarthen' and should have two sheriffs. This was reduced to one sheriff in 1835, and the post continues to this day.

Both the Priory and the Friary were abandoned during the dissolution of the monasteries in the reign of Henry VIII, when the land was returned to the monarchy. Likewise the chapels of St Catherine and St Barbara were lost, the church of St Peter's being the main religious establishment to survive this era.

During the Marian persecutions of the 1550s Bishop Ferrar of St David's was burnt at the stake in the market square. The square has since been renamed to commemorate General Sir William Nott.

General Sir William Nott (1782-1845) has been claimed as Carmarthen's most famous soldier. William joined the East India Company in 1800 and was posted to the Bengal European Regiment. From 1804 his military career developed, but it was the First Afghan War which saw him distinguish himself as a military leader, and resulted in his subsequent promotion to Major-General. In 1842 William won three decisive battles; at Kandahar, Ghuznee, and Kabul. As a result, he received considerable acclaim

General Sir William Nott.

and he was invested with the order of the GCB. William's health had suffered in the East, and in 1844 he returned to Carmarthen where he died soon after his return. He was buried in St. Peter's Church and honoured by the erection of a commemorative statue in Market Square (now Nott Square).

In the mid eighteenth century the iron and coal trades became much more important to the town, although Carmarthen never developed ironworks on the scale of the valley towns of South Wales, or even such

The Carmarthen County War Memorial.

as the neighbouring town of Llanelli, which grew at a much faster rate during the Industrial Revolution.

The Boy's Grammar school was founded in 1587 on the site that is now occupied by the old hospital in Priory Street, outside of which the County War Memorial now stands. This school moved in the 1840s to Priory Row before relocating to Richmond Terrace. It was here at the turn of the century that a local travelling circus was given permission to bury one of their elephants after it fell sick and died: the elephant's final resting place is under what was the school rugby pitch.

There is supposedly another elephant buried at Carmarthen, under the foundations of the Picton Monument. This fine Obelisk was erected to the Memory of another famous West Wales soldier, General Sir Thomas Picton.

Thomas Picton had been born at Poyston in Pembrokeshire, but had another residence near Ferryside, just south of Carmarthen. In 1771 he obtained an ensign's commission in the 12th Regiment of Foot, but he did not join until two years later. The regiment was then stationed at Gibraltar, where he remained until he was made captain in the 75th in January 1778. He then returned to Britain.

The regiment was disbanded five years later, and Picton quelled a mutiny amongst the men by his prompt personal action and courage, and was promised the rank of major as a reward. He did not receive it, and after living in retirement on his father's estate for nearly twelve years, he went out to the West Indies in 1794 with Sir John Vaughan, the commander-in-chief, who made him his aide-de-camp and gave him a captaincy in the 17th foot. Shortly afterwards he was promoted major.

His career blossomed during several campaigns in the West Indies, and he was made Governor of Trinidad, a post he held until resigning the post following allegations of brutality, and Thomas returned to the Army. Again he carried on making a name for himself, culminating in his being given command of the 3rd Division of Wellington's Army in Spain. Yet again Thomas excelled, and at the end of the campaign was honoured by Parliament. Upon Napoleon's return from exile on Elba, Picton was called on by Wellington to take up a commission in the Dutch Army, with whom he was killed during the

General Sir Thomas Picton.

Picton Monument, pictured in 1920, with a souvenir tank.

Battle of Waterloo. The obelisk at the top of Picton Terrace in Carmarthen honours this remarkable man, who added so much to the rich military history of the County

Another important military figure from Carmarthenshire was General Sir James Hills-Johnes, of Dolaucothi, near Carmarthen. James was born 20 August 1833, the son of James Hills, at Neechindipore, Bengal, India. He was educated at the Edinburgh Academy and Addiscombe before entering the Bengal Artillery in 1853, with whom he served in the Indian Mutiny of 1857-8, winning the Victoria Cross for saving his battery at the siege of Delhi. He later served in the Abyssinian campaign from 1867-8, and the Lushai campaign from 1871-2, and was awarded the CB. James fought also in the Afghanistan war of 1878-80 and was made military governor of the Kabul. He was made KCB in 1881, and advanced in 1893 to GCB. In 1882 he married Charlotte, the daughter and co-heiress of John Johnes, Dolaucothi, Carmarthen. In 1883 he assumed by royal licence the additional name and arms of Johnes. James was honorary colonel of the 4th battalion of the Welch Regiment and his presence at the outbreak of the Great War was to drastically aid the recruitment of men throughout Carmarthenshire.

The County of Carmarthenshire itself comprises of a wide spread of smaller rural towns and villages. The largest town in the county is in fact not Carmarthen itself, but the industrial Llanelli, less than twenty miles east.

Llanelli was subject to a massive growth during the Industrial Revolution, with numerous coal mines in the surrounding area leading to a massive influx of workers. The rise of steel making also helped to secure the prosperity of Llanelli, and it is still a major industrial town in West Wales today. This industry also ensured that the town of Llanelli contributed more men to the war effort than did Carmarthen, and by

looking at just the statistics of men that died during the Great War; Llanelli contributed twice the men of Carmarthen.

Also, these two large towns were, and still are, surrounded by clusters of smaller towns and villages, one of the largest of which is Ammanford, another mining community in the Amman Valley, in the north of the County, which contributed strongly to the war effort in terms of men, as well as material in the form of the good quality anthracite that was mined there.

These other towns and villages are too numerous to name, but looking at the casualty lists of the 15th Welsh on the Commonwealth War Graves Commission database, it is clear that almost all of these contributed some of their sons to the battalion, and mourned their loss when they made the ultimate sacrifice.

Thus, the Carmarthen Pals were men from all over the county of Carmarthenshire, and not just from the County Town. Although strong local rivalry did exist then, as indeed it does today, in the form of hotly contested rugby and football matches every Saturday afternoon, these men bonded together to form one of the most successful battalions of the Great War, the 'Carmarthen Pals'.

General Sir James Hills-Johnes VC

August 1914, and Europe
is on the march:

*Above: German
invaders roll through
Belgium.*

*Right: Belgian soldiers
withdraw before the
onslaught.*

*Right: Britain mobilses
in defence of Belgium
and its regular
battalions head for the
Channel ports.*

*Below: French troops
surge eastwards in an
attempt to stop and
throw back their old
enemy.*

Chapter One

Raising the Battalion

FIRSTLY WE MUST UNDERSTAND the initial reasoning behind the coming into existence of the rapid expansion of the Welsh Regiment. Most people will have heard of the Great War, and also the politics that led to it, sparked by the assassination on 28 June 1914 of the heir to the Austro-Hungarian Empire, Archduke Franz Ferdinand, and his wife Sophie.

This assassination set in place a catastrophic chain of events. Austria blamed Serbia for their part in the assassination, and was backed by Germany in any action seen necessary in dealing with the Serbs. The situation thus swiftly deteriorated, with Serbia and Austro-Hungary mobilizing their armies. Germany rushed a division to seize vital railheads in Luxembourg, and France and Russia rushed to mobilize their vast armies, and the scene was now set for a European War.

On 2 August 1914, Germany insisted upon Belgium right of way to advance their now massed armies through to northern France. The Belgian King refused, and on the following day Germany declared war on France and their troops entered Belgium.

Britain had a treaty with Belgium, which tied its fate to that of the smaller country; and so on 4 August 1914 the British Government solemnly declared war on Germany, and the British Expeditionary Force was rushed to France, moving to positions around the Belgian city of Mons.

Here the British forces assembled, and took to the field against a numerically superior German Army, with momentum and confidence on their side. The first battle of the war thus occurred, the Battle of Mons. Although giving a good account of themselves, the vastly outnumbered British Expeditionary Force withdrew south, splitting either side of the Forest of Mormal, and reforming south of Mormal, at the town of Le Cateau, where they took part in another large scale pitched battle.

Again the British Expeditionary Force was pushed back, and the men carried out a long forced march over the coming days south to the banks of the River Marne, near the village of La Ferte-Sous-Jouarre, where they managed to stem the German tide. The shell shocked Germans

Left: Daily Mirror *page 3; how the British public were learning of the events in France and Belgium.*

Above: *Gordon Highlanders in Belgium.*

Below: *A crowded troopship leaves England for France.*

pulled back north, taking up positions on the River Aisne, where the British again met them in battle, stopping the German advance to Paris once and for all.

From here, the remnants of the British Expeditionary Force were moved to Flanders, where a fresh German push towards the Channel ports was stemmed at the ancient Flemish city of Ypres, and from here the lines of the Western Front were formed.

Due to the terrible losses incurred by the British during these initial stages of the war, the Territorial Battalions were sent to France to reinforce them. Lord Kitchener, the new Minister for War, had realised that this war would be a long and bloody one, and he was the instigator to the vast expansion of the army which followed.

As part of this expansion, a growing political force in Wales had come to see the chance of creating a Welsh Army Corps. The first steps towards this came into being as a result of a speech made by David Lloyd George at the Queen's Hall, London, on 19 September 1914:

> I should like to see a Welsh Army in the Field. I should like to see the race that faced the Norman for hundreds of years in a struggle for freedom, the race that helped to win Crecy, the race that fought for a generation under Glyndwr against the greatest Captain in Europe- I should like to see that race give a good taste of their quality in this struggle in Europe; and they are going to do it!

This patriotic speech helped to get the wheels turning in motion which ultimately led to the forming of the Executive Committee, with its dream of raising a Welsh Army Corps of two Divisions, which would take to the field together.

The inaugural meeting to form the committee was held at Cardiff on 24 September 1914, and invitations were sent out

David Lloyd George.

to various peoples of high standing throughout Wales. The new committee knew that enough Welshmen had already been recruited to form an Army Corps, and it was soon realised that to raise another large number of men to fulfil the requirements for a complete Army Corps of their own would take a lot of hard work.

Nonetheless, this work involved in the first stages of recruiting the men began, and in addition to the men already serving with the regular army, and the men of the 53rd (Territorial) Welsh Division, a further Army Corps of between 40,000 and 50,000 men was asked for.

Using figures gathered from the 1911 Census, the County of Carmarthenshire had been counted as containing just over 26,000 men of military age, ranging from twenty to forty years old. The Carmarthenshire County Committee was formed in order to draw from this group of men the numbers required not only to raise a local infantry battalion, but also to recruit enough men to supply reinforcements to this battalion, and indeed to both the Regular and Territorial Army.

Over the coming months the first part of the dream of a Welsh Army Corps turned into reality, and thus part of Lloyd George's dream came into being, with the formation of the 43rd (Welsh) Division. Raised as part of this new division, was the 15th (Service) (Carmarthenshire) Battalion of the Welsh Regiment.

The battalion was first raised at St. Helens football ground in Swansea during the months of October and November 1914 by the Carmarthenshire County Committee, and was attached to 129 Brigade, 43rd Division. It was composed at first of an original nucleus of seventy-one men coming from the 10th Welsh on 21 November 1914. Recruiting began in Carmarthen that same month, with, intriguingly, a strong recruiting campaign around the industrial town of Bolton, in Lancashire.

The local Carmarthenshire newspaper, the *Welshman*, had an interesting article within its pages on Friday 18 December 1914 relating to the progress of recruiting for the Carmarthenshire Battalion:

> Good progress is being made in raising the Carmarthenshire Battalion of the Welsh Army Corps. Since August the numbers who have enlisted at Carmarthen for Kitcheners Army up to the end of last month was 567.

Not all of these men reached the ranks of the 15th Welsh though, with many joining other Service battalions of the New Army instead. To remind us of the difficulty recruiting Carmarthenshire men for the 15th Welsh, the same edition of the *Welshman* also carried the following report:

> Recruiting for the Reserve Battalion of the Pembroke Yeomanry at Carmarthen is going strong, with only 60 more men needed to complete its establishment of 469 Officers and men.

The Reserve Battalion of the 4th Welsh, stationed at the time at Carmarthen Barracks, had just received the honour of being inspected

An early batch of recruits outside York House, Pontyberem, 1914.
(Jon Stubbs)

by Lieutenant-General Sir James Hills-Johnes, VC. The Welshman reported:

> *After brisk recruiting locally it was only 100 men short of its full complement; of the number locally recruited, Llanelli had contributed 350, Llandeilo 100, Carmarthen 78, Haverfordwest 64, Cardigan 45 and Pembroke 24.*

[Recruiting for this battalion had in fact been carrying on in earnest since the outbreak of war, and many officers and men recruited for the 4th Welsh were later posted to the 15th as reinforcements]. Although a considerable number of men had hurried to enlist into the 15th Welsh, the same issue of the newspaper also had news of several men from local villages who had travelled to Chatham to enlist into the Royal Engineers, and the maritime heritage of towns like Llanelli and Carmarthen was shown by the large numbers of men serving with both the Royal Navy and the Mercantile Marine.

As a result of these concerns, recruiting events were held around Carmarthenshire. At one such meeting at St. Clears, presided over by Sir James Hills-Johnes, VC, Mr H H Philipps of Picton Castle spoke to the gathered crowd:

> *As true Welshmen they must all realise the great crisis which had*

overtaken us as a nation, and he felt that as gallant Welshmen they would not be behind, but would, as in the past, still maintain the noble traditions gained by them in their great days gone by. He asked the older people to encourage the young ones to come forward and to respond to their country's call and join the new Welsh Army Corps… Without in any way prejudicing the new Welsh Army Corps, he asked why Wales should not also have its own Welsh Guards Regiment?

In October 1914 a campaign had begun to lobby the War Office to create a battalion of Welsh Guards, to serve alongside the existing Scots and Irish Guards Battalions.

Campaigners in West Wales such as H H Philipps worked hard to lobby for their cause, resulting in the formation of the Welsh Guards by Royal Warrant of the 26 February 1915. This new unit was to be another drain on depleted resources of manpower from West Wales, although its core was made up of 300 men transferring from the Grenadier Guards. Nonetheless, even with the competition for men, during the coming weeks the strength of the 15th Welsh grew. A draft of 350 men from Porthcawl joined the battalion on 23 January 1915, with a further 250 men joining who had enlisted in Lancashire (mainly from the Bolton area).

The administrative side of the battalion on the other hand was rapidly built up, with many seasoned soldiers, having had experience of fighting around the Empire, and especially in South Africa, re-joining the colours and taking up posts with the battalion.

Chosen to command the 15th Welsh was the experienced Lieutenant-Colonel Mackay John Graham Scobie, CB. Mackay was born at Hereford on 27 March 1852 and at the age of nineteen

Another drain on depleted resources of manpower from West Wales – a poster recruiting for the Welsh Guards.

joined the Herefordshire Volunteers. He served as their Commanding Officer during the Boer War, and was the first Commanding Officer of the 1st Battalion, the Hereford Regiment until his retirement in 1911.

Lieutenant-Colonel Mackay John Graham Scobie, CB

Mackay was prominent in Hereford life. He practised as a solicitor there and was a former Mayor of Hereford prior to the Boer War. Mackay was very actively involved in recruiting in Herefordshire at the outbreak of the Great War, which led to him being selected to command and form the 15th (Service) Battalion of the Welsh Regiment. He was to play an important role in building the 15th Welsh, and in forming the battalion into an efficient fighting unit from a bunch of raw recruits.

Not all of these officers were seasoned soldiers like Colonel Scobie though. Two men with no previous military experience were the young Second Lieutenants Herbert and Alexander Lewis, two of the ten sons of the well known Carmarthen gas engineer and artist, Benjamin Archibald Lewis, and of his wife Mary.

The ten young brothers were all of an adventurous nature, and by early in 1915 five of them had joined the colours. Herbert and Alexander took up commissions in the 15th Welsh, Jack was a Corporal with the Welsh Field Company, Royal Engineers, and Gwynne and Rex were Ordinary Seamen in the Royal Naval Division, although Gwynne later received a commission into the 13th Welsh, and then to 114 Trench Mortar Battery, where he fought alongside his two brothers.

In January 1915 Herbert and Alexander were settled in well with the battalion at Rhyl. From his billets at the Morville Hotel, Herbert sent Olive Marsden (who later became his wife) a postcard to say that he was sorry he would not be coming home after all; he had been expecting to be sent to Carmarthen on a recruiting campaign, but this was not necessary as 300 new recruits were arriving the next day.

15th Battalion Welsh Recruiting Party outside Carmarthen County Hall.
Carmarthen Archives

Recruitment drive around Bolton throughout November 1914

In fact it was not until the end of February that the Battalion was finally made up to full strength by men enlisted in Carmarthenshire, after a heavy recruitment campaign in the county. The centre-piece of the recruitment effort had been a motor car that had been donated to the battalion, which had been instrumental in the recruitment drive at Bolton, adorned with banners urging men to join the 15th Welsh.

After a successful recruitment drive around Bolton throughout November 1914, the party drove the car southwards to Carmarthenshire, where they campaigned hard for more recruits, finally ensuring that the full strength of the battalion was achieved.

The decision as to why a Welsh Regiment should have campaigned for recruits around Bolton is a strange one, but at the time the cotton trade was in full swing, and so it was quite possible that Bolton had received a large influx of Welsh workers, whose resources could be tapped into to provide men to fill the gaps not just in the ranks of the 15th Welsh, but also of the other Kitchener battalions, especially the 10th Welsh.

The *Farnworth Journal* of 5 November 1915 reported on a group of young men from the Farnworth All Saints Church Football Team who had all decided to enlist together into the Welsh Regiment after watching the Welsh recruitment men in action.

Fifteen men from the team attended a recruitment drive at Farnworth Town Hall, and the following Monday they all met at Moses Gate Station to catch the train to Rhyl, where they were to join the 12th Welsh Training Battalion at Kinmel Park. A large crowd of 200-300 people gathered at Moses Gate train station to see their young heroes off that day.

Almost the first letter home from one of the lads was a request for a football, which was duly supplied by courtesy of the *Farnworth Journal*, who had received a similar letter from another Farnworth man, Herbert Bithell, the husband of Edna Bithell, of 37, Longcauseway, Farnworth, Bolton.

Herbert had been born in Holywell, and had moved to Farnworth prior to the war, where he worked at Denmark Mill as a warehouseman. He taught Sunday School at Farnworth Baptist Church, and had played football for Atherton, Bolton Wanderers and Macclesfield as a professional before the war. Herbert had enlisted at Bolton, and joined the 15th Welsh at Rhyl. He was not to survive the war.

Bolton was, and still is, a fanatical hotbed of football, and the football was a most welcome distraction from the daily rigours of army life for the young men at Rhyl over the coming months of intense training. Sport was, as it still is, used very much by the army to keep bored young men's minds occupied, so whenever the young recruits weren't training, football and rugby matches often took place. The sport took on a new importance for the men after the end of the war.

The importance of rugby in the British Army, especially in the Welsh

A group of Bolton recruits at Rhyl.
David Rawsthorn

Regiments, is summed up in the words of a St Clears man, Ira 'Taffy' Jones, a Territorial with the 4th Welsh at Carmarthen prior to the war. Ira joined the Royal Flying Corps in 1915, where he became the highest scoring Welsh fighter pilot of the war:

> *When war was declared in August 1914, and the four Rugby Unions cancelled all fixtures, I well remember what a blow it was to me. I felt as if the end of the world had come. When I went to the war I took a rugger ball with me, and great was my joy when I heard that matches were being played in the fighting zone.*
> (An Airfighters Scrapbook, 1938).

One member of the newly formed 15th Welsh was a pre-war regular, James Alfred Daniel, who had won the Army Rugby Cup while playing for the 2nd Welsh in 1912. This was just the second time that the Welsh had won the cup, with 1st Welsh the victors in 1909.

Lieutenant Daniel, along with five former Llanelly R.F.C. rugby players who had enlisted into the 15th Welsh, Lieutenants D.H. Thomas and T.L. Stewart, and Privates D.J. Rees, Arthur Howells and Hendy Evans, soon formed the basis of a very competitive 15th Welsh Rugby Team, which played Llanelly R.F.C. at Stradey Park on 12 March, 1915, before taking on Ammanford and Neath the following week

Lieutenant James Alfred Daniel would play a big part in the history of the 15th Welsh during the war, with his gallantry leading to his being awarded both the Distinguished Service Order and the Military Cross before the end of the conflict.

Another man who was to play a vital role in the raising and training of the battalion during those early months of their formation was their veteran Regimental Sergeant Major, Isaac Jones.

Isaac had been born in Liverpool, the son of Ann Jones, later of Ystrad Farm, Lanwbra, Denbigh. He had attested into the Depot Battalion of the Welsh Regiment at Chester on 11 December 1884, aged nineteen years and five months, and had then served with the 1st Welsh from

Regimental Sergeant Major, Isaac Jones.
Mark Collins

December 1884 until September 1888, when he joined the 2nd Welsh for two years. He then moved back to the 1st Welsh, and fought with them during the Boer War in South Africa, gaining the Queen's South Africa Medal with three Clasps, 'Relief of Kimberley', 'Paardeberg' and 'Driefontein'.

Isaac served continuously with the Welsh until his retirement in February 1909, by which time he had been promoted to Colour Sergeant with the 4th Welsh, the Carmarthenshire Battalion of the Territorial Army. He had by then married Miss Selina Jane Littlejohn at Plymouth, and had set up home with her at 49, Margaret Street, Ammanford, where they raised their young family.

On his retirement in 1909 from the Territorial's, Isaac was awarded a gold watch and pendant by his Company of Volunteers, and took up employment at Ammanford Colliery as a surface foreman. At the outbreak of the Great War, the old soldier re-attested into the Welsh Regiment as a Private, joining the 15th Welsh on 9 December 1914. He joined up with the rest of the Battalion at Rhyl the following day, by then aged forty-nine years and five months old.

The veteran was promoted to Company Quarter Master Sergeant just two days after joining, and on 22 May 1915 was promoted to Regimental Sergeant Major, a pivotal role in a newly formed Battalion of civilian soldiers. His wealth of experience and knowledge of soldiering was to prove of great benefit to the 1,000 odd fresh recruits over the coming months.

After the Welsh Division had completed its formation at the end of February 1915, the division had the honour of an inspection by the then Chancellor of the Exchequer, David Lloyd George, whose brainchild it had been. During his tour, Lloyd George visited Rhyl where the 15th Welsh mounted a guard of honour.

In a proud speech to the gathered soldiers, Lloyd George proudly read the following stirring words:

> *I have seen now about 15,000 Welsh Infantry. I never thought I should live to see the day when there would be 15,000 Welshmen once more ready to meet the foes of liberty. But there they are, always ready to the call as they were in the past. They are only part of an army of 80,000 turned out by Wales in this crisis, and I am certain that the 80,000 is only a beginning to the much larger force that our country is going to contribute to the greatest struggle that has ever taken place for human progress. (Cheers). I congratulate the Officers on the appearance of the men. Lord Kitchener and those responsible for the creation of these great armies will, I have no doubt, be duly grateful for the elements which have so much contributed to the efficiency of this fine force. I am*

sorry I must return to town. The whole of us are very hard worked as Ministers (hear, hear) and I shall have to resume work as soon as I get back.

It was a proud beginning for the new Welsh Division, but the dream of a Welsh Army Corps, consisting of two full divisions, was sadly never to be fulfilled, as too many Welshmen had already been absorbed into other units, and the reality was to be just the one Welsh Division in the field in France.

Recruits from Carmarthenshire continued to join the battalion while they were at Rhyl. One of these was the nineteen year old Harry Montague Allen of Whitland. Harry was the son of Thomas Allen, a plumber with the Great Western Railway. The family had moved from Haverfordwest to Whitland, which was at that time a large railway depot, and the young Harry was to follow in his fathers' footsteps, becoming a fireman on the railway, based at Llanelli.

Harry was called up for service in April, and was posted to the 15th Welsh. His service papers show that he attested on 17 April 1915, and arrived at Rhyl five days later, his papers being counter-signed by the Adjutant, Lieutenant Aneurin Rhydderch. He was examined by the battalion medical officer Lieutenant Wilfred Soden, who recommended that Harry's teeth should be worked on before he would be passed as fit for duty.

Harry Montague Allen

Harry's teeth were easily cured, and he was accepted into the battalion soon after. Interestingly the complaint of bad teeth was a common condition among young men in those days. In fact it was quite common for thrill seeking young men to fail their initial medical exam as a result of bad teeth, and then to have all of their teeth extracted so as to pass their examination the second time.

In a short note home to his parents at Whitland after having his teeth repaired, Harry wrote a brief note:

> Dear Mother,
>
> *I have arrived safely at Camp. The journey was quite long, and I am tired. It is very busy here, so as soon as I get the chance I will write you some more.*
>
> *Your Loving Son, Harry.*

Another of the recruits, the only known man within the photo overleaf, is Private Joseph Larkin, who stands in the back row, ninth from the left. Joe Larkin was born in Bolton on 29 April 1893. He joined the 15th Welsh on 3 February 1915 while they were at Rhyl, and was part of another batch of Bolton men. Joe was allotted the service number

No.3 Platoon, A Company, 15th Welsh on the sands at Rhyl, March 1915.
Martin Southern

20357, and was to survive the war, although he was invalided out of the army after being gassed and receiving shrapnel wounds to his arm later in the war, and discharged in 1918, gaining a pension of 16 shillings, and died in 1957.

Although initially blighted by a lack of suitable NCOs, plus a shortage of weapons and uniforms, training began on the beaches of Rhyl for the 15th Welsh. Rows of men drilled on the beach throughout the winter, and so much route marching was carried out that boots and socks fell in short supply, and so requests for equipment were placed in the local newspapers, the *Welshman* and the *Carmarthen Journal*.

The Welshman newspaper of Friday 28 April 1915 contained a small paragraph of how the fund raising for the Carmarthenshire Battalion was going:

> *Already promised: £20 each, Mr. J.H. Thomas (High Sheriff), Lord Dynevor, Messrs. Cleaves (Western Valleys Anthracite Company) and Mr. H. S. Allen, Cresselly. £10 each, Mr. J. W. Gwynne Hughes (Lord Lieutenant), Sir Stafford Howard, Lady Howard and Sir Charles Philipps (Picton). £3, Sir Owen Scourfield. Second List; 5 Guineas each, Mr. H. G. Evans (Llangennech Park), Mr. A. R. Gery (Regent's Park, London). Five Pounds each, Sir James Hills-Johnes, Mr. John Hinds, M.P., Lady Hills-Johnes, Mr. Mervyn Peel (Danyrallt). £3 Colonel Barkely-Calcott (Cheltenham). £2 each, Mr. W. P. Jeffreys (Ludlow), Mr. E. S. Protheroe (Glyntaf), Mr. Henry Williams (Llwyngwern). £1 10s. Captain H. E. E. Philipps. A Guinea each, Judge Lloyd Morgan, Mr. Ll. John (Gelly, Llanelli), Reverend J. John (Llanstephan), Principal Evans (Carmarthen), Mr. J. Tregoning,*

Colonel W. B. Lloyd (Brunant), Mr. F. A. Davies (Llanelli), Mr. G. R. Brigstocke (Ferryside), Mr. S. Morgan Evans (Dalston), Mr. T. Howell Davies (Penllwyn Park, Carmarthen), Colonel W. Gwynne Hughes (Glancothi, Nantgaredig), Colonel J. H. W. Pedder (Gwynfe House, Llangaddock). £1 each, Mr. D. E. Davies (Gelly, Llanwrda), Mr. Edward Davies (Craig Evans, Trelech), Mrs. Stokes (St. Botolphs), Mr. J. Lewis (Morfabach, St. Clears), Mr. A. C. Lewis (Pontyberem), and Mr. J. P. George (Kilgerran). Ten Shillings and Sixpence each, Mr. A. Morgan (Burry Port), Dr. Williams (Carmarthen), Mr. D. Howell Thomas (Auctioneer and Estate Agent, Carmarthen), Mr. C. Chapman (Carmarthen), Mr. J. E. Lewis (Brynamman).'

There was another article stating the need for razors for the troops of the Carmarthen Battalion, and a comprehensive list of who had donated them was also published that same day, doubtless meant to shame local businesses that hadn't helped the effort.

At that time, the 15th Welsh was funded by the Carmarthen County Committee and that in turn by the Executive Committee. In fact it was to be the only battalion of the New Armies raised by County Committee. Uniforms, equipment, even rifles and ammunition were all in short supply, and the County Committee worked hard to raise funds to purchase such items as required by the battalion, even to the extent of being donated such items as rifles, bullets and personal equipment like the razors mentioned above.

This fund-raising was not always an easy task. Businesses across Carmarthen had already been asked to contribute heavily to the 4th Welsh and the Pembroke Yeomanry, and many private homes in Carmarthen town gave up rooms to accommodate troops stationed at Carmarthen Barracks. In fact this gave much cause for concern at the early part of 1915, when it was discovered that those town folk billeting men of the Pembroke Yeomanry were being paid more by the army than those people who had 4th Welshmen billeted with them. [17s 6d compared to 23s 7d – *The Welshman* – 16 April 1915].

Also, as a rural, mainly farming area, the County of Carmarthen had a lot less money, mainly due to a smaller population, available to spend on equipment for the Carmarthen Battalion than did for example the neighbouring prosperous cities of Swansea and Cardiff, whose Battalions, the 14th Welsh (Swansea), and the 11th and 16th Welsh (Cardiff) received a lot more in regard of donations of money and equipment.

Equipment and monetary problems aside, the building of the Welsh Division, and the 15th Welsh, carried out at full pace. From 28 April 1915 the 15th Welsh became attached to 114 Brigade, 38th (Welsh)

The grave of Albert Francis of Llanelli
Sarah Bassett

Division, part of K5, (Kitchener's 5th New Army). Its commander was the former Liberal Member of Parliament, Major-General Ivor Philipps, brother to Lord St. Davids of Pembrokeshire. It wasn't until May of 1915 that all three brigades of the Welsh Division managed to combine for an exercise at Colwyn Bay, and by now talk was rife of a move to camps in the south of England.

In the meantime, the battalion suffered its first death on 14 June 1915, whilst at Rhyl. The veteran forty-two year old Private Albert Francis of Llanelli had taken ill. He had sadly died of sickness on 14 June, and was brought home to Llanelli for burial at Box Cemetery. Due to his age, it is highly probable that Albert had served in the Boer War and was a reservist who had rejoined the colours.

Just a week later another Llanelli born recruit died of sickness whilst in hospital at Bangor. David Griffiths was thirty-five years old when he died on 22 June 1915. He is buried in north Wales, at Bangor (Glanadda) Cemetery.

The *London Gazette* of 6 July 1915 noted the promotion of the young Carmarthen man Herbert C Lewis, when he was made a full lieutenant, as well as his fellow officers John D Sampson, Eric Walker, and John C MacDonald. Lieutenant and Adjutant Aneurin Rhydderch was promoted to temporary captain.

Another man who was to play a pivotal part in the wartime service of the battalion was the Padre, the Reverend Lewis Arthur Hughes. Sadly he is not pictured with the Officers outside the Morville Hotel, (overleaf), but Reverend Hughes was a well known and respected Carmarthen man, having prior to the war been the Pastor of Zion Presbyterian Chapel at King Street, Carmarthen.

During July and August 1915 the battalion moved south with the remainder of the Welsh Division to Morn Hill Camp, Winchester. There was still a shortage of rifles, but training commenced there as best as they could manage. Until the arrival of enough rifles, training concentrated on brigade and divisional manoeuvres, and the men found it very hard going, with long forced marches, incessant training, and wet weather and sickness plaguing the battalion over the coming months. Amazingly it was not until November 1915 that the full quota of rifles [the Short Magazine Lee Enfield Number 4, Mark 1] reached the division, and a hurried course on the Salisbury rifle range was put into place.

Morn Hill Camp was at that time still a tented camp, which had been used in the summer of 1914 as a summer camp for the local militia. Due to the lack of proper accommodation, soldiers were billeted in any

Standard issue British infantry rifle, SMLE No.4, Mark I.

31

*Photographed outside their quarters at the Morville Hotel in Rhyl, is a group of the Officers of the 15th Welsh. The photograph was taken just prior to the move south to Winchester. The men pictured are, from left to right, **back row:** A Lewis, T Landman, F Roberts, D S Davies, W Reese, G Hamilton-Lloyd, A G Corser, J Skelding, T L Morgan, W B Protheroe, Douglas Jones, R Burgess, B A Lewis. **Middle row:** Captain H Gardiner (QM), Lt W Soden, (RAMC), Lt J McDonald, Lt P L Humphreys, Lt A E Edwards, 2nd Lt G A Griffiths, Lt E Walker, Lt H C Lewis, 2nd Lt T L Stewart. **Front row:** Captain P Anthony, Major J H Rees, Major W S R Cox, Lt Colonel M J G Scobie (CO), Lt & Adjt A Rhydderch, Major J K Williams, Captain A P Sprague, Captain D Powell. At the front are the Goat Mascot [Copthorne Ghost], and the Goat Major.*
(Courtesy Welsh Regimental Museum)

Men training on the rifle range.

house or building that could be commandeered, and even the famous Winchester College and the local schools were crammed with soldiers.

Scattered all around Winchester were several other army camps, and they played host to men from all over the world; Indians, Canadians and also Americans by the end of the war. This huge number of energetic young men played havoc in Winchester itself, where they would often go for a drink at night. The Welshmen of the 38th Division gained themselves quite a reputation during their stay at Winchester, as Stanley Richardson of Winchester recalled years later:

> *I recall the riots in the 1914-1918 war. The Welsh were the worst. They attacked the police station in the Broadway, smashed all the windows and tried to get out one of the Welshmen who had been arrested. But they were beaten off, or held back by the police, and then the Rifle Brigade from the depot marched down the High Street with fixed bayonets – straight down the High Street in line abreast to clear it – and the Welsh went out one end while the Rifle Brigade came in the other. I actually saw that happen.* Winchester Voices-Sarah Bussy

Quite a reputation then, but aggression was soon to be sorely needed,

Rioting Welsh troops being moved on by police. Summer, 1915. Winchester Voices

and the army was instilling it into the men day after day through their rigorous training regime.

In the small Township of Laugharne, on the western edge of Carmarthenshire, the retired Mariner George Roberts of Fernhill Cottage received a letter from his son James, stating how much he was enjoying his new life. James had volunteered into the 15th Welsh when recruiting first began, along with his friend Fred Richards of Hugdon, and was given the service number 22750.

James' two brothers George and John had already enlisted into the Royal Marines, but James decided to enlist into the 15th Welsh, and his eagerness paid off during the first week of July 1915 when he received his first promotion to Lance Corporal. The young man ended up as a Colour Sergeant by the end of the war, and was to be Mentioned in Despatches for his courage.

Lieutenant-Colonel Thomas William Parkinson, DSO.

Lieutenant-General Sir Archibald Murray made an appearance as the inspecting officer in September, and he 'reported so favourably that the Division was placed in the fourth 100,000, though it really belonged in the fifth 100,000, and it was warned to be ready to proceed to France about the end of November'. Plainly speaking, the 38th Welsh Division was being moved from the 5th to the 4th New Army. It had been judged as being ready for war.

Throughout the summer of 1915 the 38th (Welsh) Division received an influx of seasoned officers, mostly from other regular army units, but also many officers from the Indian Army. As a result, some officers who were deemed to be too old for overseas service were replaced by younger men. This probably explains why on 10 November 1915 Lieutenant-Colonel Scobie retired from the command of the battalion that he had worked so hard to build, and it came under the command of the newly promoted Lieutenant-Colonel

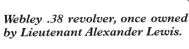

Webley .38 revolver, once owned by Lieutenant Alexander Lewis.

Thomas William Parkinson, DSO.

Parkinson had been born on 8 July 1880. He had been commissioned into the York and Lancaster Regiment in 1899 and had fought with them in the Boer War, although he was seconded to the 2nd Welsh for a spell. Thomas Parkinson continued on the ladder of promotion from then on and, in April 1915, moved to the Western Front as Captain and Adjutant of the 1/5th Battalion, York and Lancaster Regiment.

In November he was promoted to Temporary Lieutenant-Colonel, and was asked to take command of the 15th Welsh, so he returned back to Winchester to meet his new command. By this time he had been awarded the Distinguished Service Order for his work in France. Thomas was to remain in command of the 15th Welsh for most of the Battalion's time at war.

Around this time the Battalion lost its third man; the first Lancashire casualty from their ranks. Charles Frederick Stephenson is recorded as having died of wounds on 4 November 1915. He must have been wounded in a training accident involving live firing, as accidents with these had become commonplace. Charles had married prior to the war, and was buried back in his home town of Nelson, in Lancashire.

While at Winchester, the two Lewis brothers of Carmarthen seized the chance to meet up with two of their other serving brothers in London. Herbert and Alexander met up with Jack and Gwynne, and had tea together at Victoria Station, having arrived just after 14.00 hrs. It was a short time they had together as Gwynne had to catch the 18.10 hrs train, and Herbert and Alexander the 18.40 hrs back to Winchester.

This was the brothers last meeting before they all headed to war. Luckily, although they were not to know it at the time, all the brothers were fated to survive the conflict.

The 38th Division was almost ready for war, and it was reviewed at Crawley Down on 29 November 1915, by Her Majesty the Queen Mary, as King George had been taken ill. The time for the divisions move out to the Western Front was nearly here, and so the men of the division gathered at Winchester Cathedral for a service.

A report in the *Welshman* stated: 'It may be interesting to learn that the 15th Battalion, Welsh Regiment are now at Winchester', and the *Hampshire Chronicle* reports the proceedings in camp as follows:

> *Last Sunday afternoon a Welsh service was held by the Divisional Chaplain near King Alfred's statue in the Broadway when 3,000 soldiers attended. The band of the R.W.F. played selections and the hymns. An* eisteddfod *was also held on Thursday evening "Agored I'r byd." The organisation of this was admirably carried out by Captain Anthony of Kidwelly, the Divisional Chaplain, Rev. P.J. Roberts, Lance Corporal Rees and Private W.J. Owen. Dr. Prendergast, organist of Winchester Cathedral, was the musical adjudicator, and the Reverends P.J. Roberts, Divisional Chaplain R. Jones (Llandinam) and Arthur Hughes (Carmarthen) adjudicated on the recitations and poetical compositions.*

Fifty years later Captain Herbert Lewis wrote of this service held in Winchester Cathedral before the troops' embarkation. His account, which was published in the Western Mail, described how the cathedral was filled with so many Welsh soldiers and:

> *For the first and perhaps the only time the walls of this great and magnificent House of God reverberated with strains of hymns sung with true Welsh fervour.*

Herbert no doubt reflected his own feelings when he added:

> *The memory of this wonderful service alleviated the trials which the Division was to undergo in the next few years.'*

Just days later, on 4 December 1915, the first parties of the battalion entrained at Winchester, bound for Folkestone. During the march through Winchester it rained, giving the men a taste to come of the conditions they would soon be facing. Upon reaching Folkestone, the battalion marched down Slope Road (later renamed the 'Road of Remembrance' due to the thousands of soldiers who trod its path) to the harbour. For many this would be their last steps on British soil, but even with this knowledge, the men were still cheery and looking forward to their adventure.

The Road of Remembrance, Folkestone.

Chapter Two

The Western Front – Nursery Sector

AT AROUND 10.30 HRS ON THE MORNING of 4 December 1915, the 15th Welsh sailed from Folkestone, and arrived at Boulogne at 12.35 hrs. For most of the young men in its ranks this was the furthest they had been from home, and many of them would sadly have said their final farewells to loved ones and homes that they would never see again.

After safely disembarking in France, the battalion was assembled at La Porte de Calais, and then organised and marched to Ostrohove Camp on the eastern side of Boulogne, where they remained until midnight, before moving on to Pont de Briques, about five miles south.

Soldiers of the Welsh Regiment en-route to France.

The Port de Calais, Boulogne-the 15th Welsh Assembled Here in December 1915.

Welsh Troops transported by cattle truck.

They entrained there at 04.00 hrs for Aire in northern France. Here, the 38th (Welsh) Division came under the wing of XI Corps, under the command of Lieutenant-General Sir Richard Haking, KCB, DSO.

Came the day when we marched to the station, to the cattle vans all labelled 8 Hommes 8 Chevaux, I think it was. What a journey it was, now December and cold. There was no heating of course, and the train crawled along with frequent long stops. Even when the train was in motion, we could run up to the engine, beg some boiling water to make tea,

38

then wait till until your van came along, hand up your dixie and jump aboard. There were several trains ahead, I suppose, for it took the train two days to travel there although it could not have been seventy or eighty miles. We arrived at the rail head at midnight, men shouting "All out, all out", and it was pitch dark. No preparations were made for the reception of the troops.

We got out of the van, half frozen with cold and all left there miserable, hungry and cold, wandering and stumbling in the dark. I at last crept into a space in a huge stack of timber but not for long, for it was too cold. So another search, and at last I opened the door into a long wide timber hut. By the light of candles alight here and there I could see the whole area was covered with sleeping men. Seeing just enough space for me to lay down, I was soon down and asleep.'

Private William Shanahan

The train was indeed made up of cattle wagons, built to take eight men and eight horses, as the name suggests.

After disembarking at Aire the now weary men marched two miles west through the pleasant French countryside, to billets in the village of Rincq, about thirty miles behind the British front line, where they settled down for a welcome nights sleep.

The move into billets at Rincq was completed by 5 December 1915, when the Division became part of the XI Corps under the command of Sir Richard Haking, KCB, DSO.

The situation in France at the time was not good. The British had suffered casualties during the First Battle of Ypres and in 1915 had lost heavily at the disastrous Battle of Neuve-Chapelle and at the Battle of Loos. The campaign in Gallipoli, which had been intended to open up a second front, had also stalled, and little did the men know it at the time, evacuation of the Allies from Gallipoli was imminent.

The Commander-in-Chief of the British armies in France, Field Marshal Sir John French, had been sacked and replaced by General Sir Douglas Haig, the former commander of the First Army. Haig was to remain in command for the duration of the war.

Now in France, further training began in earnest for the Welshmen. The men were instructed in the wearing and use of gas masks, and the battalion specialists received training in their allotted new professions; bombers, machine-gunners and stretcher-bearers were all put through their paces by battle seasoned instructors, readying the men for their first spell in the trenches.

Daily route marches took place, in almost continual rain, and the men were introduced to the new Mills hand grenade, which replaced the previously amateur jam tins stuffed with nails and explosives. These new Mills grenades in fact turned out to be almost as dangerous for the handler as they were for the intended victim, with many reported incidents of casualties amongst the men of the 38th Division.

The memoirs of Private Shanahan of Llanelli show the dangers surrounding the handling of the Mills Grenades;

> *We were busy fusing Mills bombs, whilst older servicemen were never capable of fusing bombs. Others had not fused a bomb before and to even handle the fuse one had to be extra careful, especially in how you treated the fuse which was a copper tube containing detonating powder. We were warned that this needed careful handling and was liable to explode merely by handling it too long before inserting it into the centre of the bomb. The bombing, when demonstrated, seemed straight forward, but when you were standing in the trench, the pin holding the lever in one position, the arm poised to throw, a sort of paralysis seemed to affect the hand which became unwilling to leave the bomb go. You were sometimes so nervous that you would be liable either to drop it at your feet or throw it only as far as the trench top. I suppose that's why the instructors got into the next bay of the trench, to be out of danger.*

Orders now arrived, with the effect that from 10 December 1915 to 6 January 1916, battalions of the 38th Division were to be attached in turn to units of the two divisions in the front line, to learn the dark arts of trench warfare. XI Corps was to hold the right flank of the Second Army, from Givenchy in the south to Laventie in the north. Lieutenant Wyn Griffith of the 15th Royal Welsh Fusiliers, part of the sister 113 Brigade, wrote of his feelings as his battalion awaited their move into the trenches;

Cut-away section of a training Mills Grenade.

> *Less than twenty-four hours stood between us and the trenches; there were two kinds of men in the world- those who had been in the trenches and the rest. We were to graduate from the one class to the other, to be reborn into the old age and experience of the front line, by the traversing of two miles over the fields of Flanders.* Up to Mametz

At 08.00 hrs on 12 December 1915 the men of the 15th Welsh, tempered with a blend of fear and excitement, set off from Rincq for instruction with 57 Brigade near Richebourg St. Vaast, north of Neuve Chapelle. A Company became attached to the 10th Royal Warwickshire Regiment in brigade reserve. B Company joined the 8th Gloucester's in the trenches, C Company was attached to the 10th Worcester's and D Company to the 8th North Stafford's. These three units formed part of

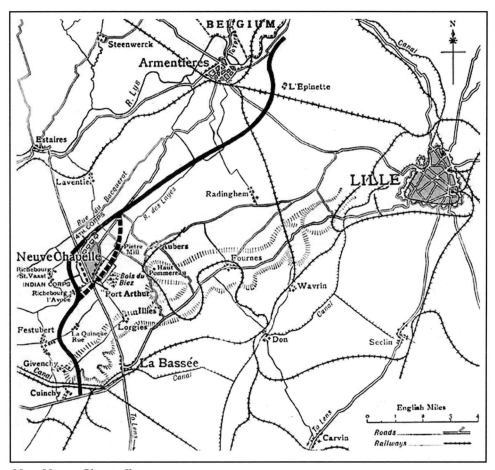

Map-Neuve Chappelle.

the 19th (Western) Division. They themselves had only been on the Western Front since July 1915, but had gained invaluable experience during the Battle of Loos, which stood them in good stead for the rest of their time at war, when they proved themselves amongst the best of the British Divisions in the field.

Here the real training began in earnest, and the men were to have their first taste of the devastated landscape at the front. This was the so called 'Nursery Sector' of the Western Front. It was deemed ideal for training new units as it was by now a relatively peaceful sector of the front. However, just two days into their training, on 14 December 1915, two men of the battalion were killed by German sniper fire, and a further three were wounded.

The two dead were the first real casualties of war for the battalion. William John Waite was from Tidworth, and had enlisted at Mardy, then a flourishing mining town in the Rhondda Valley. He is buried at St Vaast Post Military Cemetery. The other man, Frederick Ward was from Henley. He had also enlisted in the valleys. Sadly his grave was lost during the course of the war, and he is listed on the Loos Memorial. In fact Frederick turned out to be the only 15th Welsh casualty to be listed on the Loos Memorial during the course of the war.

From quite early in the war, the British had adopted a defensive system comprising of three basic lines; a Front Line Trench, a Support Trench and a Reserve Trench, each connected by Communication Trenches. Where geology and conditions allowed, the trenches were dug into the ground, and inside they were generally fitted with wooden 'A' frames, which held a planked walkway or duckboards above a drain. The side of the trench facing the enemy was known as the Parapet, and in it were fire steps, lookout posts, sniper posts and sometimes dugouts to house men. The rear was known as the Parados, and that sheltered the back of the soldier from shrapnel. The earthen sides of the trench were usually revetted with wood, sandbags, wire mesh or corrugated iron to keep them from falling

A View of a typical trench in Flanders (the 1st Monmouths at Le Bizet). With kind permission of The Regimental Museum of The Royal Welsh, Brecon

in, but maintenance on these structures was high.

The trenches referred to in Flanders were not pure trenches, but breastworks built up to a height of around seven feet, as the ground here was too waterlogged to allow the digging of deep enough trenches to afford protection. They were constructed from massive breastworks of sandbags (usually filled with clay). Initially, both the parapet and parados of the trench were built in this way, but a later technique was to dispense with the parados for much of the trench line, thus exposing the rear of the trench to fire from the reserve line in case the front was breached.

Now conditions were starting to turn difficult. The notorious Flanders winter had kicked in. Even though constructed above ground trenches were waterlogged, and it was almost impossible to keep warm and dry; bloated corpses lay out in No Man's Land, sickness and disease drained the men in the line. Strict instructions were therefore issued, and strictly maintained whilst in the trenches to guard against trench foot; feet were rubbed with whale oil, dry socks were to be worn, and spare socks to be carried, gum boots were issued, and regular foot inspections of the men carried out.

The section of the line held now ran from Quinque Rue to Farm Corner. The war diary reported: 'Impossible to visit trenches without going through 4 feet, sometimes 5 feet of water'.

It was not in the least a pleasant place to be posted, as was reported in this letter home from an anonymous British Officer:

The damp has got into my pockets. I am wet from head to heel. My hands are caked in mud; I am wet through, and have nowhere a chance to dry myself. Everything and every pocket is ruined, and my money is nothing but a lump of coloured paper. I have tried to dry the lead pencil I am writing with by candlelight in my dug-out, but it is no use. The water is trickling down the walls and gives me a shower-bath all the time.

My breeches are thick with mud. I don't suppose even my mother would recognise me at this minute. I have tried in vain to dry my hands. I have blown on them and held them round the candle, but it is no good. They are inches deep in mud. My revolver case has turned into putty, and my muffler is more like a mud pie than anything else. The paper I am writing on I found round some chocolate in my dugout. Somehow it had kept dry. My watch has stopped at 5, as the wet and mud have penetrated it. I have lived on chocolate all day long.'

At 01.30 hrs on 19 December 1915, the now weary battalion was relieved from the front line, and marched to a rest house at Rue Des Chevattes. The following day they gathered at Le Touret cross roads and moved to Calonne-Sur-La-Lys, a small village north of Bethune, from where they marched to billets at Les Rues Des Vaches. Here they remained for the coming days, cleaning and undergoing regular inspections to keep them on their toes.

On Christmas Day 1915, their first in France, the entire 38th Division was given the day off, with voluntary religious services for all denominations catered for. During the previous night the divisional artillery had begun to arrive from England, and the 38th Division was finally complete by 27 December 1915.

Silk aeroplane postcard sent by Peter Boardman. Courtesy of Mary Curtis

Somewhere in Flanders – a ruined canal lock and cottage.
With kind permission of The Regimental Museum of The Royal Welsh, Brecon

One of the Bolton recruits, 20492 Private Peter Boardman, found time to write a quick note home to his Mother on the back of a silk postcard, wishing her a 'Happy New Year, from your affectionate son Peter'. He continued this tradition of sending back silk postcards to home at every birthday and Christmas afterwards, also adding a note on each card to his sister Lillie, whose birthday was on 23 December.

Silk postcards were the soldiers preferred method of sending quick notes home to loved ones. The official Army version was the 'Field Service Postcard', which was a lot more formal, giving the sender only the options of deleting pre-written lines of text, and the writing of any notes, however small or trivial, were harshly censored, leading to many cards being destroyed.

On 27 December 1915, after two pleasant days of rest, Lieutenants Morgan and Corser and nine other ranks attended trench mortar training at St. Venant, and the remainder of the battalion was instructed in bombing and field engineering. The

Private Peter Boardman
Courtesy of Mary Curtis

45

final days of December and the first days of the New Year also saw the men under instruction in grenade class, more trench mortar tuition and a gas demonstration by the Royal Engineers. Gas was a new and very unpleasant innovation, which the Germans had used to good effect at Ypres the previous year.

This brief respite was soon over however. On 4 January 1916 a party was sent to Pont Du Hem to arrange billeting for the battalion, and a party of officers visited the front line trenches there, where on the following morning the 15th Welsh relieved the 2nd Battalion, Coldstream Guards in the line between Min Post and Lonely Post. The battalion frontage extended from the Moated Grange to Elgin Street.

At the beginning of January 1916 battalion headquarters moved to Winchester Post, just north of the Moated Grange. It was heavily shelled on 7 January 1916, but luckily there were no casualties except for two other ranks receiving shrapnel wounds.

The following day saw the entire line held by the battalion heavily shelled for most of the day, killing one man and wounding two others.

A Field Service postcard sent home by Private Harry Allen of Whitland.

Welsh Troops in Reserve-Flanders 1915. With kind permission of The Regimental Museum of The Royal Welsh, Brecon

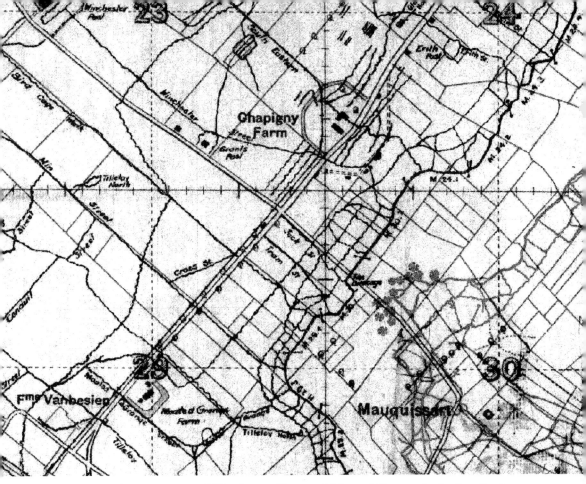

The 15th Welsh sector around Winchester Post and Moated Grange Author's collection

During these days, the battalion traded places with the 14th Welsh in the front line, spending in turn a day in reserve and a day in the line. Experience of trench warfare was being gained, but slowly the battalion was losing men, with another two men killed and four further men wounded before their final relief on 13 January 1916, when the Battalion marched out to Robecq.

Dinner was gratefully eaten at Riez Ou Vinage at 14.00 hrs, before the weary men reached their billets at 18.00 hrs. A bath house had been set up here, and the men were treated to a bath and clean clothes, before spending the afternoon of 15 January on the rifle range.

They remained for the next few days. On 20 January 1916 the machine gun and billeting parties moved out of camp to Croix Barbee, and the following day the remainder of the battalion joined them there, relieving the 10th Worcester's in the front line, taking over positions at Croix Barbee, Euston Post, Loretto Post and Curzon Post.

Two Welshmen 'brewing up' in the reserve lines.
By kind permission of The Regimental Museum of the Royal Welsh, Brecon

On the morning of 22 January 1916 the battalion came under heavy enemy shellfire, but luckily the trenches weren't hit, and no casualties were suffered. That afternoon they moved to relieve the 10th Royal Warwick's in the front line from Oxford Street to Sign Post Lane, and also Chateau Post, Church Redoubt, Hills Redoubt and Hoggs Hole. The war diary noted the dangerous condition of the trenches around the Neb position. Battalion headquarters was stationed to the rear, in a position known as 'Carmarthen Castle', which was shelled during that afternoon.

The following few days were pretty quiet, with the odd episodes of machine-gun fire, and the odd shellfire, but no further casualties were suffered until 25 January 1916, when a Llanelli man, Sergeant Ernest Frederick Bush, was shot by a German sniper. Ernest is buried at St. Vaast Post Military Cemetery, Richebourg-L'Avoue. He is remembered on the war memorial at Llangennech, a small town on the outskirts of Llanelli.

By 15.00 hrs on 26 January 1916 the battalion was relieved by the 14th Welsh, and moved to the reserve positions at Euston, Loretto and Curzon Posts and they remained here until leaving the line three days later, when they first moved to Croix Marmeuse.

On 31 January 1916 the battalion was relieved from reserve billets by the 10th South Wales Borderers, and went into reserve again, busying themselves with yet more training, after the usual spell of bathing, cleaning up and tidying of kit and de-lousing.

Lice were a common problem to the soldier in the Great War. They infested all clothing, and could only be removed by an intensive session, comprising of either 'popping' them with the fingernails, or burning them with the flame of a candle, which the soldiers referred to as 'chatting'.

Again, this was a brief respite from the rigours of trench life. On 6 February 1916 Lieutenant-Colonel Parkinson took his Company Officers out to visit yet another new line of trenches due to be taken over by the battalion, and the next day the 15th Welsh machine gunners moved into positions at Richebourg, relieving the 15th Royal Welsh Fusiliers of 113 Brigade.

The following day of 8 February 1916 saw the remainder of the battalion marching to Richebourg, and they took up positions at Mole Street and Copse Street. The night was relatively quiet, and in the entry in the war diary, the Adjutant, Aneurin Rhydderch stated that the Germans opposite were 'quite cheery'!

The following day also began quietly enough, but a salvo of German shells hit the battalion's position at No. 4 Rest House, killing another two men, Private Harry Jones and William John Williams, both of whom were buried at St Vaast Post Military Cemetery. Casualties were now up to twelve men killed, and the 15th Welsh was still in the 'Nursery Sector', learning the black arts of trench warfare.

Captain Aneurin Rhydderch

The war diary entry for 10 February 1916 makes note that a shell crashed near No. 4 Rest House, and smashed the officers' crockery. Strangely no note was made of the loss of the battalions' Company Quartermaster Sergeant Mansel Davies, from Llangeinor in Glamorgan. Mansel had been wounded during the previous days shelling, and had been moved for treatment to the hospital at Merville. Sadly he died there on 10 February 1916, the unlucky thirteenth casualty of the battalion.

In a letter sent home to his parents in Haverfordwest, which was published in the *Western Telegraph* at the beginning of 1916, Jim John of Prendergast wrote:

> *The weather the last few weeks has been very miserable and the trenches are in a very bad state. It's impossible to walk without getting knee deep in mud and water, and it is also very cold, while to make things worse our dug-out is leaking so that we find it difficult to get a dry place to rest in. Well, never mind, we're not downhearted, and what*

is more we don't intend to be. It is some consolation to know that Fritz has to put up with the same. We are working one week in the trenches with four days rest and so on. We have been served out with fur coats now, and they are also going to give us jack boots, and the sooner these come the better, as we shall then enjoy dry feet. Last week we were billeted in some empty houses in the ruins of a town about a mile behind the firing line. It was rather draughty and a bit hard, but all the same quite a luxury after the dug-outs.

Jim had been eager to get into the war at its outbreak, and as the Service Battalions of the Welsh Regiment weren't to be sent to France for a while, he enlisted into the Rifle Brigade. However, his regret at his lack of patience can be seen further into the letter:

Our battalion has been specially mentioned in dispatches, so we really should be proud to belong to such a good old corps, though I sometimes wish that I had joined one of the Welsh regiments. But as we are out for the same thing it really does not matter much. I remember well when the recruiting officer asked me what I wished to join, I replied, "Anything, so long as it is the Army".

A typical trench occupied by the 15th Welsh, showing the sandbagged parapet and duckboards.
With kind permission of the Regimental Mueseum of the Royal Welsh, Brecon

On 12 February 1916 the battalion was relieved again by the 14th Welsh, and moved into reserve billets at Richebourg. Over the next few days the battalion sent working parties to assist the Royal Engineers, laying duckboards and sandbagging dugouts in the locality, before being again sent to the front on 16 February, relieving the 14th Welsh in positions at Boars Head, Farm Corner and Mole Street. Attitudes were beginning to harden to casualties by now.

Eighteen year old Private Harry Wilkinson was killed during the relief of the 14th Welsh. He is

No. 3 Platoon, 15th Welsh in Flanders, early 1915- Private Joe Larkin of Bolton is to the right of the Regimental Goat wearing a German cap. Note the 'souvenir' pickelhauben worn by two men, and the German felt cap worn by Joe himself. Also in the photograph, the last man on the right in the back row is Peter Boardman, and (probably) the second man on the left in the back row is Private Harry Taylor, also of Bolton. Harry was later to become captured by the Germans at Ypres.

Martin Southern/Mary Curtis

buried alongside his comrades at St. Vaast Post Military Cemetery. He was another Bolton lad to fall while proudly wearing the badge of the Welsh Regiment.

The following day a minor operation was carried out by the 15th Welsh. The line was evacuated save for the trench mortar, bombing and sniping parties, and a bombardment of the enemy trenches followed, supported by the Royal Artillery. The Germans replied in kind, but no casualties were suffered during the operation, and so the remainder of the battalion moved back into the line.

Operations were scaling up slowly now, as confidence and experience within the ranks grew. On 18 February 1916, Lieutenant-Colonel Parkinson and Lieutenant Lewis, the Carmarthen man, crawled through No Man's Land at 04.00 hrs, and listened in on the Germans. No information was gleaned, but it was discovered that no working parties were active on the German front at the time.

Tit-for-tat bombing and sniping sessions followed during the next few days, culminating in a small, yet successful trench raid on 20 February led by Lieutenant D A Jones, who, with a small bombing party, got within five yards of the German trenches, and threw four bombs into a gathering of sentries. They returned safely with no losses.

The 23rd Manchester's joined the battalion in the trenches on 20 February for instruction, and two days later a fall of snow covered the shell pocked battlefield. A peaceful few days followed, with some shelling of the British positions on 25 February, and on 26 February the 15th Welsh trench mortars opened up a combined attack on the German trenches, breaching the parapet and provoking a spell of retaliatory German shelling on the British positions at Rue Du Bois and Pall Mall.

During this period, Tom Ebsworth, a Serjeant in another Welsh battalion, wrote home to his mother at the Beach Hotel in Pendine:

> I am glad to say I am so far tip-top. Well, I am writing you this now, and my word it is an experience. We are only 75 yards away from the Germans, and our chaps and they are blazing away. It is fairly quiet in the day for rifle fire, but the artillery shells are getting over our heads. At night it is like hell. God help anybody where these shells drop, but we are in very nice trenches- 7ft. high, with steps and periscopes. When you fire if you stop about a minute with your head up you are a goner. The snipers are on you, bang. It is fine to see the aeroplanes out and the fights with them. It is good weather so far, but we are afraid we are going to have rain. There is an awful mess here when it is raining. My pal has just popped up and had a shot. He just shouted to me 'I've sent them another souvenir, Tom. I hope they like them'. You'd not believe you can nearly get lost in these trenches! They are marvellous. One would not think, sitting where I am now, that to jump up suddenly would mean instant death. We are on a flat field with long grass and barbed wire between us. Our chaps caught two Germans cutting it, but they will never cut again. Next time you send, please put in a box of liquorice tablets as my throat is a little sore today.

> Hoping you are all well, and with fondest love to all, etc., etc.

Tom went on to gain a commission into the 6th Welsh, and gained the French Croix-de-Guerre by the end of the war. By 1939 he had built up a successful bus company at Laugharne, Ebsworth Brothers, and regained his commission, helping to raise the local Home Guard battalion at Laugharne.

This dreadful shelling continued for the next few days, and it was a relief to the tired men to be relieved again by the 14th Welsh on the afternoon of 28 February. Another member of the battalion lost his life while they were being withdrawn from the line that day. The dead man, Private Joseph Cunningham, was from Bolton, the seventeen year old son of Catherine Cunningham, of 66, Sidney Street. He was the last of the battalions' casualties to be buried at St. Vaast Post, as the 38th Division was due to move to another sector of the line soon.

On 1 March 1916 the battalion began their move to their new sector, with companies spaced at regular intervals, as laid down by the Field Service Regulations, via a route through La Couture, Locon and La Pannerie. Battalion headquarters set up on the La Bassee Canal, south of the 'Nursery Sector'.

A pleasant few days were spent at La Pannerie, cleaning kit and bathing, and the Commanding Officer of 114 Brigade, Brigadier-General Thomas O Marden, CB, CMG, DSO inspected the battalion. Marden was a regular officer who had served with the Welsh during the Boer War.

He had commanded the 1st Welsh at the outbreak of the Great War, and as the army expanded, Marden had gained promotion to command 114 Brigade of the new 38th (Welsh) Division. His recruitment to the 38th Division had added some much needed 'Regular Army' experience to the juvenile division.

On 5 March 1916 Lieutenant-Colonel Parkinson and the Company Commanders visited the new section of front line which the battalion was set to take over, and Major Cox, Lieutenant Williams and Lieutenant Morris attended a demonstration of the use of the new flame throwers and rockets. Flame throwers had been used by the Germans at Ypres, where they annihilated the British defenders at Hooge on 30 July 1915.

Brigadier-General Thomas O Marden.

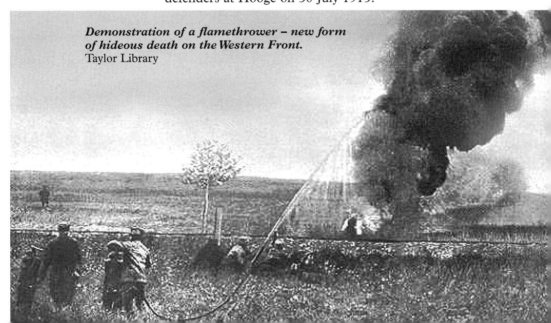

Demonstration of a flamethrower – new form of hideous death on the Western Front.
Taylor Library

At 09.00 hrs on 8 March 1916, the battalion machine gunners left for the front line, and the remainder of the battalion moved out at 10.00 hrs, relieving the 16th Royal Welsh Fusiliers of 113 Brigade at Grenadier Street. After a successful relief, the men of the 15th Welsh settled down for a deserved nights sleep. They were rudely awoken by a terrifying noise on the following morning of 9 March, when a German mine was blown opposite 'I' Sap and the Germans launched a heavy trench mortar and artillery attack on the Welsh positions.

The La Bassee Sector Author's collection

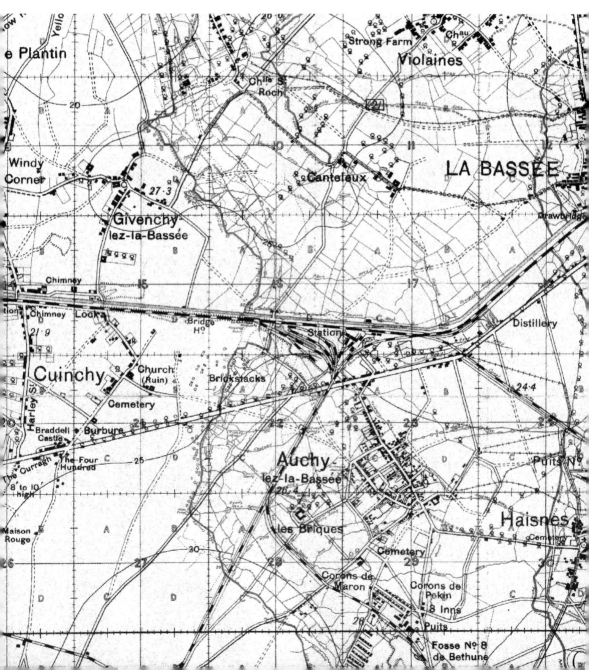

This was the battalion's heaviest losses in a single day so far, with seven men killed and fifteen wounded and evacuated for treatment. The seven fatalities were all buried at Guards Cemetery, Windy Corner, Cuinchy.

One of these casualties was Private Nathaniel Davies, the son of Mr and Mrs Edward Davies, of 2, Market Street, Lampeter.

Lampeter is a large market town on the road from Carmarthen to Aberystwyth, and lies about three miles north of the Carmarthenshire border in Ceredigion. Nathaniel had enlisted at Ammanford into the Battalion, and was just nineteen years old when he died.

Lampeter had a long affiliation to the Pembroke Yeomanry, and many men from the town served in their ranks, but Nathaniel was one of two men of Lampeter to die in the service of the 15th Welsh.

Another of the dead men was Private John Henry Dodd, the second son of George Robert and Alice Dodd of 29, Back Turton Street, Bolton. John had been born on 27 April 1897 and had attended Folds Road Council School at Bolton.

Private Nathaniel Davies

He had volunteered and enlisted into the 15th Welsh on 9 November 1914 along with his brother Thomas, and the boys had consecutive service numbers of 19908 and 19909. Thomas survived the war, but was transferred to the Royal Engineers after the death of his brother.

Also killed was the twenty-two year old Private Arnold Cecil Ewart Lewis. Arnold was the son of Benjamin and Elizabeth Lewis, of Pontycymmer, a mining town in the Garw Valley in Glamorgan. Benjamin and Elizabeth were both from Saundersfoot, and had moved to Pontycymmer looking for work, which is where Arnold was born.

Sadly, when Arnold was just six years old his parents died from tuberculosis, and so Arnold and his sister Elizabeth went to live with their Uncle and Aunt Bill and Ann Frost, at Stammers, in Saundersfoot. Bill was a carpenter, and was a local celebrity, having built his own wooden and canvas aeroplane in 1894; at least seven years before the Wright Brothers flew their own aircraft.

According to an article in the *Tenby and County News* of 9 October 1895, it was reported that 'Mr

Pioneer of flight, Bill Frost.

The grave of John Henry Dodd, with his photo inset.
Author

55

William Frost, Saundersfoot, has obtained provisional protection for a new flying machine, invented by him, and is supplying designs to secure a patent.'

Local legend has it that Bill did indeed fly his invention for at least ten seconds at some time in 1894, and so today Bill Frost is regarded in many circles as the first man to have ever flown an aeroplane.

Arnold grew up in Saundersfoot with his pioneering Uncle, doubtless being party to his work, and lived there until enlisting at Bridgend into the 15th Welsh. Just after enlisting, Arnold arrived in Camp at Rhyl. From here he had sent a short note to his Aunt and Uncle at Saundersfoot:

> *To Dear Aunty.*
>
> *Just a line to say I received your parcel this week. I expected to hear some news but was disappointed. I have been very bad since I come back from Saundersfoot so that is a sure thing the place do not agree with me. Hope you are in the best of health like myself at present. No more news to tell you so now I will close with best love to Uncle and accept the same,*
>
> *From Arnold.*

Arnold is buried alongside his fallen colleagues at Guards Cemetery, Windy Corner, Cuinchy. His war medals, the 1914/15 Star, British War and Victory Medal were posted to his sister after the end of the war, and are still proudly held in the family today. Arnold Cecil Ewart Lewis is commemorated on the Saundersfoot War Memorial, outside St. Issell's Church.

That wasn't the last action of the day however, as at 07.30 hrs another mine was blown between 'K' and 'T' Sap, and a larger mine blown at 13.30 hrs at Duck's Bill. No further casualties were inflicted on the battalion with these further explosions however, and the rest of the day passed quietly after the solemn burial of their seven comrades.

Arnold Cecil Ewart Lewis
David Harries

The battalion was relieved by the 14th Welsh on 12 March 1916, and relieved in turn the 13th Welsh in brigade support, taking over Givenchy Keep, Moat and Redoubt, Hilders and Le Plantin South. The war diary stated that it was very quiet the following day, but it still saw the death of another Private, Thomas Eynon of Hundleton in Pembrokeshire. Thomas had been born at Cosheston, and had worked prior to the war as a coachman at nearby Pembroke. He was thirty-nine years old.

On 16 March, the battalion moved back into the front line, relieving the 14th Welsh. The relief went smoothly, but the following day saw three men killed by German sniper fire, all three of whom were buried at Guards Cemetery, Windy Corner, Cuinchy.

The following day saw Private George Evans of Treherbert die of wounds at Bethune French Hospital. He was buried at Bethune Town Cemetery, and was the twenty-seventh casualty of the Battalion thus far in the war.

Jim John, a machine-gunner, took the chance to write home to his mother in Haverfordwest:

> The machine gun I am attached to has recently been in an emplacement we call a "dead end" so styled because it projects from our main line of trenches towards the enemy's for about 40 yards. We are on the extreme end and are therefore liable to be surrounded and cut off from our main line unless we keep our eyes very wide open indeed, which I assure you we generally manage to do as we have no particular fancy to fall into their hands and don't intend to (alive). Fritz is very anxious to know what we have there and he comes creeping up to explore. We are only 75 yards apart and sometimes at night when on sentry we get some lively times. One night about mid-night it was my turn. The night was exceptionally dark and wet and I fancied I heard someone tampering with our barbed wire in front. I could not fire at the moment as I had just before had the order passed along that some of our men were out so all I could do was to listen, with fixed bayonet.

> Its not very pleasant standing on a "dead end" in the dead of night in inky darkness with two or three of the enemy creeping about only a few yards away while all the time ones eyes keep playing fanciful tricks and magnifying two or three into twenty, and all you are allowed to do is to watch and wait. And wait for what? Perhaps to be the target for a couple of deadly bombs. Personally I much prefer a good charge. Well I waited and listened for about an hour, but it seemed endless. Then the "flying sentry" as he is called came along and whispered "all patrols and working parties in". I almost jumped for joy. And then the machine gun spoke, and I more than repaid Fritz for all the agony of suspense I had endured and we had no more trouble that night. This is the kind of thing that plays havoc with ones nerves....

> There is the usual daily routine, unless there is some extraordinary on the slate. Snipers watch from dawn until dusk for targets. Trench mortars, rifle and hand grenades, shells of all descriptions and sizes, come at intervals.

> At night, machine gun fire sweeps the parapets, communication trenches, roads near firing lines etc. Bombarding is in the daily routine and nightly. You see the flash of guns, hear the report, and then wait for

the explosion; thoughts run riots in your brain; a flash, boom, and a crunch, and one, three, or perhaps twenty human beings, are gone to the skies.

A machine gun catches a working party; a star shell goes up, a rattle of death dealing lead: shrieks, curses, moans, and then silence. A solitary sniper haps- a crack, thud and groan, another poor devil bites the dust. The cry runs along "stretcher bearers". Such is the daily routine of trench warfare, yet "There is nothing to report on the Western Front." Some poor mothers, wife's, sweethearts, or sisters heart is broken. The news comes so and so "Killed in action", still there is "nothing to report on the Western Front".

While the battalion was enduring another spell in the trenches, yet another Private died of wounds. Private Robert 'Bob' Balderson was another of the Bolton men who had joined the battalion in 1914.

Bob was only sixteen years old, barely old enough to hold a rifle, but he lies in a soldiers grave at St. Venant Communal Cemetery, on which his name is wrongly spelt. He was the Son of Joseph and Hannah Balderson, of 18, Lenora Street, Deane, Bolton, and he was to be the youngest casualty suffered by the 15th Welsh during the course of the war. On his grave is inscribed the simple verse 'For God Took Him'.

By 20 March 1916 the battalion was again relieved by the 14th Welsh, and moved to billets at Gorre, where the men enjoyed a well deserved bath and clean up before marching to Les Harisoirs on the morning of 23 March, where cleaning of clothes and equipment became the priority, due to the terrible state of the men.

The grave of Robert 'Bob' Balderson in St. Venant Communal Cemetery with mis-spelt name.

A further two men died during this spell. On 20 March, Private William Foley of Cardiff and Sergeant Eli Mumford of Rhondda died. Both are buried at Guards Cemetery, Windy Corner, and both men are listed purely as 'Died', which could really mean anything. Nothing is mentioned of their deaths in the war diary for the day. One of the Carmarthen men, Private William Howells from Kidwelly, died of wounds on 21 March at Bethune Hospital. He is buried at Bethune Town Cemetery.

After a relaxing days rest at Les Harisoirs, working parties were sent out on 25 March to Le Touret and Loisne defences. The following day saw the battalion treated to baths at Locon, before witnessing a flamethrower demonstration, which must have struck fear into the hearts of the young soldiers, after hearing of the destruction caused by these terrible weapons at Ypres the preceding year, when horrific casualties were suffered by the men of the 20th (Light) Division stationed near Hooge.

On 30 March 1916 the battalion was inspected by the General

Officer Commanding First Army, and returned to the line on the following morning, first taking up reserve trenches at Rue L'Epinette, and then moving to the front at La Quinque Rue.

Just two days later, the 15th Welsh relieved the 16th Royal Welsh Fusiliers at Festubert, in the line running from Grenadier Road to La Quinque Rue. The Germans shelled the trenches during the relief, but no casualties were suffered. The following morning saw another artillery attack on the battalion lines. After it had calmed down, half of the battalion was put on wiring duties in the front.

No casualties occurred during this short tour of duty, and the battalion was relieved by the 14th Welsh on 5 April 1916, and moved into reserve at Le Touret, where the men enjoyed another spell in the bath house, and two days of relative peace before moving back to the front on 9 April, relieving the 14th Welsh, who moved into reserve.

The month of April 1916 passed by quietly enough for the 15th Welsh. They were relieved on 13 April by the 14th Welsh, and moved into support at Festubert, before marching to billets at La Gorgue on 18 April. Rest days on the Western Front were not easy however, and the battalion constantly supplied men to working parties while out of the

Welsh Regiment soldiers at rest during a march to the front.

line, and the remaining hours were spent training.

Life was already pretty miserable for the troops, as an extract from a letter sent home reads:

We are having plenty of rain here, we should be living in boats. Every man has his kennel, we are living like rats in a hole, it is worse than being in clink. I have lost my cooking things. I only wish the war was at an end, but we will be here another 12 months. I would like a decent drink.

The 38th Division had been on the Western Front just five months, and morale was already low.

The 15th Welsh returned to the line on 24 April 1916, taking over the line from Erith Street to Lonely Trench. Apart from the odd German shell flying over, the line had quietened down, and after an uneventful few days the battalion was relieved again on 28 April, moving into reserve at Pont Du Hem. Three men were wounded by shell splinters before the battalions' relief, and another fell onto his bayonet. The wounded were evacuated to Merville Hospital.

On 1 May 1916 the battalion was at bombing practise, when Lieutenant Evans and three men were accidentally wounded. This was a regular occurrence at the time, with many a man wounded due to faulty grenades, careless handling or just plain mistakes.

The following day the battalion moved back into the front line at Rue Tilleloy, and two more men were wounded that afternoon by stray bullets.

Another Bolton man died of his wounds on 3 May. Private Joseph Ramsden was only seventeen years old, and was the son of Mr and Mrs J Ramsden of 7 St. Joseph Street, Bolton. He is buried at Merville Communal Cemetery. The twenty-two year old Private Charles Thickens of Miskin died three days later on 6 May, and was also buried at Merville. These two men were possibly the casualties of the stray bullets.

The Germans were very quiet now. A burst of fire by the Welsh towards the German trenches on 4 May drew no response, but this lack of response was welcomed.

On 5 May, three men were wounded by German shells, and the following day the battalion was relieved, sending 260 men to supply working parties behind the lines again with the Royal Engineers.

The morning of 9 May 1916 saw the 14th Welsh under heavy attack. Two platoons of the 15th Welsh were sent up in support, and the Germans were forced to withdraw.

Sadly Private David Reginald Morgan from Llanelli was killed during

the desperate fighting. He was just nineteen years old, and was the son of Daniel and Eliza Ann Morgan of 4, Woodend Road, Llanelli.

That same morning saw the remainder of the 15th Welsh march out to Robermetz, near Merville into brigade reserve. The two other companies rejoined them there at 22.00 hrs, and the men settled down for a good nights sleep, remaining here for the next few days, in relative peace and comfort in a local barn.

On 18 May 1916 the men returned to their support billets at nearby Laventie. Three days later they relieved the 16th Welsh, and that night drove off a German patrol that was attempting to cut the barbed wire belt in front of their section of the line. The battalion captured a German torpedo from a party of Germans who had tried to lay it in the barbed wire defences, but quickly returned to the safety of their own lines when faced by a hail of accurately aimed British .303 bullets.

This was a similar weapon to the well known 'Bangalore Torpedo', a steel tube filled with explosives and fitted with a delayed fuse, which was used to cut a path through the maze of barbed wire in front of the trenches which would then allow for the German infantry to cross the wire and attempt the capture of a section of the British line.

This latest stint in the trenches passed reasonably quietly for the battalion, and on 25 May they were relieved again by the 14th Welsh. One man was killed before the relief, Private Andrew Ward of Farnworth, Lancashire. Andrew was the son of Andrew and Elizabeth Ward, of 32, Princess Street, Wigan. He was also a married man with two children, and prior to enlisting into the 15th Welsh was a wageman at Brackley Pit, living with his wife and two young children at 76, Leach Street, Farnworth. Andrew was attached to a wiring party when he was shot by a sniper and killed. His body was carried back to Laventie, where he was solemnly buried by his comrades at the Royal Irish Rifles Graveyard.

Private Andrew Ward.

The Battalion remained at Laventie in reserve for the next three days, providing Working Parties for the Royal Engineers. A shell struck one of these working parties on 29 May, wounding two men, one of whom, Sergeant Thomas Harris of Gelli in the Rhondda, was evacuated to the Hospital at Merville where he died of his wounds on 1 June 1916.

In the meantime, the 15th Welsh moved back into the front line on 29 May, and were hit that night by a shower of German rifle grenades. Life was hard, but there were moments of merriment at times, as can be seen in this extract of a letter sent home:

> *One night a Saxon shouted across,*
>
> *"Is there anyone from Swansea?"*
> *Tommy replies "yes"*

Saxon: "I used to work in the smelting works"

Tommy "Hmm – warm place?

Saxon "yes"

Tommy: "show yer face, see if I knows yer and I will send you to a f*****g slightly warmer one"

Again on 1 June 1916 another batch of German grenades flew into the Welshmen's trenches, killing Lance Corporal Thomas Thomas of Port Talbot. He is buried at the Royal Irish Rifles Graveyard, Laventie, and became the last man of the battalion to lose his life in French Flanders – during this spell at least.

Wounded during these last few days in the line in Flanders was 2nd Lieutenant Frank Roberts of Llanelli. He was evacuated from the line, and sent to No. 20 Base Hospital at Etaples, where he underwent several operations to remove shrapnel fragments from his body. In his first letter home to his parents at Llanelli, Frank wrote:

No. 20 General Hospital,

BEF

My Dear Mam and Dad,

Don't be alarmed. Its nothing serious. I'd have written before only I have not had the opportunity. A Chaplain promised to write the day before yesterday, so I expect you know all about it.

Since it happened I've been miles on a stretcher, had about 5 motor rides and one train journey of about 12 hours. So you see, since I have about 9 pieces of bomb distributed over different parts of my anatomy I couldn't very well write.

It was an unfortunate affair altogether. I had been out patrolling for an hour and a half. We couldn't see 10 yards in front of us owing to shell smoke and fog. Things had been a bit busy – as a result one of our listening posts got a bit nervy and bombed us as we were coming back without challenging.

Well, the first one hit me before it exploded and gave us warning and so I escaped with my life by turning my back on it. I thought I was done for, I can tell you - but I managed to crawl into the trench and find it was one of ours and then got assistance.

They disturbed me halfway through this to put me under the X-Ray. I had five photos taken.

I'm pretty comfortable now and am getting all the attention necessary in a hospital so don't worry – Cheerio! Yours Lovingly Frank

P.S. Sorry my leave is knocked on the head but still I should get home sometime now. Tata, Love to All Frank.

Frank survived his treatment, and wrote a short series of graphic letters

Lieutenant Frank Roberts.

home detailing his time at hospital. He was transferred to the 2nd Southern General Hospital, Maudlin Street, Bristol, King's Side Ward, where he recovered fully, and spent a short spell at home in Llanelli, before returning to the battalion later in the war, gaining promotion to Captain, and being awarded the Military Cross.

On 2 June 1916, the battalion was again relieved by the 14th Welsh, and moved to brigade reserve. While the 15th Welsh was in reserve, one company of the 14th Welsh raided the German lines to try and gain some intelligence. As a reprisal, the German artillery opened up a storm of high explosive shellfire on the Welshmen's trenches, which overshot the front line, with the result that the reserve line was hit and two men

A typical view across No Man's Land from the British trenches. The lip of a mine crater which has been fortified by the Germans can be seen about 300 yards away.

of the 15th Welsh were wounded as a result. The battalion was then relieved from reserve on 5 June by the 16th Welsh, and moved into divisional reserve at Robermetz, with two companies being sent on a 'special training course' in trench raiding.

Little did the men of the 38th (Welsh) Division know, but their days in the relatively peaceful French Flanders were rapidly drawing to a close as the British built up their forces on the Somme in preparation for their great offensive.

It was a desperate stage in the war. The French forces at Verdun had been hammered for months, and lived in a field of corpses. The situation was so bad that the French Army was close to mutiny, and as a result,

Sir Douglas Haig had been put under heavy pressure to try and draw German attention away from Verdun.

The answer was to open up a large scale offensive by the British, and the ideal place was in the, up until then, relatively peaceful Somme sector. The lines had been almost stagnant on the Somme since the British had taken over from the French, and in the ensuing tranquillity the Germans had created a complex defensive system, comprising of hundreds of fortified dugouts, bunkers and redoubts.

By the middle of June 1916 the entire 38th (Welsh) Division pulled from their positions in Flanders, and begin the move south to the Somme. On the morning of 12 June 1916, the men of the 15th Welsh marched to Le Pierriere, near Busnes. They were slowly marching to the Somme sector, where their lives were to change forever. After a much deserved nights sleep, they marched to Cauchy la Tour the following day. On 14 June the men marched to Bethencourt, a small village near Savy. For ten days the division remained there, and trained hard for the forthcoming offensive.

It was here, on 15 June 1916 that the 38th (Welsh) Division joined the XVII Corps in the Third Army, and began training following a strictly laid down programme, which GHQ had issued. The troops were being trained in what was at the time thought of as revolutionary tactics.

The 38th Division was to be trained in the techniques of attacking on a large scale against the German trench lines, and in following through the attack once the lines had been broken.

From 16 June onwards the troops of the division were busied digging a system of trenches to train in. The constituent platoons and companies practised attacking over open ground in waves, with successive waves coming through them once the first had checked their attack, and the whole regime worked in conjunction with the assorted support arms; artillery, machine gun companies, the service branches of signals, engineers and intelligence, and the Royal Flying Corps.

On 26 June 1916 the battalion marched twenty miles to Barly, a small village sat on the main road from Arras to Doullens. Here they bivouacked for the night, in continuous rain. Over the next few days the 38th Division marched ever closer to their objective of Heilly, in the luscious green Somme Valley.

During May 1916 the 38th Casualty Clearing Station had set up camp at Heilly, preparatory to the coming Somme Offensive, and the predicted heavy casualties. This was to be the main dressing station for the forthcoming Battle of Mametz Wood, and many of the men now camped peacefully here were to see this place again, but in rather more unpleasant circumstances.

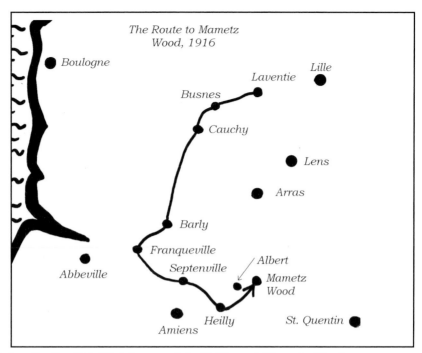

The Route to Mametz
Wood, 1916

The route taken by the 38th Division south to Heilly and Mametz Wood.

Sophia John

A British battalion marches on its way to take up position on the Somme.

Taylor Library

Slowly marching southwards, The 15th Welsh arrived at Franqueville by 27 June, and then the following day marched on to Septenville. Here the 15th Welsh were when the awesome artillery barrage that marked the opening of the first attacks of the Battle of the Somme opened up, over the night of 30 June/ 1 July 1916.

The terrible sound of thousands of artillery pieces of varying calibre was noted in the diaries and letters home of several of the men, and must have struck fear into the hearts of even the bravest soul.

On the following morning, the day of 1 July 1916, deafened by the almost constant roar of artillery, and the sound of gunfire from the front, the Division marched on to Herrisart.

The first Somme Casualty for the 15th Welsh occurred on 1 July 1916, during this march toward the Somme Battlefields. Private Thomas Jones, a farm worker from Talybont, near Aberystwyth, was listed as killed in action somehow that day.

There is no mention of a death in the war diary, but records show that he was killed in action, and so it was possibly as the result of a long range shell burst. His grave was lost during the course of the war, or possibly even as a result of the possible explosion that killed him, and Thomas is commemorated on the Thiepval Memorial. He is in fact the earliest casualty of the battalion to be commemorated on the Thiepval Memorial, but many more of his friends were to join him, their names engraved into the Portland stone panels that adorn the pillars of this vast memorial.

Early in the morning of 3 July the men marched on to Franvillers, reaching Heilly in the Somme Valley on 4 July 1916, at 09.15 hrs. This was then, and is today, a beautiful and tranquil part of France, and the men set up camp here overnight alongside their medical counterparts, near to the railway line at the bottom of the valley.

Dawn along an unspoilt valley behind the British front line on the Somme, 1 July 1916. Taylor Library

Chapter 3

The Somme – Mametz Wood

THE BATTLE OF THE SOMME had opened at 07.30 hrs on the morning of 1 July 1916, with the explosion of a series of massive underground mines, the chief ones in positions at Beaumont Hamel and at La-Boiselle. The massive craters thrown open by these mines are still highly visible today. From positions stretching eighteen miles, from Hebuterne in the north to Maricourt, south-east of Albert, the British Third and Fourth Armies went over the top, and began their slow march across No Mans Land to destruction.

By the end of the day almost 60,000 casualties had been incurred by

On 1 July 1916 the British and French walked across No Man's Land into a hail of death.

Taylor Library

the British, with almost no gains. The German defenders had not been wiped out as planned. They had sheltered safely in deep underground bunkers during the artillery bombardment, and had rushed to the surface and taken up their posts as soon as the barrage had finished. The British and Commonwealth troops had walked into a hail of red-hot lead. It was slaughter on a scale never seen before or since.

One of the rare successes of that first day was south-east of Albert, where the 7th Division, containing the 1st Battalion, Royal Welsh Fusiliers, had advanced, and had captured the villages of Fricourt and Mametz. This resulted in the staging positions for the next phase of the offensive on this sector of the battlefield being attained.

On 3 July the 38th (Welsh) Division had joined XV Corps, and had moved into XV Corps reserve while at Heilly. They left the beautiful greenery of Heilly behind at 14.30 hrs on 5 July 1916 and marched on to Albert, through the ancient market square and filed past the ruins of the famed Basilica, with it's 'Golden Madonna' hanging precariously from its spire. Through Albert along the Roman Road towards Bapaume they marched that day, reaching the original front line of 1 July at Ovillers-La Boiselle, where they marched down the road toward Contalmaison, over the scorched and battered battlefield of the previous day's fighting.

During that night 5 July 1916 the 38th Division took over the front from Bottom Wood to Caterpillar Wood from the 7th Division, and the 15th Welsh, in reserve, bivouacked for the night on the road between La Boiselle and Contalmaison, in trench map reference F15a.

View across the battlefield near Contalmaison
Courtesy Library and Archives Canada/PA-000198

The sound of the terrible fighting, and the continuous shellfire which echoed around the area of the battlefield must have been terrifying for the men. They had taken part in trench warfare, but the trials facing them now where to be totally different from what anyone in the battalion, most probably within the whole division, had ever faced in their lives. The ground they were now treading had just recently been taken, with huge loss of life, and the bodies of men of both sides lay scattered over the ground.

Slowly the front had been pushed north from the villages of Mametz and Fricourt, and by the end of 5 July, while the men of the 15th Welsh were asleep; XV Corps had taken Bottom Wood and White Trench, just south of Mametz Wood. During the coming days the positions here were strengthened, ready for the next phase of the offensive. This phase, the task set for the 38th Division, was to be the capture of Mametz Wood.

The 15th Welsh bivouacked on the road from La Boisselle to Contal maison in square 15 on the night of 5 July 1916.

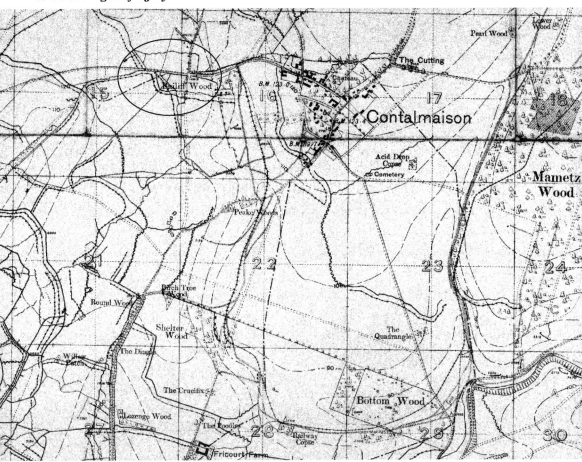

A camp of the 2nd Royal Welsh Fusiliers on the somme, July 1916.
Courtesy of the Royal Welch Fusiliers Regimental Museum. ID 7003g

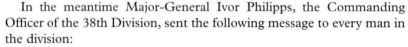

The site where the 15th Welsh camped for the night of 5 July 1916. Bailiff Wood is in the distance.

It was well known that wood fighting was a specialised and dangerous task, but how deadly it was had yet to be discovered.

In the meantime Major-General Ivor Philipps, the Commanding Officer of the 38th Division, sent the following message to every man in the division:

> *You have worked hard for many months with an energy and zeal beyond praise to fit yourself for the task you have voluntarily undertaken. You have forgone the hardships of a winter campaign with fortitude. You have earned the praise of your corps commanders for your courage, discipline and devotion to duty. You have now held for six months a section of the British line in France, during which time you have not allowed one of the enemy to enter your trenches except as a prisoner, and on several occasions you have entered the enemy's lines. Eleven officers and 44 NCOs' and men have already received awards from the King for gallant and distinguished conduct in the field. Your*

fellow countrymen at home are following your career with interest and admiration. I always believed that a really Welsh Division would be second to none. You have more than justified that belief. I feel that whatever the future may have in store for us I can rely upon you, because you have already given ample proof of your worth. During the short period in the training area you worked hard to qualify yourselves for still further efforts. I thank you most sincerely for the loyal and wholehearted way in which you have all supported me and for the way in which each of you has done his utmost to carry out the task allotted to him. With such a spirit animating all ranks we can one and all look forward with confidence to the future, whatever it may have in store for us. You are today relieving the 7th Division, which has attacked and captured German trenches on a front of little less than one mile and for a depth of about one and a quarter miles. In this attack the village of Mametz was captured, the enemy have suffered very heavy casualties, 1,500 German officers and men were taken prisoner and six field guns were captured.

The 1st Battalion, Royal Welsh Fusiliers and the 1st Battalion, Welsh Regiment of the 7th Division have both distinguished themselves in this attack, and I am confident that the young battalions of the famous Welsh regiments serving in the 38th (Welsh) Division will maintain the high standard for valour which all three Welsh regiments have been renowned throughout the war.

On 6 July 1916, Officers of the 15th Welsh first visited the ground in front of Mametz Wood. They spent the next few days exploring the ground, and preparing for the planned assault on the wood. Mametz Wood was, and still is, the largest wood on the Somme, covering an area of over 200 acres with a maximum length of about a mile. It is situated on a low spur of the Bazentin Ridge and is overlooked by the valley which separated the two forces in the early days of July 1916.

Due to its situation at the opposite side of the valley, any attack made by the British forces would be initially downhill from their starting positions, then down a steep chalk bank ranging from thirty to fifty feet in height, and uphill across 'Death Valley' to make contact with the enemy in the wood itself. The Germans were also able to bring flanking fire to bear on any approach to the wood from Flatiron and Sabot Copses to the east. Also the German second line was 300 yards beyond the northern edge of the wood and therefore it could be reinforced easily, since much of the movement would go unobserved through the cover of the wood.

To the left was the area held by the 17th Division. To the right was the 18th Division, spread from Caterpillar Wood eastwards. The capture of Mametz Wood was to be the responsibility of the 38th Division, though support from the 17th Division on its left flank was essential. Facing the Welshmen was the Lehr Regiment of the Prussian Guard holding the line from Mametz Wood to Flatiron Copse.

The task facing them was indeed immense. The Lehr Regiment was an elite unit, having seen action on the Eastern Front against the Russian Tsarist forces. They were concealed within the fringes of an unkempt, overgrown wood, which offered the benefits of a good defensive position with minimum effort. The wood itself was split by several overgrown pathways, or 'rides', which bisected the wood both north-south and east-west, and the tangled mass of trees and undergrowth

A trench sign displayed at the Imperial War Museum.

View towards Mametz. Courtesy Library and Archives Canada/PA-000440

eliminated any real need for trenches and fortifications, as machine-gun crews and snipers were easily hidden behind fallen trees and bushes.

If the Welshmen were to be able to successfully cross the open ground between themselves and the outskirt of the wood, any fighting that would then take place would be of a brutal, almost medieval hand-to-hand nature, with bayonet, knife or trench club. The scene was set for a brutal encounter, which the survivors of neither side would ever forget. Unknown though to the British, the outlook was also bleak on the side of the German defenders. An excerpt from the diary of a German officer captured at Mametz Wood on 13 July 1916 read:

> The troops who had so far held the lines south of Mametz and south of Montauban (Prussians, among them Regiment No...) had sustained severe losses from the intense enemy bombardment, which had been maintained for several days without a pause, and for the most part were already shot to pieces.

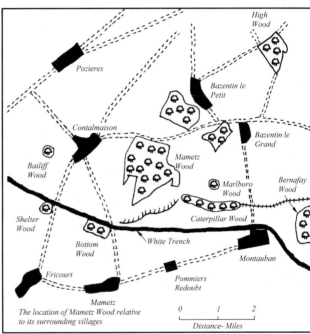

The location of Mametz Wood relative to its surrounding villages

Sketch map of the sector concerning the 38th (Welsh) Division. This tiny portion of the Somme battlefront was to cost countless lives during July 1916. The Welshman approached Mametz Wood by way of a track from La Boiselle, which is just off the map to the left. They marched to Contalmaison, then south to attack the wood from positions north of Pommiers Redoubt.

75

The plan for the attack of 7 July was that the 17th Division would attack Acid Drop Copse on the left flank of the wood and act as support for the 38th Division whose task was to attack the Hammerhead on the right. Both divisions were to advance to the central ride and then turn north to sweep through the wood. In the 38th Division the responsibility for the attack was to rest on the shoulders of Brigadier-General Evans and his 115 Brigade.

Evans had surveyed the ground, and had decided to attack with two battalions squeezed into a single battalion frontage, with one spearheading the attack and one immediately following to the rear. A third battalion was to be in support at Caterpillar Wood and the fourth in Reserve.

However Evans' plans were not met with approval at XV Corps headquarters. They told him to assemble no more than two battalions at the western end of Caterpillar Wood, as any more would cause overcrowding, and increase the risk of casualties from German artillery. The third battalion should be in support at

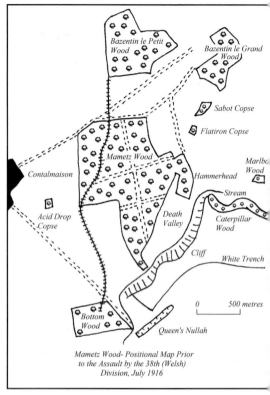

Mametz Wood- Positional Map Prior to the Assault by the 38th (Welsh) Division, July 1916

Mametz Wood. Positional map prior to the assault by the 38th (Welsh) Division, July 1916.

Montauban, and the fourth further back. This compromised his plans somewhat, but Brigadier-General Evans had no choice but to comply.

His revised plan put the 11th South Wales Borderers on the left, near Caterpillar Wood, and the 16th Welsh on the right, on the ridge above the valley. The 10th South Wales Borderers were in reserve at Montauban Alley. Each battalion would have no more than a 250 yard frontage for the attack. It was also planned that the problem of flanking fire from the Germans was to be eased by the use of a smoke screen, which would cover the attack.

On the night prior to the attack it rained heavily, and movement became very difficult in the resulting mud. The attack was planned for 08.30 hrs on the morning of 7 July and 115 Brigade went into the attack as planned, although the planned smoke screen did not appear. The 11th South Wales Borderers and 16th Welsh rose to their task as soon as

Mametz Wood
The Hammerhead

Flatiron Copse

Caterpillar Valley

Present-day view looking up 'Death Valley' towards Caterpillar Valley, the ground crossed by the 38th (Welsh) Division in the assault on the wood.

the artillery stopped and immediately came under fire from the German machine guns in Flatiron and Sabot Copses. As a consequence, the casualties mounted and the attack died out some 250 yards short of the wood.

By 10.00 hrs the situation had deteriorated as the Germans increased shell and machine gun fire across the approaches to the wood. The 10th South Wales Borderers were ordered up in support but did not reach the battle area until after noon. Artillery support was offered but actually fell on the men of the 16th Welsh as they tried to push home the attack. The arrival of the 10th South Wales Borderers did help a little in the afternoon but their Commanding Officer, Lieutenant-Colonel Wilkinson, was killed in Caterpillar Wood as he brought his men forward. Gradually the attack faltered.

Brigadier-General Evans received another order telling him that an attack was to be carried out at 17.00 hrs when the wood was to be entered at all costs. He reported the gravity of the situation to Divisional Headquarters and they in turn reported to Corps Headquarters who ordered a withdrawal to allow reorganisation.

The attack by the 17th Division also failed, and so the co-ordinated effort also failed. It had cost 400 casualties in the three battalions engaged, and nothing at all had been achieved as these battle weary units were withdrawn to lick their wounds and count the cost. General Haig was unimpressed by the performance of the division. At the end of the day Lieutenant-General Horne of XV Corps informed Haig that he was not happy with the conduct of General Philipps of the 38th Division who was removed from command on 9 July 1916. This was probably not helped by the fact that Philipps was a close friend and confidant of Haig's nemesis, David Lloyd George, who had in fact negotiated his command of the 38th Division as a result of alleged family and political ties. Ivor Philipps didn't fade away though. After a successful business career in the City, he retired to the family seat at Cosheston, from where he supervised the restoration of the mighty Pembroke Castle. He died in August 1940.

However, the attack was to carry on. A plan for an attack on 9 July 1916 had been worked out by the 38th Divisional staff. The unused brigades, 113 and 114, were to be used. The whole of 114 Brigade, including the Carmarthen Pals, were to provide the main attack on the central ride while 113 Brigade were to capture Strip Trench. This plan was cancelled when Philipps was replaced and nothing of significance happened that day except for the command of the division passing to Major-General Watts. An unsupported attack by the 17th Division on 9 July was completely unsuccessful.

The following day it was to be the turn of the 38th Division again. Major-General Watts had taken over command of the division in the afternoon of 9 July 1916 and immediately set about organising an attack on the wood. The attack was essentially the same as that which had been worked out by Philipps the day before, but Watts placed importance on the equal status of the two brigades to be engaged, 113 and 114. The artillery plan, however, was changed, and contained two novel features:

The first was that the initial barrage was to lift off the main German trenches to their rear, as if an infantry attack was to commence, and then to resume on them after a few minutes, to catch the Germans as they emerged from their dugouts. This approach had been used successfully by the French further south, and was an innovation for the British. Secondly, the use of a creeping barrage to accompany the attack was also planned. This was a timed lift of the artillery, keeping a screen of shellfire ahead of the advancing troops.

That apart, there was no complexity to the attack and the plan was simply relying on the weight of numbers to overpower the German defenders. In this area it has been estimated that the Germans were outnumbered by as much as three to one and so the weight of numbers argument looked sensible. However, these figures took no account of the fact that the Germans were fighting from prepared defences and had numerous machine guns in supporting positions about the wood and, in general, had better trained and experienced men in the front line who had been on the Western Front for almost a year longer than the men of the 38th Division, who had limited trench experience.

However, the plan for the attack went ahead:

The 14th Welsh and the 13th Welsh of 114 Brigade were to attack from the right.

The 16th Royal Welsh Fusiliers of 113 Brigade to be leading the assault, and the 14th Royal Welsh Fusiliers of the same was to be close behind on the left.

The 15th Welsh was in reserve at Triangle; supplying work parties which carried Royal Engineers material, as well as being tasked with moving supplies to the front line, and bringing German prisoners back with them as and when required.

At 03.30 hrs on 10 July 1916 the artillery barrage opened up, followed twenty minutes later by the planned smoke screen which drifted from Strip Trench towards the north-east. Just after 04.00 hrs 114 Brigade started to move, as they were further from the wood than 113 Brigade. This created confusion in 113 Brigade area but Lieutenant-Colonel Carden, of the 16th Royal Welsh Fusiliers, sorted this out in short order and the attack was carried out with 'perfect steadiness'. In the time this took to sort out, the 16th Royal Welsh Fusiliers lost some of the cover offered by the creeping

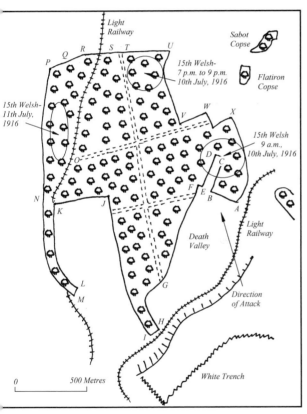

Mametz Wood. 15th Welsh positions 10th-11th July, 1916.

artillery fire and subsequently the battalion lost heavily in the advance to the wood. Amongst the casualties was Lieutenant-Colonel Ronald Carden himself. He had been wounded at the start of the attack but carried on right up to the edge of the wood where he was killed. He is buried at Carnoy Military Cemetery.

On the right the 13th Welsh came under fire from the German machine-gun posts placed in the Hammerhead. They suffered heavy casualties and were beaten back on two occasions but a third attempt was made and they managed to get a foot hold in the Wood. The 14th Welsh were attacking in the centre and were to some extent covered from enfilade fire by the flanking battalions and managed to reach the wood more or less as the artillery barrage was lifting from the edge. On the left the 14th Royal Welsh Fusiliers had suffered heavily as it attacked close behind the 16th Royal Welsh Fusiliers, and Brigadier Price-Davies committed the 15th and 13th Royal Welsh Fusiliers to the attack almost immediately so that they were then in close support to the battalions already engaged.

On the right the 10th Welsh were added to the attack, making a total of seven out of eight battalions of the two brigades engaged in action. The attack was a reasonable success with all the objectives being taken ahead of the schedule. It had not been without cost. Casualties had mounted throughout the first hour of the attack such that in the seven battalions that went into battle five of the commanding officers had been killed or seriously wounded. Added to this was the loss of many of the junior officers which resulted in the control of the thousands of men in the wood becoming increasingly difficult.

The Royal Welsh Fusiliers were held up at point 'J' by machine gun fire, and Price-Davies ordered the last two companies of the 13th Royal Welsh Fusiliers forward to assist in the situation.

To the right the Germans reinforced the Hammerhead, and this created havoc for a while amongst the attacking Welshmen. To ease this situation the 15th Welsh, the eighth battalion to be committed, was ordered from reserve at around 07.00 hrs to occupy the Hammerhead, and to be prepared to meet any German counter-attacks.

The Germans were skilled in the siting and operating of their heavy machine guns.

Major Percy Anthony led the Battalion into their positions, leaving 'A' Company behind in reserve, and set off to aid 13th Welsh at point D-X.

The 15th Welsh were met with heavy machine-gun fire, but reached the wood with few casualties, and pushed through the Hammerhead, establishing their positions on the eastern side. Major Anthony ordered two platoons of 'B' Company to establish contact with the 13th Welsh on their left. No contact could be made, so a further platoon from 'A' Company was sent forward under Major Phillips, to push to points V W X.

However, during this time the Germans had entered the northern edge of the Hammerhead at point X, bringing with them a machine-gun team, and another group of Germans had massed at Flat Iron Copse ready for a counter-attack.

The German machine-gunners separated the two platoons of B Company from the platoon of A Company, and annihilated them, leaving only four survivors, who were led out of the wood by Captain Bertie Lewis of Carmarthen. During this initial carnage, Major Percy Anthony fell dead, killed at around 08.00 hrs by a sniper. His death was a sad loss to the battalion.

Before the outbreak of the Great War Percy had given up military life, and was in Malaya, where he took up rubber planting. At the end of 1914 Percy returned to Britain, and was gazetted Captain in the 15th Welsh, fighting with them until his death at Mametz Wood. His grave was lost during the continued fighting in the area, and so he is today commemorated on the Thiepval Memorial to the missing.

Percy Anthony was born on 3 May 1880. He was educated at Dulwich School, where he played cricket for the School XI. The talented batsman played for Herefordshire after leaving school, and was invited to play first class cricket for both Surrey and Worcestershire. However, Percy decided on a military career, and was commissioned into the Army. The Boer War was raging in South Africa, and he served in South Africa attached to the 2nd Battalion, King's Shropshire Light Infantry.

One of the other ranks killed during the massacre in the Hammerhead was the young Private Harry Williams. Harry was one of the original Bolton enlistees, and was the son of James and Lettice Williams, of 28, Ormrod Street, Bolton. He had joined the 15th Welsh with a bunch of his friends from Bolton and had arrived in France with the Battalion in December 1915.

The survivors of the 15th Welsh pulled back to points D E where they consolidated. In the meantime, the 14th Welsh, under the command of Lieutenant-Colonel Hayes, had succeeded in capturing the central ride through the wood, though their right flank was held up since there was little by way of support.

The remaining company of 15th Welsh was sent in to aid 10th Welsh, who had lost a company that had been attached to 113 Brigade. At 10.30 hrs, 15th Welsh were at a line running from D E, but were hit by a strong German counter-attack, and driven back to D C, where Lieutenant J Evans rallied the men, organising a counter-attack which secured their positions [This earned Lieutenant Evans the Military Cross]. The attack then ground to a halt, and the next few hours were spent desperately clinging on to their precarious footholds in the wood.

Harry was twenty-three years old when he lost his life within the mayhem of Mametz Wood that day. Sadly, after the further fighting that took place in the wood over the coming days, his grave was lost forever, and Harry is today commemorated on the Thiepval Memorial. His memory has never been forgotten by his family, as his younger brother Albert, who was just thirteen years old when Harry went to war, idolised his older brother, and kept his memory alive within the family, who still visit the Mametz area today.

As a result, Lieutenant-Colonel Marden committed the reserves at his disposal to the attack. These were the 17th Royal Welsh Fusiliers, who went to support 113 Brigade on the left, and the 10th South Wales Borderers, who went to support 114 Brigade on the right of the attack. They arrived in the fighting by about 14.40 hrs adding fresh impetus to the attack, and the 10th South Wales Borderers soon reached a point to the north of the second cross ride and were able to get patrols out to the northern edge of the wood.

In the meantime, 114 Brigade was pushing further into the eastern half of the wood led by 14th Welsh. The undergrowth was so thick that progress was only possible in single file, and so 14th Welsh dug in, preparing positions ready for the next phase of the assault. The fragmented 15th Welsh was now moved up to replace 14th Welsh at this new line, and was hurriedly organised under Captain J.R. MacDonald, and dug a trench parallel to the northern edge of the wood, while 14th Welsh was pulled back.

By 18.30 hrs that day the 17th Royal Welsh Fusiliers had reached to within twenty to thirty yards of the northern edge of the wood and the Hammerhead had been taken by the 10th South Wales Borderers as the German troops were forced to withdraw. The bulk of the wood east of the central ride was in the Welshmen's hands, though to the west it was necessary to turn a flank along the railway line facing the north-western corner of the wood.

The rest of the division came under heavy fire from the German second line and withdrew to the cover of the wood for some 200 to 300 yards. The day's fighting ended there but it left the men tired and jumpy, and throughout the night there was much wild firing.

At 05.00 hrs the following morning of 11 July, Brigadier Evans of 115 Brigade took over the command of all the troops in Mametz Wood, establishing his headquarters on the junction of the central ride with the first cross ride. He brought up into the wood the 16th Welsh and the remaining companies of the 11th South Wales Borderers to replace some of the tired units of 113 and 114 Brigade.

Evans was expected to complete the capture of the wood with the remaining tired troops at his disposal. He established a line, from the left, as follows:

16th RWF – 16th Welsh – 17th RWF – 11th SWB – 10th SWB

An attack was planned for 15.00 hrs with the 16th Welsh, 17th Royal Welsh Fusiliers and 11th South Wales Borderers taking the lead. The centre left was expected to meet with the greatest difficulties. Evans had planned the attack without artillery support, but at 14.45 hrs an artillery barrage was opened which could not be stopped and Evans' infantry units began to suffer from the drop shorts of eighteen-pounders firing on the limit of their range. This bombardment carried on until 15.30 hrs.

As soon as the bombardment stopped the battalions moved into action. The 11th South Wales Borderers reached the north east corner of the wood by 17.40 hrs, relieving the battered 15th Welsh, who moved into support roughly on the line YX. The other two attacking units of 115 Brigade had much less luck and were held up.

With the attack again stagnant, Brigadier-General Evans brought up the remnants of the 10th and 15th Welsh, and the 16th Royal Welsh Fusiliers at around 18.30 hrs to renew the attack, but after heavy fighting, and reaching positions just sixty yards south of the wood's northern edge, heavy casualties due to artillery fire among these three battalions forced a withdrawal at around 02.30 hrs on the morning of 12 July. The attack had not been a success, though there was fierce fighting throughout the rest of the day. The German reaction to the attack though was that they had realised that to continue to defend the wood was fruitless and costly and at 20.00 hrs orders had been issued for their withdrawal.

Unknowingly though to Brigadier-General Evans, the evacuation of the 38th Division began as darkness fell, leaving only a few patrols

British artillery moving through Mametz Wood following its capture by the 38th (Welsh) Division. Taylor Library

within the boundary of the wood. As dawn broke on 12 July 1916 the units of 62 Brigade of the 21st Division entered the wood to relieve the tired troops of the 38th (Welsh) Division and in no time at all they had moved through it, which was hardly surprising since the Germans had already left the area after being soundly beaten by the Welshmen.

The fighting for Mametz Wood was over. It had cost the 38th (Welsh) Division around 4,000 casualties, about a third of their total infantry strength.

The 15th Welsh alone had lost a quarter of its strength, with over 240 casualties, including almost seventy dead, and a high proportion of the losses were officers and NCOs. Most of these men were lost during the attack of 11 July, with others dying of wounds in the coming days. The majority of the dead were buried within the wood where they fell, at

Mametz Wood Cemetery. Many of these graves within the wood were lost during the continued fighting in the area during the course of the war. They are today remembered on the Thiepval Memorial to the missing of the Somme. Five men of the 15th Welsh gained the Military Medal as a result of their part.

There are scattered burials throughout the battle area; at Heilly Station Cemetery, Caterpillar Valley Cemetery, Flatiron Copse Cemetery, and at Dantzig Alley Cemetery, Mametz. One man whose grave was discovered after the war is now buried north of Albert, at Serre Road Cemetery Number two. Private John Bryant Collins was a twenty-one year old man from Cardiff. His father had died before the war, and his mother had re-married a Sidney Wheadon, settling at Arabella Street in Cardiff.

Private Harry Montague Allen of Whitland, who had been conscripted on 17 April 1915, was shot in the chest by a German sniper on 10 July during the fighting at the Hammerhead. The bullet passed through his pocket Bible, leaving it holed and bloodstained, and entered his chest. Harry was quickly evacuated to the 38th Casualty Clearing Station at Heilly, where he died the following day. The medical staff at the Casualty Clearing Station at Heilly, were so inundated with casualties during the opening days of the fighting on the Somme that Harry, along with many others from the fighting in the early part of the Somme offensive, was buried there in a grave shared with two other men.

Benjamin Evans is another of the missing men of the fighting within Mametz Wood, and the second Lampeter man to die with the battalion. He is commemorated on the Thiepval Memorial.

Lampeter War Memorial Book, Ceredigion Archives

Another Mametz casualty was the twenty-one year old Sergeant Benjamin Evans of 8, Market Street, Lampeter.

Also commemorated on the Thiepval Memorial is Private Joshua Hall of Nelson in Lancashire. Joshua enlisted in February, 1915 and moved to France with the division in December that year. On the night of Sunday, 2 July he wrote his last letter home to his wife:

By the time that you receive this letter you will see by the papers that the biggest battle in history is beginning.

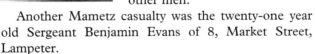

Harry Montague Allen's scarred New Testament, showing the damage caused by the bullet that killed him.

Denise Lodwig

Sadly Joshua was killed and buried within the confines of the wood on 10 July by his Platoon Sergeant, J Norman, who wrote to Joshua's widow two weeks later, informing her of the death of her husband. He had worked prior to the war at Mathers Mill, Nelson, and left a wife and two young children. Joshua's grave was lost during the course of the war, and so he is commemorated on the Thiepval Memorial. (Nelson Leader).

John Hirst was the Son of Mrs M King, of 55, Villa Road, Oldham. He had moved to Llanelli prior to the war and lived at 13, Water Street. John had enlisted into the 15th Welsh on 17 March 1915, and joined D Company. John was originally posted as wounded and missing on 11 July, during the Mametz attack. He was buried in the wood by men of the 1st South Wales Borderers, but sadly his grave was lost during the war and he is now commemorated on the Thiepval Memorial. John was thirty years old.

Private Joshua Hall.

Another man killed during the assault on 11 July was the twenty-one year old Private Daniel Cokley, of 1, New Century Street, Trealaw, a coal mining town sat in the Rhondda Valley. Daniel had worked as a collier prior to joining the 15th Welsh at Rhyl on 23 January 1915. He moved to France with the battalion in December 1915 and fought with them until his death at Mametz Wood.

Private John Hirst.

Daniels' body was found after the battle for the wood was over, by soldiers of the 2nd Gordon Highlanders, and he was buried about 300 yards north of Caterpillar Wood. The burial service was read by Reverend F D Langlands of the 2nd Gordons. Sadly as so often happened during the war, Daniel's grave was lost during further fighting in the area, and he is now commemorated on the Thiepval Memorial alongside so many of his comrades.

One of the saddest known incidents among the men who died during the battle for Mametz Wood was one of the two pairs of brothers from the 15th Welsh to die during the battle, Corporals Henry and Thomas Hardwidge, of Ferndale. Thomas had been shot by a German sniper during the fighting within the Hammerhead, and his brother Henry rushed to his side to give him water, but was himself shot by the same sniper. Both men died in each others arms.

Henry and Thomas Hardwidge died in each others arms.

The brothers are now buried side by side at Flatiron Copse Cemetery, Mametz. Both men were married. A third, elder, brother,

86

Morgan was killed later that year while serving on the Somme with the 2nd Welsh. Tom left behind his wife Annie and three children, at 17, High Street, Ferndale and Henry left his wife Jennie and one child, at 13, Lake Street, Ferndale.

A letter sent by their company commander to the widows of both men read:

> *I had known them for nearly 12 months, for they were in my platoon. More cheerful, willing and capable soldiers I do not think it possible to find, and their presence is greatly missed by everyone in the platoon and by myself.*

The horrific carnage caused by the desperate fighting at Mametz Wood brought tragedy to the industrial town of Farnworth, near Bolton. During the attack on 11 July, five men of the town were killed within hours of each other, three by the same shell and two by sniper fire.

William Gerrard, Herbert Walmsley (not pictured) and James Walsh were the three men hit by the same shell. The mortally wounded James Walsh was cradled in the arms of one of his friends, and with his dying breath whispered to him to write home and say that he had done his best. The lads had all worked as colliers prior to enlisting into the 15th Welsh, and the news of their deaths spread gloom over their friends and families back home.

Herbert Walmsley and James Thornley were just seventeen years old, and Joseph Coleman was the oldest of the five, at twenty-two. All five men are commemorated on the Thiepval Memorial as their graves were lost in the continuing fighting in the area. Their names are also inscribed onto the Farnworth War Memorial.

On 12 July 1916 the 15th Welsh had been withdrawn from the wood, after their positions had become untenable due to intense German artillery fire. The battle weary men withdrew through Strip Trench, and returned to positions at the Citadel where they set up camp. The war

Four of the men are pictured right: from left to right, are Privates William Gerrard, James Walsh, Joseph Coleman and James Thornley.

Farnworth Weekly Journal

diary shows the following list of casualties among the battalions officers:

Major C G Phillips, Killed

Major Percy Anthony, Killed

Captain T B Phillips, Wounded

Captain D H Thomas, Wounded

2/Lieutenant H E Simmons, Wounded

2/Lieutenant J R Hall, Killed

2/Lieutenant P H Davies, Wounded

2/Lieutenant C M Lucas, Killed.

The most senior officer of the battalion to be killed at Mametz was Major Christian Gibson Phillips, who had been attached to the 15th Welsh from the Kings Own (Royal Lancaster) Regiment. Christian was the Son of the late R E Phillips, MD, of Burlington House, Bromley, Kent, and had been commissioned into the 2nd Royal Lancaster Regiment on 5 May 1900. Christian was promoted Captain on 18 December 1907. He had gained the rank of Temporary Major on 1 June 1916, and led the attack against the wood on 10 July 1916. Christian sadly fell at Mametz aged thirty-six, during the fighting of 10 July, and is now buried at Caterpillar Valley Cemetery, Longueval. His temporary second in command, Major Percy Anthony was killed that same day.

After the capture and consolidation of Mametz Wood, the entire 38th Division was relieved to a quiet part of the line. In spite of the effort that had been expended in the capture of the wood it was to get no credit for the work. The division was considered by some regular officers to have been of an inferior quality for a number of various reasons and all neglected the fact that the wood had fallen to them in a relatively short time. It was a political situation which the men of the 38th (Welsh) Division had no control over, and wild tales spread of the Welshmen's cowardice under fire.

This was blatantly untrue. Cowards don't run into machine gun fire and die like those gallant Welshmen did over those bloody days; the amount of casualties suffered by the division at Mametz shows this. Also a succession of chances to capture the then lightly defended wood after the initial advance of 1 July were not taken, and by the time that the 38th Division had moved into position to attack the wood, it was heavily defended, and any momentum had been lost. If any blame was to be attached to the 38th Division, it was not the fault of the men who had spilt their blood on the battlefield.

Interestingly, later on in the Somme offensive, the smaller High Wood was to take two months and several divisions to clear. No blame was laid at the feet of those divisions.

Partly due to the unfounded criticism which followed the battle for

Mametz Wood over the coming months and years, it took over sixty years for the efforts of the 38th (Welsh) Division to be properly remembered. After a lot of hard work by members of the South Wales Branch of the Western Front Association, a splendid memorial in the form of the Welsh Dragon was erected at the spot from where the Division attacked. This magnificent piece of metalwork was aptly created by a Carmarthenshire man, the artist blacksmith David Peterson of St Clears.

The only Welsh language road sign in France, pointing to the 38th (Welsh) Division Memorial at Mametz Wood.

38th (Welsh) Division Memorial at Mametz Wood. The red dragon glares in defiance over the ground of attack.

On the battalion's first parade after being evacuated from Mametz Wood, the following 'Special Order of the Day' was read out to the men, written by Brigadier-General T. O. Marden CMG, Commanding 114 Infantry Brigade:

> *The Brigadier General congratulates all ranks on their achievements of the 10th of July when they firmly established the fighting reputation of the 114th Infantry Brigade by capturing the portion of the Mametz Wood allotted to them by the Divisional Commander, thereby gaining the thanks of the Commander-in-Chief for the performance of a task which called for a special effort.*

> *Wood fighting is recognised as the most difficult form of fighting and it reflects the greatest credit on all engaged, that at the end of the day all Units in the Brigade were under their own Commanders.*

> *'The advance to the attack was carried out in perfect order by the 13th and 14th Welsh, to whom fell the majority of the Wood fighting, the severity of which is shown by the Casualty Lists.*

The 10th and 15th Welsh showed equal steadiness in the advance when called on to support. The thanks of the Brigadier are especially due to Lieutenant Colonel J H Hayes, Commanding 14th Welsh, for his special work throughout the day, and to Captain A P Bowen, Brigade Major, for his Staff work and organising work in the Wood.

They are due to Lieutenant Colonel P. E. Ricketts, Commanding 10th Welsh, to Major D. A. Howards, Commanding 13th Welsh, and to Major C. G. Phillips, Commanding 15th Welsh who all, unfortunately, became casualties during the action.

They are due, too, to those Officers and Non Commissioned Officers who assumed Command of Battalions, Companies and Platoons, when their leaders fell, and to others whose names have not yet been ascertained.

With such a splendid start, the 114th Infantry Brigade can look with confidence to the future, and with pride to the past.'

Signed T O Marden, Brigadier-General, Commanding 114 Infantry Brigade, 13 July 1916.

A note at the bottom stated 'This Order will be read on Parade to every man of the Brigade.'

Just days after the 38th Division left the battlefield, on 15 July 1916, troops of the 2nd Royal Welsh Fusiliers passed the wood, while advancing towards the new front line near Bazentin le Petit. Various accounts written after the war by Siegfried Sassoon and Frank Richards of that battalion spoke of the horrors that met them during their march, with the lingering smell of gas filling the valley; the shattered bodies of Welsh and German soldiers scattered over the tortured ground; and even the grisly sight of a South Wales Borderer and his German foe who had bayoneted each other at the same time – both stiffened and propped up by a tree. Torn bodies hung from branches and the stench of death was awful. The grounds within the woods are still scarred with the remnants of battle; trench lines and shell holes are scattered throughout the wood, in testament to the men who died taking them

The Medals and memorial plaque issued to the family of 35079 Private John Robert Noyes. John was the son of John and Mary Noyes, of 37, Taff Street, Pontypridd, and was killed in action within Mametz Wood on 11 July 1916. He was twenty-two years old, and is commemorated on the Thiepval Memorial.

Robin Mellor, Great Nephew

Chapter 4

Withdrawal from
Mametz and the move north

AFTER PULLING BACK from Mametz Wood, the 15th Welsh spent the night of 12 July at Dernancourt. From there they entrained for Longpre the following morning, where they bivouacked for the night. The following day the men marched to Buigny, where they again had a nights rest before spending the coming days marching through Domqueur and Couin to positions at Hebuterne, on the Serre to Puisieux Road, where they relieved the 1/5th Gloucestershire Regiment on 16 July 1916.

This sector was relatively quiet. The main Somme battle was raging on further south, and all attention by the Germans had been diverted there. Casualties had almost ceased by now within the 38th Division, with just a few men dying of wounds suffered during the Mametz battle, at hospitals both in France and at home.

Although by then a peaceful sector, Hebuterne had seen its fair share of death and destruction.

The devastated village of Hebuterne.

The whole area had been turned inside out and upside down-disused and partially filled up trenches abounded. Spread about everywhere were the bodies of our chaps and the Germans. They lay about in all postures and were mutilated beyond description. They lay around like swedes the farmer had turned up from the soil and strewn around to dry. Some large shell holes were all but full of soldiers, bodies completely decomposed but the uniforms keeping some semblance of the shape of a man.
Shanahan

The remainder of July was a peaceful time, trading places in the front line with the 13th Welsh, until on 30 July the battalion marched to Doullens to

Hebuterne sector held by the Division after withdrawal from Mametz.

Author's collection

entrain for Arques. By 1 August 1916 the battalion was back in northern France, in billets at Merckeghem, and on 3 August marched to Tatinghem, on the western side of St Omer, where they became attached to the Second Army Central School of Instruction, possibly meant as a slight after the Battle of Mametz.

King George V and General Blackader on the occasion of the inspection of 38th Division. IWM.

Although rumours had abounded in some quarters of the Welshmen's lack of conviction during the capture of Mametz Wood, many more were impressed by their courage, and the fact that a division comprised solely of 'Kitchener's Men' had achieved such an important success. This fact was not lost on His Majesty, King George V, who was so pleased with the work of the 38th (Welsh) Division that an inspection was ordered.

On 13 August 1916 the battered but proud Welshmen gathered along the roadside near Wormhoudt, where they eagerly awaited their King. King George was greeted by Major-General Blackader, the Commanding Officer of 38th (Welsh) Division, who introduced His Majesty to some of his Staff, before the King inspected the men himself.

It was a proud day for the men, but they were quickly returned back to their training camp at Tatinghem, where the remainder of August 1916 was spent under instruction. The division remained around Tatinghem until 29 August 1917, when the constituent units moved out. The 15th Welsh marched to St Momelin, where they entrained for Poperinghe. After disembarking at Poperinghe, the men marched to a camp just north of the town, within earshot of the constant artillery being fired over the now nearby Ypres Salient. This was the part of the line most dreaded by the British soldier, and it was to become home to the 15th Welsh for the next twelve months.

Poperinghe itself was known as the 'gateway to the salient'. Almost every soldier who served at Ypres passed through 'Pop' as it was known, bound for the trenches, many never to return. Allied forces had commandeered the town as a base from the early days of the war, and since then a sprawling array of camps, hospitals and supply depots had

Poperinghe town square. Taylor Library

sprung up around the it. Located in Poperinghe was the famous soldiers' rest place run by the Reverend 'Tubby' Clayton; Talbot House, popularly known to the men who frequented it as 'Toc H'. The town was firmly established by the time of the arrival of the 38th Division as a favoured recreational area for resting soldiers, and over 250,000 men were in fact billeted in the area.

The first week of September was spent in divisional reserve, supplying working parties to the front line and burying cable. On 6 September 1916 the battalion relieved the 14th Welsh in brigade reserve.

A and B Companies set up in positions on the east side of the Yser Canal. Battalion Headquarters, C and D Companies set up in

The rest place in Poperinge with the sign above the door which read: 'Talbot House 1915–? Every Man's Club'. Taylor Library

94

positions at Machine Gun Farm, and these remained their positions until 10 September, when the 15th Welsh relieved the 14th Welsh in the front line. A Company took up position on the right, C Company in the centre, D Company on the left and B Company in support.

This first spell in the trenches at Ypres was to prove relatively peaceful. On 14 September the battalion was relieved by the 14th Welsh, and moved back to brigade reserve, with two companies on the Canal bank and headquarters and the other two companies at Machine Gun Farm.

On 18 September the battalion returned to the front line, where it remained until the 22 September. This swapping of positions with the 14th Welsh continued for the remainder of the month.

As September drew to a close, shelling and machine-gun fire became more frequent, with the Germans shelling Turco Farm and Clifford Towers almost daily. On 2 October 1916 the battalion moved into divisional reserve at 'P' Camp near Elverdinghe.

The area around Poperinghe and Elverdinghe was packed with military camps, holding the men needed to man the front line at the Ypres Salient. Although ranging from distances between three to six

Positions of the 15th Welsh during their first week at Ypres.

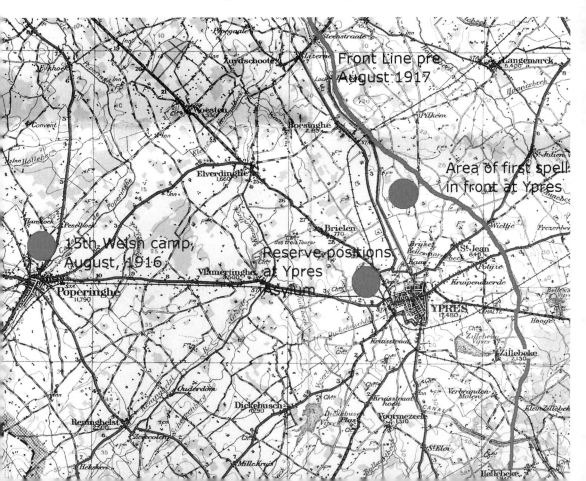

French   German trenches   British trenches

Northern most position of the British line. 15th Welsh had the Yser Canal to their rear and No Man's Land was only a few yards across. Taylor Library

miles behind the front line, these camps could still be hit by long-range German shellfire, which one Company of the 19th Welsh were to sadly find to their cost in January 1917.

The 15th Welsh remained at 'P' Camp until 14 October 1916. In the meantime, working parties were supplied to the front line, and on 12 October the battalions first proper trench raid was carried out. Second Lieutenants Landman and Davies and seventy other ranks were sent into the line, and from there entered a German sap, looking to identify the German units stationed around Morteldje Estaminet, and to eradicate a troublesome German machine-gun post. However the sap was found to be un-occupied and so no intelligence was gathered, fortunately with no casualties suffered.

On 14 October 1916 the battalion moved back to brigade reserve, relieving the 17th Royal Welsh Fusiliers at Machine Gun Farm and the Canal Bank, and the following day took over the front line from the 16th Welsh, in the same positions as before. The weather had now turned. It rained heavily during the first night back in the front line, and the trenches soon began to turn into mire, giving the men a preview of the conditions that were to be facing them in nearly twelve months time.

The same cycle of time in the front line, alternated with relief and time in brigade reserve, again continued throughout the remainder of October, and the month was to see just one casualty. Private James Chadwick, another Bolton man, died at the French hospital at St Omer on 20 October 1916. His cause of death is listed at just 'died', and so it must be presumed that he had died of sickness. He is buried at Longuenesse (St Omer) Souvenir Cemetery.

On 5 November 1916, 114 Brigade moved back into divisional reserve. The 15th Welsh remained at the front, in support of 115 Brigade, near La Belle Alliance, and remained here until rejoining 114 Brigade at 'P' Camp on 9 November. On 14 November 1916, A and B Companies became attached to the 14th Welsh, and together relieved the 17th Royal Welsh Fusiliers in 'Left Support'. The companies moved back to the line via train from Peselhoek to Brandhoek, where they came under the command of the 14th Welsh.

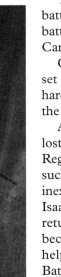

Regimental Sergeant Major Isaac Jones

The following day saw the remainder of the battalion relieve the 14th Welsh, and so the complete battalion was together again in positions along the Canal Bank near Boesinghe, in brigade support.

Conditions were getting quite poor now with the on-set of winter, but the men of the 38th Division were hard at work grading the trenches to attempt to drain the water from them.

At the beginning of December 1916 the 15th Welsh lost their most experienced soldier, the respected Regimental Sergeant Major Isaac Jones, who had been such a large influence during the training of the inexperienced recruits at Rhyl and Winchester in 1915. Isaac's services were now required elsewhere, and so he returned to England on 9 December 1916, where he became attached to the South Lancashire Regiment, helping to raise their 16th (Transport Workers) Battalion. He finally retired from the Army on 28 February 1919 after serving a total of nearly thirty-one years. Isaac had been mentioned in Sir Douglas Haig's Despatches of 13 November 1916 for his work at Mametz Wood. He also gained the Meritorious Service Medal for his work on Home Service. Isaac died on 18 April 1940 at home in Ammanford. He was seventy-five years old, and was buried at Bethany Chapel, Ammanford. [Details of his MID and MSM are in the Awards section at the rear of the book.]

The work of draining the trenches continued throughout the

remainder of December 1916, with the only offensive work being carried out in the form of the odd trench raid, and the battalion machine gunners occasionally firing barrages towards the German High Command Redoubt. Nightly patrols investigated the positions of the German trenches and redoubts, but otherwise all was quiet, with only one man killed during the final weeks of 1916.

Lance Corporal John Thomas Hill, a married man from Farnworth in Lancashire, was killed on 3 December 1916. He had worked at Proctor's Machine Works at Cawdor Street prior to the war, and is buried at Essex Farm Cemetery, alongside the Canal Bank. John's widow Catherine was left alone to bring up their eighteen month old daughter Mary Ellen.

By 12 December 1916 the 15th Welsh had been placed in corps reserve at 'Z' Camp, safely behind the lines, and here the men celebrated their second Christmas, and another New Year on the Western Front. Here they remained for the next two weeks, until on 12 January the battalion moved to relieve the 1/1st Hertfordshire Regiment in brigade support on the Canal Bank. The following day the 15th Welsh moved in to relieve the 1st Cambridgeshire Regiment in the front

Essex Farm Cemetery when it was first formed next to a dressing station. Taylor Library

line, and the four companies spread into position. The usual pattern of front line, brigade reserve and divisional reserve followed with little excitement bar some sporadic German shellfire. During the night of 29/30 January, the battalion was in positions around La Belle Alliance, when it came under heavy German artillery fire.

The first two men of the battalion, and certainly not the last, to die during 1917 were killed by shell fire that night. Private Thomas Haydn Davies of Ammanford had been awarded the Military Medal for bravery in the field during the fighting at Mametz Wood the previous year. He is buried at Bard Cottage Cemetery alongside the other man to die that night, Private Henry Morgan Richards of Aberystwyth.

Captain E McCawley was wounded during this latest spell in the trenches, and on 2 February 1917 three other ranks and Second Lieutenant R J Gibson were wounded while the battalion was moving into brigade reserve on the Canal Bank.

Lieutenant William Reese.

Private Thomas John Griffiths.

Private James Dunn.

Back home in Wales, one of the original officers of the battalion, Lieutenant William Reese, one of the Carmarthen men, died of sickness on 2 February 1917. William is buried at Carmarthen Town Cemetery.

On 4 February, one of the battalion wounded from the latest spell in the trenches died of his wounds at the hospital at Hazebrouck. Private Thomas John Griffiths of Llwynhendy was twenty-six years old. He was buried at Hazebrouck Communal Cemetery, where his grave is still visited by relatives today.

The battalion moved back into the line on 7 February 1917, and came under heavy German artillery fire throughout the day, with two men being wounded. The following afternoon at 16.30 hrs the Germans shelled them again, and another two men were killed, and five wounded, when a direct hit fell on Coney Street. The two dead men were the cousins George and Herbert Farrow, of Bolton. Herbert was a married man of thirty-one with five children. His widow Catherine gave birth to their sixth child just weeks after Herbert's death. His cousin George was twenty-three years old. They are buried next to each other at Bard Cottage Cemetery.

It was under these terrible conditions of intermittent shelling of their muddy trenches that the men remained, with Captain Lord becoming another casualty. They were relieved on 11 February, and moved back to the Canal Bank in brigade reserve until 14 February, when they moved back into the line. On the morning of the following day, at 01.30 hrs, the Germans launched a heavy artillery and trench mortar bombardment on the positions held by the 15th Welsh. The bombardment was immediately followed up by several German trench raiding parties, and some isolated posts were hit, resulting in what was thought at the time, two men killed, four missing and sixteen wounded, including Second Lieutenant J W Evans.

In fact four men were killed during the German trench raid, and some of the missing must have been taken prisoner by the German raiders. The dead were Lance Corporal John Demaine of Bolton, whose body was never recovered from the battlefield, Private James Dunn of Farnworth, Lance Corporal David Killeen of Bolton and Corporal George Roblings of Ferndale died of wounds that same day at Ferme-Olivier Dressing Station. John Demaine's death must have foxed the Army authorities for a while after the war, as he is listed on the Addenda Panel of the Menin Gate Memorial at Ypres. This was the worst spate of casualties for the battalion in Belgium so far, yet the men remained in the front until their relief on 20 February 1917.

James Dunn had been born in Colne, Lancashire. He moved to Farnworth, where he worked at Ashton Field Pit, and had enlisted along

A Field Hospital In Belgium.

with his brothers John, Thomas and Joseph. James was attached to the Machine Gun team in D Company when he was killed on 15 February 1917, and was just eighteen years old. James is buried at Ferme-Olivier.

Sadly another man wounded during the trench raid died of his wounds later that day. Private Ebenezer Davies of Talley, near Llandeilo, had been evacuated to the 46th Casualty Clearing Station, which was situated at Mendinghem, near Proven. He was thirty-six years old, and is buried within the military cemetery at Mendinghem.

After a brief respite from the sodden trenches in brigade reserve, the men returned to the front line on 24 February. The following day saw a heavy German trench mortar barrage come down on the positions to the left of the 15th Welsh, but the expected attack didn't follow, and no German infantry were seen at all. On 27 February German activity was noted to have become considerably heavier, as transport movement behind their lines increased, and a heavily laden train was spotted pulling out of Morteldje. During the night, much activity, shouting and talking had been heard from the German positions, especially around the High Command Redoubt. It was a very nervous time for the front line soldiers, but later in the day the battalion was due to be relieved by the 14th Welsh.

The same evening, during the time when the relief was in progress, the enemy guns opened up and plastered heavy shell fire around and about our strong points. These shells did not explode. The cap blew off with a distinct plop, releasing the gas- sometimes it was phosgene gas, other times chlorine gas which had a strong smell like the familiar chloride of lime added to the washing bleach used at home in laundry work and for disinfectant use.

This was a deadly gas and, if inhaled over a short period, it proved fatal. So there we stood on the trench edge, for there in the trench the old guard was about to climb out. As soon as we smelt gas, we began to put our gas masks on. The latest box respirator had not yet been issued and our mask consisted of a flannel bag with eye pieces and a rubber tube which was attached to a mouth piece and held by the teeth or in the mouth. We quickly got out the flannel bag from the cotton bag usually worn over the shoulders. We shook the bag, which was saturated with some protective oil, over our heads and tucked the end into the collar of our coat. You then held the dummy like valve in your mouth and hoped for the best. You had to remember all this amid the gun fire, and usually then trouble began.

We exhaled by the mouth through the rubber valve and inhaled by nose in the bag which smelt of disinfectant of a kind new to us. But the hot breath escaping at the edge of the valve outside froze instantly, and we found that although we could inhale in the bag, the outside of the valve was sealed. Our breath of course, and the intense cold, sealed the end. We could not hold our breath forever and to inhale the fumes was fatal. Quickly, we took off the bag, popped the frozen end of the rubber valve into our mouth to unfreeze and then it was back on with the bag. All this was in the dark or in semi-darkness. It was quick work, no second chance. The gas all-clear was signalled, and by now the old guard had gone and the new taken over.

To have some sort of shelter, a few tin sheets or sand bags were stretched over the portion of trench occupied. Both ends were similarly covered and with two on duty, the other four would be able to sit down on the firestep and snatch some sleep, no Horlicks required. Came sleep to the just and the unjust, a burning candle stuck fast in the wall of the trench providing a homely glow. A few hours later, the gas being heavier, it sank to the ground and to the bottom of the old trenches, where it was wafted along. This gas by now had reached our post and would have been blown further along. However, when it passed the section over which we had arranged some sort of shelter, the enclosed section must have altered conditions. The gas rose high as soon as it got there and the men who sat there were soon in trouble, struggling to put on their helmets. No room to move around and half asleep, they must have inhaled a little gas before they got their mask on. One chap, I believe his name was Morris and he was a cobbler from Trimsaran – how correct this was I don't know, but I must have heard something about him to know where he hailed from - he was in a bad state and before he could be taken to the first aid post, he died.

Shanahan

The dead man was Corporal William Morris, who was in fact from Ammanford. He died of wounds at Mendinghem that same day, and was buried in the cemetery there. He had been with the battalion since landing in France on 4 December 1915 and was a veteran of the fighting at Mametz Wood.

On 28 February 1917, the battalion made the short march from their overnight billets at Roussel Farm to 'D' Camp in Owl Reserve, near Elverdinghe. Here they remained for the next ten days, in divisional reserve, and returned to brigade reserve at the Canal Bank on 10 March, relieving the 13th Welsh. The following morning saw the battalion move into the front, relieving the 14th Welsh for another spell in the trenches. Two men died during the relief, Sergeant David Lewis Jones who died of wounds on the morning of 14 March at Mendinghem, where he is buried, and Private William David John of Amroth, who is buried at Bard Cottage.

During the preceding night 13/14 March, artillery had sporadically rained down on the British lines. This bombardment again hit the lines on the afternoon of 14 March, causing more casualties to the weakened battalion. This spate of shelling continued until the 15th Welsh was relieved at 18.30 hrs on 15 March, by the 14th Welsh, and the weary men moved back into brigade reserve until 19 March, when they again traded places with their sister battalion in the front line.

This pattern again continued throughout the remainder of March 1917, with just the odd casualty being suffered by the battalion. The only notable entry on the war diary shows the launching of a trench raid at 00.15 hrs on the morning of 29 March 1917, led by Lieutenant Landman. The raid was a total failure. The intent was to place a Bangalore Torpedo in the German wire, and blow it to create a gap. However, due to the darkness of the night, and the failure of the fuse of the torpedo, the raid was called off, and the torpedo dismantled and brought back almost four hours later by Lance Corporal Bamber, who was awarded the Military Medal as a result. The German defenders had noted the presence of the raiding party though, firing a spread of Very Lights at intervals over No Man's Land to try and spot them, but luckily no casualties were suffered.

A fatigue party bringing up duckboards used for the bottom of trenches

On the following morning a salvo of heavy shells was fired towards the Welshmen's positions, but luckily fell short, injuring just one man. Enemy activity now heightened, and shells fell across the line in the Boesinghe area. Observers of the battalion spotted several British SOS signals being fired from the positions there, and the German shelling continued throughout the morning, wounding another five men of the 15th Welsh in the process. One of these men died of wounds at Mendinghem on 1 April 1917. Private Francis John Saunders was from Stotfold in Bedfordshire. He was laid to rest in the military cemetery at Mendinghem.

On the night of 31 March 1917, the battalion sent another raiding party over the top with a Bangalore torpedo. The raid was supported by an artillery barrage which opened at 23.55 hrs and the torpedo was successfully fired. The party then crossed into the German trenches, killing several Germans, and bringing back three prisoners, two of which died on the way back. The only casualties suffered during the raid

A source of water when desperate. Taylor Library

were two officers, one of whom had only suffered minor wounds. This raid earned Serjeant Schofield a Bar to the Military Medal which he had gained at Mametz Wood.

Retaliatory German shelling badly damaged the lines of the Welshmen, but amazingly no further casualties fell upon the 15th Welsh that night, and the battered battalion moved quietly back into reserve at Merckeghem. Unknown to the men of the 15th Welsh, while they were in reserve another of their number had succumbed to illness and died on 5 April 1917. Private Horace Dash had been born at Wood Green in Middlesex. He had enlisted at Llanelli into the battalion, but had been taken ill during his time at the front, and returned to London for hospital treatment, where he died. Horace is buried at St. Pancras Cemetery in London.

That same day, the battalion relieved the 10th Northumberland Fusiliers in the 'L' Line defences, west of the Canal Bank. The 'L' Line defensive system ran from a position by due south of Boesinghe, at Wagram Farm, down through Brielen, and south toward Ypres. The battalion remained here for the next few days, until their relief on 11 April by the 17th Royal Welsh Fusiliers. From here the 15th Welsh moved into the front line at Lancashire Farm, relieving the 15th Royal Welsh Fusiliers. Sadly another member of the battalion had been wounded during the short spell at 'L' Line. Private Jesse Froy, of Hitchen in Hertfordshire, had been evacuated to the 46th Casualty Clearing Station at Proven. He died of his wounds on 11 April 1917, and is buried at Mendinghem Military Cemetery. Jesse was thirty-seven years old, and left a wife and young family behind.

This latest spell in the front saw several casualties suffered by the battalion, while under sporadic shellfire from the German artillery. Late on the night of 14 April the tired men were relieved by the 13th Welsh, and moved to brigade reserve at the Canal Bank. Just three days later

Devastation in the Ypres Salient. Taylor Library

the battalion was relieved by the 14th Hampshire's, and moved back into the front, taking over the line from the 15th Royal Welsh Fusiliers in the Zwaanhof sector.

On 20 April 1917 the battalion was again relieved, and moved to brigade reserve for two days, before moving into divisional reserve on 22 April at Machine Gun Farm. Here the men remained for the next week, enjoying a relatively relaxing spell away from the direct fire of the German artillery and machine gunners, but this short spell was soon to come to a bloody end.

The only source of water around hereabouts were the shell holes so shell hole water it had to be. After carefully parting the green algae that flourished on the top, we filled our dixies, cut a ribbon of sandbag, rolled it around about one and a half inches of candle, cut a tiny trench in the floor and placed the candle and sacking in it. The combination of sacking and wax blazed away and soon boiled the water. It never failed, and ignoring dire warnings as to the dangers of drinking such contaminated water, we still boiled the water, drank the tea, and as far as I remember, contracted no fevers. Often, such water was rendered safe by the authorities by chlorination, when it was sometimes sent up to the front in petrol tins with brass screw caps. It tasted like chloride. I think they used to fill them up with water without bothering whether the tins contained petrol or not. No tea could be brewed with it. Even with smelly water, tea was not much sought after, but again, one got accustomed to it.

Shanahan

Chapter 5

The First Large Scale Trench Raid

BY 29 APRIL 1917 THE 15TH WELSH had been in divisional reserve at Machine Gun Farm for a week. It had been decided to send a raising party into the German positions within the Morteldje Salient to gain intelligence, and to bring back German prisoners for interrogation, and the 15th Welsh were chosen for the task. That night a trench raiding party was assembled, made up of seven officers and 180 other ranks, under the command of Captain J A Daniel.

Trench raids were particularly feared by both sides, with sentries in constant fear of the threat of enemy raiding parties crashing into their trenches. Typically, trench raids were carried out at night by small teams of men who would navigate across No Man's Land and infiltrate enemy trench systems before returning to their own lines. Trench raiding was very similar to medieval warfare, as it was fought face-to-face with crude weapons. The trench raiders themselves were lightly equipped for quiet, speedy, unimpeded movement and armed themselves not only with modern weapons such as pistols and grenades, but also notably with bayonets, knives, brass knuckles, and deadly homemade maces and clubs for swift and silent killing.

Trench raiding had multiple purposes: typically, the intention would be either to kill, wound or capture enemy troops; destroy, disable or capture high value materiel such as machine guns; gather intelligence by seizing important documents (maps, plans etc.) or enemy officers for interrogation; reconnaissance for a future massed attack during daylight; keep the enemy feeling under threat during night-time hours, thereby reducing his efficiency and morale; or to maintain aggressiveness in troops.

Private William Shanahan brings some reality to life of the severity of a trench raid in his memoirs:

Our trenches were five to six hundred yards ahead and the German trenches were two hundred yards further forward. The men wore no kit, were armed with a rifle, revolver and Mills bomb, and carried the handle of their entrenching tool on which a steel cog had been threaded. Even that weapon was deadly when used on the head of a half awake German soldier, peering towards the English lines thinking, I'm sure, exactly what we were thinking – "How long, how long". No reply would

British troops readying for a trench raid.

be vouchsafed, for if it was us he enquired of, we did not know, for we were asking the same question. So the men stood around until the time to move up drew near, their faces blacked over, the whites of their eyes betraying them in the night. However the colour of one's eyes was unimportant, and to have a raiding party looking down upon you in the trench at 2:30 or so in the early morning when your wits were supposed to be at their lowest, with their blackened faces, waving their knobkerries and intent on crushing your head into your shoulders was calculated to sharpen your awareness and banish all thoughts of sleep. It's wonderful how quickly time passed whilst the raid was on. One minute you were stood up on the fire step, staring after hundreds of different soldiers all scurrying here and there, each following someone else who had no idea where he was going. These soldiers never were hungry or fatigued and could be relied upon.

Sometimes they seemed to be sitting down, then again all were advancing, but after opening and closing your eyes a few times, blinking in fact, your "soldiers" were the screw pickets or wooden stakes on which the barbed wire was hung. I never fired at them, but for a few seconds they looked just as soldiers would. By now the raiding party were gathered in the front line, and if the raid was to be preceded by a short bombardment, they would have got as near as possible to the spot to be raided.

The bombardment usually lasted a few minutes. The occupants of the trench would have taken cover, shelling would cease, and they would speed up from their shelter, ready to receive the raiders, but the raiding party too would have risen. The drill was to be in their trench before they *got to their position, for before a soldier could collect his wits together, he was hustled over the top and away on the long journey to a concentration camp. Those who made a fight of it got killed, and the raiding party more often than not suffered as well. If perhaps wounded, a soldier might be laying in a shell hole with no idea where his trench lay. He would spend the long night anxiously awaiting dawn, when he looked carefully around trying to recognise familiar features. That done, he makes a bee line for the trenches he left earlier on, and if wounded, is sent off to the First Aid post.*

The scheme had been dreamt up on 19 April, and so on 22 April Captain Daniel led his specially selected party to Burgomaster Farm, where the men commenced training for the task in hand. This training was in accordance with the 'SS143-Instructions for training of Platoons', which was a new document, issued in February 1917 by the BEF.

A scale model of the Mortjelde trenches had been constructed at Burgomaster Farm in readiness for the men, and over the coming days they practised assaulting the positions throughout day and night, soon becoming accustomed to their new instructions. Nightly patrols by the men over the ground which they were to assault also helped them to familiarise themselves with the nature of the ground, and by the night of 29 April 1917 the men were ready and waiting.

As a pre-cursor to the raid, at 21.30 hrs that night, a special patrol was sent out to ensure that the Germans were still in their positions. At 23.25 hrs they returned with the news that the unsuspecting Germans were in the line working as usual, with a wiring party at work near No Mans Cot. The codename 'Bridge' which signalled that the raid was to be carried out was relayed to Brigade Headquarters, and the raiding party moved into the line.

It was by now 22.45 hrs, and a pre-arranged salvo was fired in the area of the German lines by the waiting Royal Artillery, killing the German wiring party as they worked. The route was now open for the assault, and at 23.00 hrs two columns of men moved off into the front line, arriving at their points of exit at just after midnight. The ready signal was sent back, and at 00.28 hrs on the morning of 30 April 1917 another artillery barrage opened up on the Germans, sending them into their dugouts, and the raiders moved out of the trenches into No Mans Land, carefully following their trench maps towards their targets.

The artillery barrage was raining down still on the German front line, and the raiding party remained forty yards back from the maelstrom, awaiting the lift of the artillery fire onto the German support trenches. By 00.35 hrs the barrage had lifted and the trench raiders swarmed into the German front line. The only opposition met was when a party of German bombers was driven off on the extreme left, and on their retreat they fell into the artillery barrage and were annihilated. The Germans had now been roused, but by now the raiding party had positioned their Lewis Guns onto the support line in readiness for a counter-attack, while the artillery still crashed down on the same positions, keeping the Germans in their dugouts, and unable to respond.

In the meantime, the German dugouts were being cleared one by one, and any defenders who didn't surrender were killed mercilessly. By 01.00 hrs this work was complete, and the order to withdraw was sent to the Lewis Gun crews, which resulted in a successful withdrawal, wave by wave, from the German lines back to the original starting positions in the line held by the remaining companies of the 15th Welsh.

The raid had been very successful, with ten German prisoners and a machine-gun captured. This had been just the tip of the iceberg though. Accompanying the 15th Welsh raiding party were men of the Royal Engineers, who were experts in defensive systems and demolition. They had been allotted other tasks that night. The following is an extract from the Official Report on the raid, which tells the story:

'F' Party – Centre. O. I/C. Second Lieutenant Lloyd, 15th Welsh. Lance Corporal Whittington and Sapper Wenham, Royal Engineers.

This N.C.O. and man under Lieutenant Lloyd demolished a concrete Ammunition Store and Machine Gun Emplacement. The Ammunition Store was apparently used as a dugout as well. This store contained rifle cartridges, Very Lights and Rockets. The size of the building was about 8' by 8' inside measurements and apparently strongly built. One 2 Gallon petrol tin of Ammonal was used for this. The M.G.E. contained 4 dead bodies, apparently killed by a bomb from Lance Corporal Whittington. The walls were about 3' thick, the roof was also concrete, and the height of the dugout from the bottom of the Trench appeared about 9' overall. The charge used was one 2 Gallon tin of Ammonal. These structures were in the parapet of the Front Line, and were so constructed as to form a traverse. I attach a rough sketch of this position marked 'A'.

'K' Party – Left. O. I/C. Second Lieutenant Lloyd, 15th Welsh. Sappers W.E.F. Williams and J. Phillips, R.E.

These Sappers in their Sub-Section saw nothing to demolish although a search was made with Lieutenant Lloyd. There has apparently been a concrete Sniper's Post, but this has been demolished by the Artillery, with the exception of the plate in position and was dismantled by the R.E. About 30 yards West of the Sniper's Post was found a large plate; it

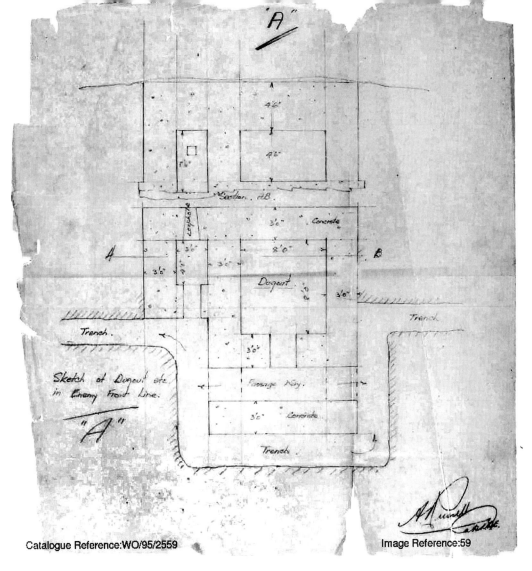

One of the sketch maps drawn as a result of the successful trench raid of 30 April 1917. This sketch clearly shows the layout of a section of the German trench system facing the Welshmen, with its dugouts also shown. (National Archives, WO/95/2559)

appeared to them like a Sniper's Plate. This was also dismantled. Two 2 Gallon petrol tins of Ammonal were carried by these Sappers, but were not used. They, however, threw them in a Shell Hole full of water. I attach a rough sketch as it appeared to these 2 Sappers marked 'B'.

'U' Party – Support Line. O. I/C. Lieutenant Morgan, 15th Welsh. Sappers E. Williams and R. Banks, R.E.

These two Sappers accompanied Lieutenant Morgan into the

Support Line, and found one Concrete Structure in course of erection. This building appeared to be 8' by 8' with 18" walls about 8' high. It was not sufficiently advanced for the Sappers to determine its use. One 2 Gallon petrol tin of Ammonal was used on the front and inside the building which was demolished. About 6 yards East was a circular iron Shelter in the parapet and parallel to it. The length and breadth of this was about 12' by 9'. This appeared nearly full of cement and was blown up with one 2 Gallon petrol tin of Ammonal. The M.G.E. which these Sappers went to demolish had been destroyed by Artillery Fire. I attach a sketch of the structure as it appeared to the Sappers marked 'C'.

'C' Party – Right Sub-Section. O. I/C. Lieutenant Lort, 15th Welsh. Sappers C.B. Stocker and W.J. Bond, R.E.

These two Sappers accompanied Lieutenant Lort in the Right Sub-Section, and found a Concrete M.G.E. and Dugout combined, 6' 6" x 8' high, the walls of which were 2' thick. The loophole was about 2' wide, 8" high, narrowing out to the front about 8" square. The height from the bottom of the Trench to the top of the Dugout was about 8'. As there were no other structures to demolish in this Sub-Section, two 2 Gallon petrol tins of Ammonal carried by these 2 men were used on this structure in the following manner- one in the loophole until it wedged itself, the other in the rear corner of the wall inside the building. During these operations Sapper Bond sustained a slight Gunshot wound. I attach a sketch of the structure marked 'D'.

Signed by Captain A. Russell, Royal Engineers,
for O.C. 123rd Field Company, 30 April 1917.

A heavy human price was paid for these sketch maps and ten prisoners, but much valuable information was gained as a result, which would stand the 38th Division in good stead in the months to come.

Records show that about a dozen men of the 15th Welsh died as a result of the raid that night. Two of these men could never be found, and are commemorated on the Menin Gate Memorial. Six were moved after the war, and are buried at Perth China Wall Cemetery, south of Ypres.

Several men died later of wounds suffered during the raid. One of them died and was buried at nearby Ferme-Olivier Cemetery, two made it out to the 46th Casualty Clearing Station at Proven and are buried at Mendinghem, and one man died at Remy Sidings Casualty Clearing Station and is buried at Ljissenthoek Military Cemetery.

Based upon trench map 28NW2 St. Julien, the sketch map of the Morteldje Salient shows the entry positions in the German front line for the sections of the raiding party on the night of the 29/30 April 1917. The letters correspond to the narrative from the war diary on the

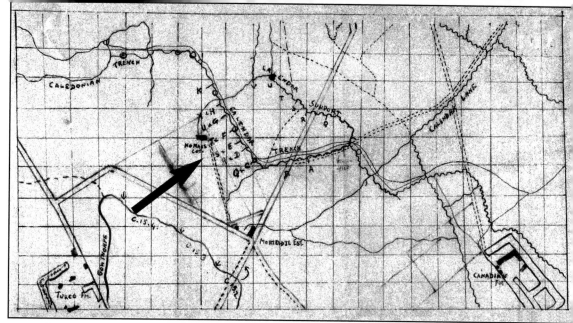

Area of the 30 April raid by the 15th Welsh on the Morteldje Salient.
WO/95/2559

Trench map of the area held by the 38th Welsh Division.

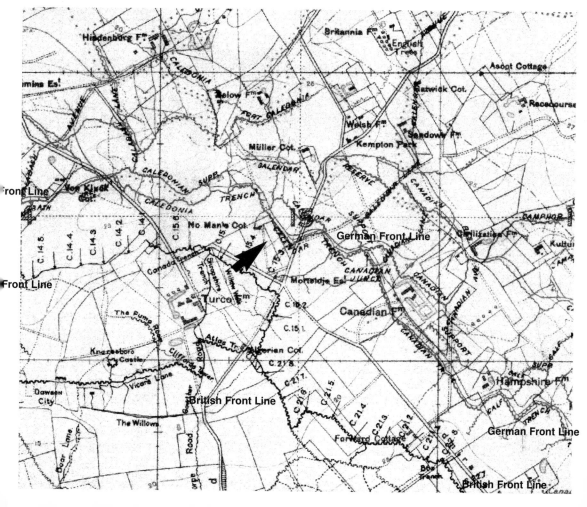

previous pages.

In relation to the British positions at Ypres, the Mortjelde Salient was sited north of the City of Ypres, directly south of Pilckem, a name that would become synonymous with the 38th (Welsh) Division.

A report by the Commanding Officer of the 15th Welsh, Lieutenant-Colonel Thomas William Parkinson, DSO mentioned in detail the work of Captain Daniel and his gallant party of trench raiders, which resulted in several gallantry awards to the men concerned.

Special thanks was also given to Lieutenant-Colonel W E Rudkin, DSO and all ranks of the Royal Artillery for their accurate work. It was indeed a good night's work done by the 15th Welsh, and helped to erase some of the unfair criticisms levelled at the 38th Division's part in the battle of Mametz Wood.

On 1 May 1917 the battalion was relieved, and moved to positions at 'D' Camp, Roussel farm and Elverdinghe Chateau. Here they remained for the next two weeks. Then followed the customary spell of brigade reserve, divisional reserve and front line duties again.

The only notable incidents were the wounding of Second Lieutenant Gort and four other ranks, by enemy machine-gun fire on 22 May, and the death in action of Captain John Chamberlain, MC, who was killed while on attachment to the 14th Welsh on 14 May 1917.

Captain John Chamberlain MC Dr Douglas Bridgwater

John Chamberlain was born on 22 December 1881, and was the younger son of Arthur Chamberlain JP of Moor Green Hall, Moor Green Lane, Moseley, Birmingham. He had initially been commissioned into the 3rd South Wales Borderers. John had been posted into the 15th Welsh, serving with distinction before being made temporary Commanding Officer to the 14th Welsh at Ypres. John is buried at Ferme Olivier Cemetery.

Chapter 6

Passchendaele – The Build Up

TOWARDS THE MIDDLE OF MAY the 38th Division was informed that it was to play a vital role in the forthcoming offensive, and so this period was to see them readying for this, and taking advantage of the diversion caused by the preparations for the Battle of Messines which was to take place south of Ypres. The 15th Welsh opened this preparatory work on the night 25/26 May when they began digging and wiring a new trench, about 275 yards long, 150 yards in advance of their original positions, and just fifty yards from the enemy trenches at Caesars Nose.

The work was carried out in utmost secrecy and quiet, but Private Arthur Pegram of Great Amwell in Hertfordshire was killed, and three other men wounded. The following day saw the battalion relieve the 13th Welsh near Caesar's Nose, and during that night, and the following morning, the line came under heavy artillery fire, wounding four more men, and killing Private George Davison Smith of Leyton in Essex. Both of these men are buried next to each other at Essex Farm Cemetery on the west side of the Canal Bank.

During the following weeks, the battalions of the 38th Division took turns digging these new trenches, covering each other in turn as the men sweated in No Man's Land, under extreme danger. The Battle of Messines was launched on 7 June 1917 near the village of Mesen, south of Ypres. A brilliant success at first, this was just a preliminary battle and in some way a diversion to the main offensive to come at Ypres, of which the 38th (Welsh) Division, and with it the 15th Welsh of 114 Brigade, were to play an important preliminary part. The remainder of the casualties to the 15th Welsh during this period came mostly as a result of artillery fire, although the other battalions of the division were active. This artillery fire was a constant fear for the men in the trenches, and even in reserve they knew they were not safe.

On 13 June 1917 the 15th Welsh left the Salient, handing over their portion of the line to the Guards Division, who were later to fight on their left flank during the forthcoming offensive, and entrained from Poperinghe for St. Omer, marching to billets at Tatinghem, in the St Hilaire area in northern France. Here, a replica of the trenches and strong points to be attacked was laid out on the ground between Enquin and Liettres and the brigades were practiced over the same in their

A section of the Poperinghe Defensive Line.

respective roles. Opportunity was also taken to practice the machine-gun barrage and this was found extremely useful, as none of the machine gunners had as yet done any firing for long periods.

Here the battalion was joined by the remainder of the 38th Division, which was relieved by the 29th Division, who took over their duties for the time being. The complete division trained hard ready for the forthcoming offensive at Ypres, and also carried out forced marches from Tatinghem to Blequin, and then from Fiefs to Witternesse. They then slowly moved back closer to the Salient, first marching to billets near Steenbecque on 16 July, then on to Hazebrouck, Proven, St. Sixtie and then finally to 'G' Camp near Poperinghe.

By 26 July 1917 the 15th Welsh were back in the 'L' Line defences, relieving the 14th Welsh in the process. That same day, two men were killed, and two wounded during the relief, with a further eight men wounded later in the day. The first was Private Rees Meredith Williams of Ammanford. He is buried at Bard Cottage Cemetery.

The other man dead was the young Benjamin Williams of St. Dogmaels. Benjamin Williams was the son of Benjamin and Margaret Williams, of 'Rose Lynn,' St. Dogmaels, and had enlisted at Cardigan

Private
Benjamin William

116

into the 15th Battalion at the outbreak of war. Benjamin was killed in action on 26 July 1917 aged just twenty, and is buried at Bard Cottage Cemetery. Sadly his brother David had been killed earlier in the War while serving in Mesopotamia, and their parents were devastated by the loss of their two gallant sons.

By now the battalion had taken up positions in the Zwaanhof sector. Patrols were sent out to reconnoitre the German front line positions, and the Germans fired retaliatory salvoes of high explosive and gas shells at the Welshmen's trenches in reply. Conditions were by now very uncomfortable. The gas shells proved to be of a new type of mustard gas, which proved to be more effective than anything before it, and the waiting British units in the front lines of the Salient suffered its effects badly.

At 17.00 hrs on 27 July 1917, two platoons from the 15th Welsh were sent out to check the German positions. They found no Germans in the front line, but their support and reserve positions were strongly held, and here the patrols met with strong opposition and were forced to hurriedly withdraw. The Germans again retaliated to this by hitting the front line trenches with an artillery barrage, mixing up some gas shells into the bombardment for good effect, and the battalion suffered heavy casualties as a result, with the war diary showing figures of three officers and twenty-one other ranks killed, three officers and sixty-one other ranks wounded, and a further thirteen men missing. The dead officers were the experienced Captain Thomas W David, Second Lieutenant Victor George Roberts of Llanelli, and Second Lieutenant Evan James. All three officers are buried at Bard Cottage Cemetery.

German artillery.

One of the missing 'other ranks' was the twenty-seven year old Sergeant Lindsay Gilchrist. Lindsay had been born at Aberdeen, and was a book keeper living at Newport, Monmouthshire when he joined the South Wales Borderers on 9 September 1915.

He had remained on home service with the Territorial's for the first eighteen months of his service career, and he married Eveline Violet Williams while on leave on 3 April 1917. Her given address was 21, North Gate Terrace in Cardigan. Lindsey was promoted Lance Sergeant in April 1917 and was posted to the 15th Welsh on 10 June 1917, joining them at Ypres soon after.

Lindsay was posted as missing after the raid of 27 July, and his body was never found. He is commemorated on the Menin Gate Memorial.

On 28 July 1917 the battalion was still in the trenches, and came under fire from low flying German aeroplanes. At 'Stand Down' that evening the German artillery again opened on the Welsh trenches, and various flares of all colours were seen in the sky, prompting a response from the British artillery.

More casualties were suffered during the night, and throughout the day, and at 17.00 hrs the following day the 15th Welsh were relieved by the 13th Welsh, moving into support at the 'L2' Defences. They remained here for the next twenty-four hours, until moving into their assembly positions on the night of 30 July 1917.

The time of their greatest test was to come.

Chapter 7

Passchendaele – The Battle of Pilckem Ridge

ON THE NIGHT OF 30/31 JULY 1917 the troops were moved into their assembly positions and were concentrated without a hitch by 02.54 on 31 July. To their left was the Guards Division, to their right the 51st (Highland) Division. To get an idea of the actions during the battle of the Pilckem Ridge, it is better to view the attack of the entire 38th (Welsh) Division.

The general dispositions of the 38th (Welsh) Division were as follows:

114 Brigade (with the 15th Welsh) on the right and

113 Brigade on the left with

115 Brigade in reserve.

Tasks allotted to the first two brigades were to capture the village of Pilckem and the Pilckem Ridge up to half-way between the River Steenbeek and Pilckem Village. On this line being attained 115 Brigade was to push through two battalions to capture the Steenbeek and its crossings, a total advance of almost two miles.

On the trench maps given to the commanding officers of the

Objectives for 38th Welsh Division in the assault on Pilckem Ridge.

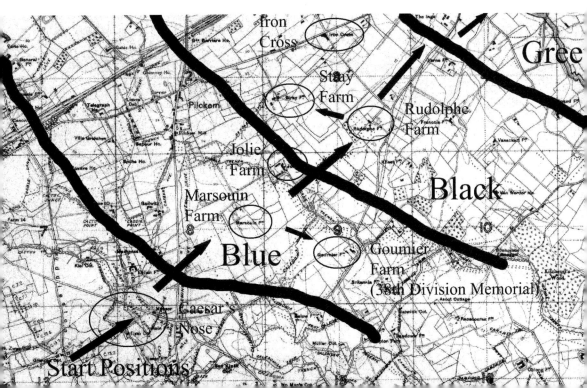

A typical scene of the dreadful conditions facing the men of the 38th Division.

battalions, the objectives were marked with a series of coloured lines; 'Blue', 'Black' and Green'. Zero hour was at 03.50 hrs and the division moved into attack, with the 10th Welsh on the right, the 13th Welsh on the right centre, the 13th Royal Welsh Fusiliers on the left centre and the 16th Royal Welsh Fusiliers on the left. The Blue Line was captured with but little opposition, most of the enemy encountered being found

in dugouts in Caesar Support. These were taken prisoners, with the exception of those who showed fight, who were killed by bayonets or shot. The advance to the 'Black Line', just east of Pilckem Village, was carried out by the 15th Welsh on the right centre and the 14th Welsh on the right.

In 113 Brigade, who had fewer trenches to encounter, this attack was carried out by the remaining two companies in both the 13th Royal Welsh Fusiliers and 16th Royal Welsh Fusiliers. Opposition made in this advance to the 'Black Line' was far more severe than that made in the advance on the 'Blue Line'. The centres of resistance were Marsouin Farm and Stray Farm on the right and the village of Pilckem on the left. In all these places there were several concrete machine gun emplacements, but the men of the 15th Welsh managed to outflank the positions at Marsouin Farm and Candle Trench, and compelled the garrisons to surrender, taking a machine-gun and over fifty men prisoner. Despite the difficulties faced, the 'Black Line' was captured on time and was immediately consolidated and held.

The advance to the Green Line was carried out by half battalions of the 15th and 14th Welsh on the right and by the 15th Royal Welsh Fusiliers on the left. The Village of Pilckem was in the hands of 113 Brigade and 14th and 15th Welsh who had joined them there.

Considerable trouble was then met from the direction of Rudolphe Farm which was in the area allotted to the 51st (Highland) Division. That division was too far to the right and consequently a platoon of the 15th Welsh under Lieutenant F.H. Jordan was detailed to attack the

A fatigue party engaged in wiring crossing the Yser Canal during the Battle of Pilckem Ridge. Taylor Library

Germans killed during an attack. Taylor Library

farm. This was successfully accomplished and the enemy, with the exception of some fifteen men who surrendered, ran away or were shot.

Their blood now up, the 15th Welsh drove on, but slightly lost their way, missing the fortified Jolie Farm and attacking Stray Farm, but the 51st (Highland) Division had now caught them up and cleared Jolie Farm, safe-guarding the flank of the 15th Welsh, who again moved on, capturing a house containing a telephone exchange and seventy Germans.

The area of Iron Cross was strongly held, and the 14th Welsh suffered heavily in taking it. They killed twenty of the enemy garrison and took forty prisoners and three machine guns from the area. This done the 14th Welsh pushed on to positions north east of Iron Cross (just off the map), where an enemy dressing station with sixteen wounded men and a further twenty-two fit men were captured. Between them, 14th and 15th Welsh had gained their objectives, and the blue line was achieved.

The 15th Royal Welsh Fusiliers meanwhile had commenced their advance from the 'Blue Line' at the correct time, but on nearing Battery Copse were met with such heavy fire that in a short time only a few officers were left, and the Artillery Barrage began to run away from the

German dead at the entrance to a concrete bunker. Taylor Library

men. The men, however, struggled forward and established themselves on the Iron Cross Ridge. It was during this attack on the Iron Cross Ridge that the Welsh poet Ellis Humphrey Evans, otherwise known as Hedd Wyn, was killed.

During the period that 113 and 114 Brigades were attacking up to the Iron Cross Ridge the 11th South Wales Borderers and the 17th Royal Welsh Fusiliers, both from 115 Brigade, were gradually working their way forward until they were close up to the Iron Cross Ridge from which they launched their attack on the Steenbeek.

This attack was successfully carried out in the face of considerable opposition from concrete machine gun emplacements which had been constructed within houses. All were, however, outflanked by the infantry and the garrisons were forced to surrender. Finally the Steenbeek was reached, and parties from the 38th Division pushed across to cover and hold its crossings.

The losses amongst the units of the 38th Division were severe, and consequently the general officer commanding 115 Brigade ordered one company of the 16th Welsh to reinforce the 17th Royal Welsh Fusiliers, and one company of the 10th South Wales Borderers to reinforce the 11th South Wales Borderers.

From 14.00 hrs onwards, Germans were seen to be massing for a counter attack, and this attack developed at 15.10. One company of the 11th South Wales Borderers which had occupied Au Bon Gite were forced to retire to the western side of the Steenbeek as a result. The remainder of the line held repelled the attack, with an artillery and machine gun barrage helping largely. Rifle fire was also successfully employed in wiping out some one hundred Germans who had got through the barrage.

During the course of the afternoon the weather, which had been dull and cloudy, changed for the worse and rain began to fall steadily and continued more or less for the next three days, rendering operations extremely difficult owing to the slippery and muddy nature of the ground, which clogged the movement of the infantry, and helped make the overall Third Battle of Ypres the hell it was to be remembered for.

The morning of 31 August 1917 was quiet as far as hostilities were concerned, but in course of the afternoon the enemy again attempted a counter-attack, which was broken up by artillery and machine gun fire before it had time to develop.

The heavy shelling, the state of the weather, and the many casualties experienced by 115 Brigade necessitated its being relieved.

On the night of l/2 August 113 Brigade took over the front line. From this date right through to 6 August there was little more action; the weather during this period being so bad that operations became impossible, and so the 38th Division clung onto its hard-won ground. On 6 August the 38th Division was relieved in the line by the 20th (Light) Division and withdrew to Proven where it rested and recommenced training. The official casualty figures for the 15th Welsh during the Battle of the Pilckem Ridge, from 31 July until 2 August 1917 were fifteen men killed, one hundred and thirty-three wounded and seven missing. In fact at least twenty seven men were killed with the battalion during this period, with a further nine killed in the days leading up to the battalions relief on 6 August 1917. These men are buried in some of the many war cemeteries that litter the area still today, and the many wounded were treated in the Casualty Clearing Stations in the area, most notably at the nearby Essex Farm Advanced Dressing Station, which still stands today.

The 38th (Welsh) Division had regained the honour which it had unjustly lost after their supposed tardiness in the capture of Mametz Wood. Both the 14th and 15th Welsh had suffered the worst, having had the more difficult side of the advance to deal with, but deal with it they did, earning them congratulations from the Prince of Wales, who had been with the Guards Division, from Sir Herbert Plumer, Commanding Second Army, from General Lord Cavan, commanding XIV Corps, and from General Sir Hunter-Weston, commanding VIII Corps.

The Battle of Pilckem Ridge was a Battle Honour carried proudly by the division, for the Welshmen had proved their worth, but a prouder hour was to come within twelve months time.

Captain Percy Lloyd Humphrey

One of the notable casualties during the advance on the Blue Line on 31 July 1917 was Captain Percy Lloyd Humphreys, the son of Cadwallader and Sara Humphreys of Llanfair, near Welshpool. He was working as a bank clerk at Llandeilo prior to the war, and was thirty-five years old when he was killed at Ypres. Percy is buried at Caesar's Nose Welsh Cemetery, near Boesinghe. He was one of the original members of the battalion.

The majority of the casualties suffered by the 15th Welsh, indeed the whole 38th Division, were caused by German machine gunners situated within strongly defended concrete pillboxes. One of the men killed during the storming of the pillboxes was the twenty year old Private Archie Potts. Archie was the Son of John Potts, of "Isledon," Trinity Place, Aberystwyth. His body was one of the many dead of Passchendaele that still lie in those peaceful fields today without a known grave, and so Archie is commemorated on the Tyne Cot Memorial.

During the taking of some of these pillboxes, there were some outstanding acts of bravery by men of the 38th (Welsh) Division.

Corporal James Llewellyn Davies of the 13th Royal Welsh Fusiliers single-handedly attacked a machine gun position and took it, although previous attempts had failed. He then led an attack on a sniper, but he died later and is buried in Canada Farm Cemetery.

Sergeant Ivor Rees of Llanelli served with the 11th South Wales Borderers. Ivor captured a machine gun post, killing its occupants with rifle and bayonet, and later went on to take a pillbox, killing five Germans and capturing a further thirty, including two officers and their machine gun. Both men of the 38th Welsh Division were awarded the ultimate recognition for their bravery in the form of the Victoria Cross.

Gallantry had not been confined to other units of the 38th Division during the battle though. The 15th Welsh gained several awards for bravery, one of which was to 22394 Sergeant Alfred Speake of Trealaw, in the Rhondda Valley. Alfred was awarded the Distinguished Conduct Medal.

Part of the front line trenches used for the attack of the 38th Division

For Conspicuous Gallantry and devotion to duty. During the operations he showed conspicuous gallantry and ability as a Platoon Serjeant and as Acting Company Serjeant-Major. On one occasion, when all his officers had become casualties, he took command of the company, and was of invaluable assistance to the new company commander.
London Gazette 17.4.18

Taylor Library

was called Yorkshire Trench. In 1992 a dugout was discovered on the site of Yorkshire Trench by a team of amateur Belgian archaeologists, and in recent years, a section of the trench and dugouts was excavated, and is now conserved for future generations to see.

During the excavation, several bodies of British soldiers were found, and discovered to have been Royal Welsh Fusiliers of the 38th (Welsh) Division. These men's identities sadly remained a mystery, and their remains were buried at nearby Cement House Cemetery. Below is a photograph of Yorkshire Trench, and a photo of fragments found during the dig. It is hard to imagine that this peaceful place was once the scene of so much pain and bloodshed for our ancestors.

Artefacts found during excavations at Boesinghe.

Part of the excavated and reconstructed Yorkshire Trench at Boesinghe.

Chapter 8

Passchendaele – Langemarck

THE 15TH WELSH WERE ENCAMPED at Poole Camp in the Proven area by 6 August 1917, and the remainder of the 38th Division was based around the immediate area. For the next week, the fatigued men rested, washed and cleaned their kit, and then began training again.

Between the end of the Battle of the Pilckem, and the time the 15th Welsh were relieved, another seven men had been killed. One was the young Private William Bailey Evans, the Son of Captain William Evans, of the Boar's Head Hotel, Aberystwyth. William had been killed in action on 4 August 1917. His body was also lost in the mire, and he is commemorated on the Tyne Cot Memorial.

Private William Bailey Evans

Another of the casualties of 4 August was the oil warehouseman, Private William Cay. William was a married man, and resided at 18, High Street, Sunderland. He was called to the colours in January 1917 and was the husband of Florence Jane Barber. They had two children, Florence Margaret, and William David Cay. William had only been with the Battalion since 11 June 1917.

William is another example of the terrible conditions on the battlefield. He was reported missing on 4 August near Langemarck. On 5 September his body was discovered on the battlefield and buried at Langemarck by a Second Lieutenant Malpas of the 7th Somerset Light Infantry, who gave a map reference to his burial place. The grave was lost after the subsequent fighting in the area, and so William is another 15th Welshmen commemorated on the Tyne Cot Memorial.

On 15 August 1917, 10th Welsh and 15th Welsh, of 114 Brigade, proceeded by train to the Malakoff Farm Area, and the following day moved to Jolie Farm, coming under orders of the 20th (Light) Division. The day of 16 August saw the launch of the Battle of Langemarck from the positions taken by the 38th Welsh two weeks earlier. During the day, the 15th Welsh sent out parties of men to survey the area around Au Bon Gite and the Steenbeek, and at 19.40 hrs the battalion moved into positions here under the command of Major Rhydderch and dug in. The battlefield by now was a quagmire of mud, shell holes and the general detritus of war, and in fact was plain hell for the men. Captain J A Davies, MC then took command of C Company, sited east of the Steenbeek, and moved them up onto the outskirts of Langemarck, suffering casualties due to the intense bombardment falling on the village. Captain Percy Hier Davies was killed during this move, along with Private Thomas Clee, of Bishops Castle in Shropshire, and also Private William Selby Hughes of Swansea. Five other ranks were reported wounded, and twenty-one reported as 'missing believed wounded'. The three dead men's graves were never located, and they are commemorated on the Tyne Cot Memorial, along with many of the men who would die within the next few days, fighting in the Flanders mud.

On 17 August 1917 the 7th Somerset's were sent forward to assist the 12th Kings at Langemarck. Captain Davies, MC with his C Company of the 15th Welsh moved up to replace the position vacated by the Somerset's, and the complete battalion then took over the front line from the 7th King's Own Yorkshire Light Infantry, 7th Somerset Light Infantry, 12th Kings and 7th Duke of Cornwall's Light Infantry of the 20th (Light) Division.

Within the 15th Welsh, Major Ernest Helme was wounded when a shell burst at Periscope House, and two other ranks killed during the relief of these Light Infantry battalions. Both of these men were of the original Bolton contingent, Privates James Coleman and Thomas Whittle. Thomas Whittle was the son of James Charles and Sarah Elizabeth Whittle, of 23, Bashall Street, Bolton. Tom was hit by shrapnel in the head and back during the relief, and died instantly. He was thirty-one years old, and is commemorated on the Tyne Cot Memorial alongside James Coleman.

The 20th (Light) Division, along with the 10th and 15th Welsh, had successfully captured the village of Langemarck. Now it was time for them to be relieved, and the remainder of the 38th (Welsh) Division moved to the front to do so, with the 14th Welsh relieving the 15th Welsh from their front line positions on 20 August. Five more men had died in the meantime, making the total casualty count for the 15th Welsh almost 250 men killed since arriving in France in December 1915.

The line taken over by the 38th Division ran through White Trench and Bear Trench, Eagle Trench being in the hands of the Germans. The 15th Welsh were now at Au Bon Gite in brigade reserve, after being re-attached to 114 Brigade.

The day of 22 August 1917 was a calamitous day for the 15th Welsh. The battalion was relieved by the 11th South

Private Thomas Whittle.

A view across the peaceful Pilckem Ridge as it is today.

Wales Borderers, and ordered back to divisional reserve at Malakoff Farm, but during the relief, Major Rhydderch was wounded by shellfire. Ten men were also killed, and twenty-two other ranks wounded, two of whom died as a result later that day.

Ten of the dead are commemorated on the Tyne Cot Memorial, one is buried at Mendinghem and the other is buried at Oostaverne Wood Cemetery. None of these were men of west Wales, but one was a promising young trainee accountant, and one of the few Scotsmen to be killed with the battalion during the course of the war. Private William Duthie Grassick had been born at Wanton Wells, Dunecht, in Aberdeenshire. William was the youngest in a large family, with three brothers and four sisters, and was just eighteen years old when he was called up in June 1916 joining the Army Reserve. William moved to Kinmel Park by the end of the year, and from there was drafted into the 15th Welsh, joining them at Ypres during May 1917. Sadly William is another of the missing of Passchendaele, and so is commemorated on the Tyne Cot Memorial to the missing.

IN MEMORY OF
COMRADES OF
38TH (WELCH)
DIVISION
1914 - 18

The bunker at Goumier Farm, Pilckem Ridge in a peaceful setting.

Inset: The 38th Welsh Division memorial plaque.

Captured German bunkers in a devastated landscape.

The 15th Welsh remained at Malakoff Farm until 29 August 1917, while the remainder of the 38th Division took part in further actions around Langemarck, and on 30 August moved back into divisional support at Hulls Farm for the next few days.

Conditions were by now atrocious. The numerous shell-holes were gradually filling with water, and the men of the 38th Division found great difficulty in getting out and advancing and keeping up with the barrage. The barrage got away from them and they came under the fire of machine guns from the direction of Pheasant Farm and were unable to reach their objective.

On the last day of August, the nineteen year old Private John James John, the son of Mr and Mrs David John, of Gosport Street, Laugharne, died of wounds suffered at Malakoff Farm, at 46 Casualty Clearing Station.

Laugharne is an ancient Township, situated on the extreme edge of the Carmarthenshire border, adjoining Pembrokeshire, and due to its situation adjoining the latter county, the majority of the men of Laugharne who served with the Welsh Regiment had joined the Pembroke Yeomanry (later the 24th Welsh). John was one of just a handful of men from Laugharne who had joined the 15th Welsh, and he is buried at Mendinghem, along with many of his fallen comrades.

No further operations were conducted on the front of the 38th Division and the remaining period in the line passed without event, except for the usual daily shelling. On 6 September the 15th Welsh were relieved in the line at Langemarck by the 14th Welsh, and moved into brigade reserve, west of the Steenbeek. On 9 September they moved back to Malakoff Farm, and the following day the battalion entrained at Elverdinghe for 'P1' Camp at Proven.

A further twelve men were killed in this short period, and twenty-four more men wounded, so it was for a well deserved rest that the rest of the 38th (Welsh) Division was relieved on 11 September by the 20th (Light) Division and moved to Proven, joining the 15th Welsh in reserve.

The successful capture of the Pilckem Ridge by the 38th (Welsh) Division was aided by excellent work done by the artillery in breaking down the wire and smashing up trenches and emplacements and also to the way in which the men rapidly outflanked numerous concrete dugouts met in the area captured. The first survey of the area after the battle stated that there were 280 of these structures scattered in the divisional area.

Opposed to the 38th Division on the morning of 31 July 1917 had been the German 3rd Guards Division, which had just relieved the 23rd Reserve Division. As part of this division were the notorious

Cockchafers, or Prussian Guards. From this elite German regiment alone, 400 prisoners were taken by the Welsh, as well as many more killed.

In all a total of over 700 prisoners were captured by the 38th Division in the capture of the Pilckem Ridge. It had been a successful enough operation to merit the praise of Field Marshal Sir Douglas Haig, the man who had so publicly damned the division after the capture of Mametz Wood just fourteen months previously.

A lasting tribute to the 38th (Welsh) Division adorns the doorway of a battered German concrete pillbox at Goumier Farm, which still stands in the pleasant pasture land which the area has reverted to. Above this doorway is a marble plaque, erected in memory of the men of the 38th (Welsh) Division.

The pillbox was actually in the sector of the 51st (Highland) Division, but a platoon of the 15th Welsh had moved out of their allotted area to assist a section of the Highlanders attacking the area around the here.

Added to the honour of the 38th Divisions attack on Pilckem Ridge, the 15th Welsh gained the honour of a special mention by the commander of the 20th (Light) Division for their part in the Battle of Langemarck.

Chapter 9

The Return To French Flanders

THE BATTLE OF PASSCHENDAELE was still raging, but the men of the 38th (Welsh) Division had done their bit, and were to be moved to a quieter sector of the Western Front to rest and rebuild their strength. On 13 September 1917 the 15th Welsh moved to the Eecke Area, and marched to Morbecque the following morning. On 15 September they marched to Estaires and by the following day had reached the Fleurbaix sector, relieving the 2/6th Kings in reserve at Bac St. Maur, near Sailly Sur La Lys; almost back to the area where the battalion tasted trench warfare for the first time nearly two long years ago, although it was a shock to the old hands of the battalion to see the damage that had been done to the area since their last spell here in early 1916.

The country was sodden. Trenches were in a poor state, and frequently flooded. The battalion's time here was to prove very trying, and the first week was spent providing working parties which maintained posts in the subsidiary line. Regular training was carried out each morning, which resulted in several men becoming wounded. On 25 September 1917 the 13th Battalion of the Corpo Expedicionário

The flooded Lys Valley.

Português, the Portuguese Army, became attached to 114 Brigade, and relieved the 10th Welsh in the Front Line. Two companies of the 15th Welsh moved up in support of the Portuguese Troops manning the line, with A and B Companies reaching their positions by 16.00 hrs. Close co-operation with the Portuguese Troops now began in earnest, with officers of the 15th Welsh becoming attached to their counterparts.

Reinforcements also began to join the battalion, to replace the many men who had been wounded or killed at Ypres. One of these men was twenty year old Private William Shanahan of Llanelli. William was already a seasoned veteran, having fought with the 9th Welsh on the Somme throughout the winter of 1916-1917. He had taken ill during the summer of 1917 when his battalion was at Messines, and had been sent back to Britain for treatment. After several weeks convalescing, William was posted to the 15th Welsh at Fleurbaix. A passage taken from his notes of his time at war reads:

> Then a move to Redcar, a resort on the east coast – more parades, drills and finally off once again via Southampton to France where I joined the 15th Welsh Battalion, known as the Carmarthenshire. It was, I suppose, a Carmarthenshire based battalion, like the 13th or the 14th which was supposed to be a Swansea formation, but as there were Welshmen in kilts and Dorset men in Yorkshire Regiments, so all counties were represented in a Welsh Battalion.

Another passage, the first of his time with the Battalion, went:

> During September 1917, while at Fleurbaix near Armentieres, the country about was well wooded with high hedges right up to the support line and one could get about freely during the day Here we used to await the ration limbers. We called this place Tin Barn Dump, and here the rations were loaded on to flat trucks running on wooden rails that ran across the land between the rear and the front line. The defence was not trenches, but earthworks built up to six feet in height. The same applied to support the narrow rail road which ran up to the support trench.

Private William Shanahan

The entire 38th Division was to be stationed in this area for the next six months, and so it was that the men of the 15th Welsh settled back into the routine of trench warfare. They had played a vital role in two large scale pitched battles, and now it was time for them to rest and rebuild their losses. For the time being, this section of the Western Front was to

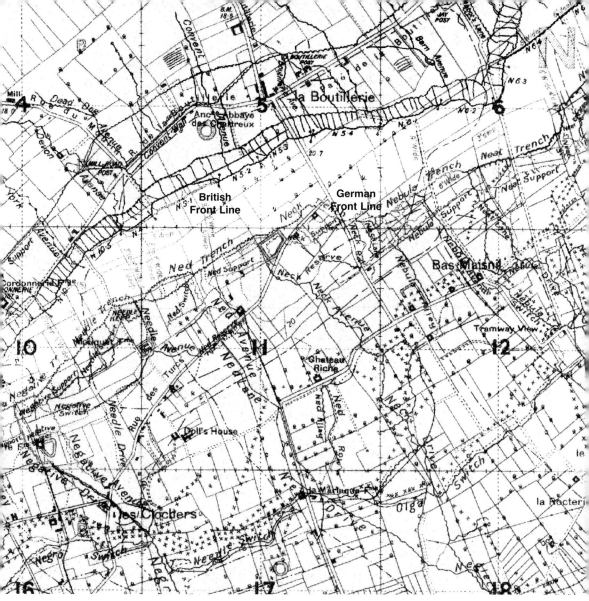

Trench map showing the La Boutillerie sector dated late 1917.

remain relatively peaceful, while other units of the British and Canadian Armies moved to the Cambrai area, where the focus of the next offensive was to come to bear during the Battle of Cambrai over the winter of 1917-1918.

In the meantime, the 15th Welsh began October of 1917 in support of their Portuguese counterparts at La Boutillerie. Apart from sporadic trench mortar and artillery fire, all was relatively peaceful here, but conditions were terrible, with trenches prone to flooding, especially when their sides were blown in by trench mortar fire.

An extract from another letter in the *Western Telegraph* shows the feelings of one West-Walian, Jim John, about life in the trenches:

> *In civil life I for one was very unsettled and always grumbling. Won't I appreciate it when, and if, I ever get back to it again! It's very easy to criticise when one has all the necessaries in life. Sometimes when there is a chance of a few hours sleep it's the usual thing when one gets down to it, to suddenly realise that you have a few hundred vermin creeping all over your body and a score of rats gambolling around your head. Such things are absolutely unavoidable out here, but still have to be put up with. When "those people" realise all this, and that there is a war on then perhaps they will understand why one writes hard things about those who are prolonging the agony, when by simply "doing their bit" they would be also hastening the end. Well, we're willing to stick it all (if we can) for the good of the cause.*

On 15 October 1917, nine men were wounded by a bombardment from the dreaded German trench mortars. One of these men, Robert Richard Owen, died at the Base Hospital at Etaples just two weeks later.

As regards life in general on the Western Front, this part of the line was a relative haven of peace compared to some. Private Shanahan wrote of this period:

A German trench mortar crew in action.

We had been in this sector in the Lys Valley some months and considered ourselves lucky to have had our lot spent in quiet places, both sides licking their wounds after the battles of 1916. Fleurbaix, where I had joined the 15th Welsh on my return to France, was indeed a lucky place to be posted and the battalion was a happy one. The time we were around and about Fleurbaix in September 1917, the trees still stood undamaged and leafy, the orchards were full of plenty of tall pear trees and walnuts. We often filled our sacks full of pears which the cooks served up stewed so often as to make us detest the sight of pears, while the soldiers away up on our left around Ypres would welcome a meal of stewed pears.

Often have I sat under an apple tree in Bois Grenier, a tiny hamlet in front of Fleurbaix and quite near to our support trenches. This was possible for nature – the trees, hedges and regular countryside – provided the best ready made camouflage. I sat under the tree reading and when I felt like it, tossed a piece of branch laying around into the tree over my head, and down came the apples and they were russets too.

It was indeed a nice break for the Welshmen. The month of October drew to a close with the men in the front line. Battalion headquarters was at Wye Farm: A, C and D Companies were in the line, with B Company in Reserve. The following month of November was also relatively quiet. The only notable instance during this period of routine trench warfare was on 14 November, when a German trench mortar attack caused six casualties amongst the battalion.

This routine of reserve and trench duty continued through the month, and only three men died in November from the battalion. Second Lieutenant Cecil Norman Jones of Lewisham died of sickness on 9 November 1917, and is buried at ANZAC Cemetery, Sailly-Sur-La-Lys.

Private Arthur Gower Jenkins, a Llanelli man, died of sickness on 23 November, and is buried at Wizernes Communal Cemetery, and on 25 November Sergeant John Pye was killed in action at Bourlon Wood, while attached to the 18th Welsh during the Battle of Cambrai. John was a twenty-one year old from Runcorn in Cheshire, and is the only man of the 15th Welsh to be commemorated on the Cambrai Memorial, at Louverval.

The month drew to a close, with just one more man wounded on 28 November, and the battalion moved back into reserve on 30 November, being relieved by the 10th Welsh, and moving into billets at Rue Biache, Rue Des Quernes and Rouge De Bout. On 5 December 1917 the area was shelled by the Germans with gas shells, and three other ranks were wounded as a result, one dying later in the day.

Private Thomas Christmas White was from the Rhondda Valley. He became the last casualty suffered by the 15th Welsh in 1917, and is buried at Croix-Du-Bac Cemetery, at Steenwerck. He is in fact the only man of the battalion buried there.

Even though it was now a routine task, burying the dead was not simple on the Western Front. Private Shanahan wrote of one such burial allotted to himself:

> We picked a spot a few yards inside the gates, but the ground was like steel and we found it impossible to dig deeper. We even now were only down eight or nine inches, so with Ted at his feet and I his head, we laid him in the grave but it was too short, so lifting him out I chopped away at the head of the grave making way for his head. Another try and this time the body lay easily. I said to Ted, "I wonder where the bullet struck him". The first few buttons had already been undone, but the blood from the wound had soaked the top of his jacket and I was not able to undo another few buttons or even open the jacket. The area around had frozen hard; blood soaked into the shirt had frozen to his chest.
>
> Now we started to fill in the grave, but to pack the soil was out of the question. We filled it in and heaped some lumps on the top, and so we buried... on a fine sunny morning with hardly a sound to disturb the operation As I remember no one asked where we had laid him, and I suppose there his remains are still.

A Welsh Christmas card.

This last sentence helps to illustrate how some of the many burials during the course of the war remain undiscovered. Many men were of course literally blown to pieces during the war, but many more were lost as a result of shelling after being buried, when cemeteries were smashed out of all recognition by shellfire. Private Shanahan also shows how other men's graves were simply lost or forgotten.

On 10 December 1917 the 15th Welsh moved into divisional reserve at Sailly-Sur-La-Lys. Here they remained until the 17th, when they moved back into brigade reserve, based at a redundant factory at Bac-St-Maur, and the following day moved back into the trenches at La Boutillerie.

Christmas and New Year passed by, with the usual trench and reserve routine carrying on throughout the New Year, with the men taking the time to write home to friends and family.

On 13 January 1918 the 15th Welsh was relieved by the 8th Royal

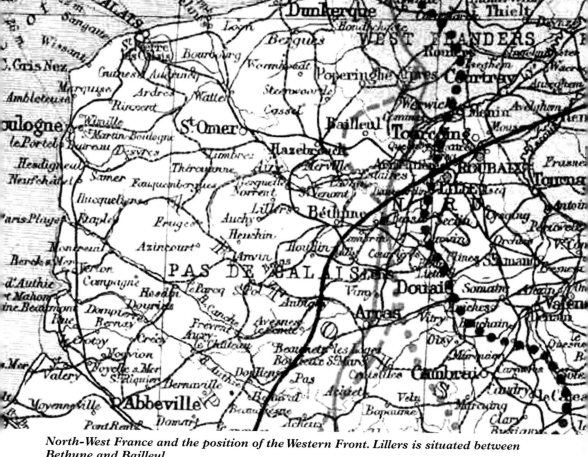

North-West France and the position of the Western Front. Lillers is situated between Bethune and Bailleul.

Fusiliers, and the whole of the 38th Division moved from the line, to the area west of Estaires. The 15th Welsh moved to the Bleu Area, north of Estaires on the night of 13 January 1918, and the following day marched to the Guarbecque sector. The following morning saw the Battalion march again, taking up billets at St. Hilaire-Cottes, a village situated between Aire-Sur-La-Lys and Lillers in northern France, where they spent the remainder of January training.

This was the first time that the entire 38th Division had been out of the line for a notable period. This period of training though was spoilt by the weather, which was so bad that for days at a time some of the farms in which the troops were billeted were completely surrounded by water, and could only be approached by wading up to the knees. This period of training was also further interfered with by the need to employ part of the division on the construction of defences.

It was to be a sad time for the 38th Division. Orders were received for all brigades in the British army to be reduced to a strength of three battalions; four of the battalions in the division were to be disbanded and the divisional commander was not given a free hand in the selection of those battalions.

The 15th Battalion, Royal Welsh Fusiliers (The London Welsh), the 11th (2nd Gwent) Battalion, South Wales Borderers, The 10th (1st Rhondda) Battalion, Welsh Regiment, and the 16th (Cardiff City) Battalion, Welsh Regiment were consequently disbanded. However, the officers and men of these battalions were not all lost to the division, for permission was given to bring all other battalions up to full strength and many of these men joined those battalions from the disbanded ones.

On 3 February 1918 the 16th Welsh received their order to disband. It was a crushing blow to the officers and men, as only the previous day they had won the Brigade Transport Competition, earning the battalion a prize of 200 francs from General Blackader, and were all in high spirits.

On the following day the men of 16th Welsh gathered for their last Church Parade together, and the system of reorganisation was read out to the assembled troops. Two companies were chosen for transfer to the 15th and 19th Welsh, and the other two were to be placed in Corps Reserve for the time being. Details were finalised in the coming days, and the entry in the 16th Welsh War Diary for 6 February 1918 showed that 15th Welsh were to gain eight officers of C Company, fifty-six Other Ranks of Divisional HQ, and ninety-four Other Ranks of C Company. A Company, officers and men, were sent to the 19th Welsh. As the names were read out, the men filed away to the tunes of the battalion band. It was a sad moment for the proud men of the Cardiff City Battalion. At the end of the month the remaining men were merged with the remainder of 15th Royal Welsh Fusiliers and 10th Welsh into No. 1 Entrenching Battalion, with Lieutenant-Colonel F W Smith in command.

Indeed, this reduction in strength could not have come at a more opportune time for the battalions which were not affected, for the machine gun companies were at this time about to be organised as a battalion, and several members of the new battalion headquarters were selected from the disbanded infantry battalions, thereby negating any detrimental effects.

On 1 February 1918 the 15th Welsh moved from the St. Hilaire-Cottes area to Le Sart, near Merville. The battalion was now back in divisional reserve, where they received their new men, before moving into brigade reserve at Pont De Nieppe on 14 February 1918.

On 18 February the battalion moved into positions at the 'Jute Factory', then on 20 February moved to Houplines. On 22 February

A view along the River Lys at Pont-de-Nieppe.

they relieved the 14th Welsh in the front line at Houplines, and remained there until their relief on 26 February, moving back into divisional reserve at 'The Laundry', at Erquinghem. The battalion war diary for this period contains some very detailed operational orders for this period, but nothing of real note occurred during this time.

Private Shanahan wrote of the Laundry:

The battalion spent some months near Houplines, taking a spell for a few days in a huge laundry on the outskirts of Armentieres. The buildings had barely been damaged and from there we provided working parties, digging and digging. Our whole period out of the trenches seemed to be spent digging reserve trenches. Often, our entire period of darkness would be spent doing fatigues of one sort or another at, or very near, where we had spent our previous four days in the trenches. More often than not in some sectors we would have preferred to remain in the line than to be relieved, but four days in, four days out was the rule, and we spent that time in working parties or shining boots, buttons and rifles for inspections.

At the beginning of March 1918 the Western Front had quietened

Back row: Privates 20456 Walter Owen and 20441 Jimmie Barlow. Front: 20457 Fred Meluish, 20459 John Roberts and 20443 James Seed (later killed at Armentieres).

Simon Jervis

down. The Battle of Cambrai, and the subsequent counter-attack by the Germans had drawn to a close, and this was a rare quiet period of the war, which was sadly fated not to last.

The 15th Welsh were still in reserve at the Laundry, when they suffered three more casualties on 5 March 1918 from German artillery fire. Two of these men were wounded, but Private Charles Trimby of Newport, Monmouthshire was killed. He is buried at Cite Bonjean Cemetery in Armentieres. Just four days earlier another man of the battalion died of sickness and was buried in the same cemetery. Private James Seed was another of the original Bolton contingent. Both men are buried next to each other.

On 6 March 1918, the 15th Welsh relieved the 13th Welsh in support at Houplines. They remained here until 10 March, suffering several casualties from gassing, and moved into the front line that day, relieving the 14th Welsh. On the following day, the trenches held by the 15th Welsh were shelled, and then hit by a strong German trench raiding party, while a box barrage prevented the 10th Welsh reinforcing the line. Considerable damage was done to the Welsh trenches, and the war diary for the day noted seven other ranks killed, three missing and twenty-two wounded. In fact nine men were killed during the raid, seven of which are buried at Cite Bonjean, one at Merville, where he had died of wounds suffered from the attack, and one man was missing and never found. No. 6 Outpost had also been lost.

The missing man was Private Daniel O'Shea of Swansea. Daniel was originally from Kerry, but had lived at Swansea prior to the war. He was twenty-four years old, and as his grave was never located, he is the only man of the 15th Welsh who is commemorated on the Ploegsteert Memorial.

More shelling continued on the following day, killing another man, Private Arthur Leonard Lewis of Aberkenfig, and wounding nine others, with one of these men dying as a result later that day. At 21.30 hrs that night Lieutenants Beech and Roberts led a strong party out to raid the German lines, but found just empty lines. The area was now beginning to really heat up, and rumours of an impending German offensive grew.

Little did the men know, but the planned German offensive, later known as the *Kaiserschlacht*, was due to be launched on the Somme on 21 March 1918 and this shelling was part of the diversion which would precede it, and also precede the launching of the German offensive that was to follow, on the Lys in April 1918. The remainder of March followed the same pattern for the 15th Welsh, with regular shelling, both of gas and of high explosive shells, continuing for the remainder of the month, providing a steady stream of casualties to the battalion. In fact a further eleven men were to die during the remainder of the battalions time in the trenches at the Lys.

On 10 March 1918 the battalion was in support trenches at Houplines, and later that day took up positions in the front line, relieving the 14th Welsh. They had not been in position long when a short barrage of forty 4.2-inch shells hit their positions, at the junction of Panama Canal and the Subsidiary Line.

Luckily no casualties occurred, but it had just been a preliminary barrage for an attack which was to follow, and early in the morning of 11 March a strong German party raided Post 6, covered by another heavy barrage on the support and subsidiary lines, and after a brief firefight the Germans withdrew taking with them three prisoners. They had left in their wake seven dead 15th Welshmen, twenty-two wounded plus the three men missing.

One of the dead was the thirty year old Private David Evans, the son of Mr. and Mrs. David Evans, of 62, Castle Graig, Landore, Swansea. David had probably enlisted into the 14th Welsh judging by his service number of 17551, but had since been transferred to the 15th Welsh. He is buried at Cite Bonjean Military Cemetery, Armentieres.

As retaliation for the attack, on the following morning of 12 March 1918 the 38th Divisional Artillery launched a heavy barrage on the German lines. This led to a burst of retaliatory fire from the Germans, and this tit-for-tat firing continued throughout the remainder of the day, killing one man and wounding nine others. This pattern continued over the following days, and on the 15th March the weary and battered battalion was relieved from the front by the 13th Welsh, moving first into reserve at the Laundry, Erquinghem.

17551 Private David Evans.
Gaenor Ev

Welshmen in the trenches in the Fleurbaix sector.
By kind permission of The Regimental Museum of the Royal Welsh, Brecon

'Y Ddraig Goch' (the Red Dragon) – a postcard sent home by Welsh soldiers.

Whilst in reserve, the battalion lost one of their most trustworthy men, Sergeant Herbert Lewis Bithell, the former professional footballer, who had been with the battalion since enlisting in 1915. He had been born at Holywell, but his parents had moved their large family to Farnworth, near Bolton, where Herbert and his six brothers and two sisters were raised.

Herbert had married his sweetheart, Edna Jackson, at the Baptist Chapel in Farnworth on 28 October 1915, and sadly he never saw his young bride again, as he remained on the Western Front until being fatally wounded, and dying at the Hospital at Merville on 18 March 1918. The very moving inscription at the base of his headstone reads: 'One of the best, my Hero, my all, and Worthy of Everlasting Love'.

A brief respite followed, and four days later, on 20 March, the battalion relieved the 13th Welsh in the front line again, and again suffered several days of sporadic shellfire. During this latest spell in the trenches, another young man from the Township of Laugharne, who had served with the battalion since 1916, was wounded and evacuated to Armentieres for treatment.

Sergeant Herbert Lewis Bithell.

Arthur Laugharne Allen was the son of William Arthur and Ellen Allen. He was born in 1897 in Seaforth, Lancashire. The family had moved to Gosport House in Laugharne, and had added Laugharne as their middle name, as they were descendants of the famed Civil War commander, Major-General Rowland Laugharne. Arthur died as a result of his wounds, aged just twenty, on 22 March 1918 and is buried in Cite Bonjean Military Cemetery, in Armentieres. His brother Cyril Allen served as a Private in the Lancashire Hussars, and won the Military Medal for bravery in the field in November 1917 whilst attached to the King's Liverpool Regiment at Passchendaele.

This tortuous period for the 15th Welsh ended on the night of 30 March 1918 when at 23.50 hrs the battalion was relieved in the trenches by the 11th Battalion, Suffolk Regiment, part of 101 Brigade, 34th Division.

Little did they know at the time, but this was the last time that the men of the 15th Welsh, and indeed the whole of the 38th (Welsh) Division, were to see the waterlogged trenches of Flanders in anger. The next period in their story was about to begin.

Chapter 10

Return To The Somme

ON 21 MARCH 1918 the Germans launched a desperate last ditch offensive against the British line stretching from the south of Cambrai down towards St. Quentin. This was known as the *Kaiserschlacht*, or Kaisers Battle, and was an attempt to split the Western Front and capture the vital Allied railhead at Amiens, forcing the Allies into an armistice before the might of the American army could make its presence felt. There were four separate German attacks, codenamed MICHAEL, GEORGETTE, GNEISENAU, and BLÜCHER-YORCK.

The Germans had launched their initial offensive against the junction of the British Fifth Army, and the right wing of the British Third Army. The artillery bombardment began at 04.40 hrs on 21 March 1918, hitting targets over an area of 150 square miles. This was to be the heaviest barrage of the entire war, with over 1,100,000 shells being fired in just five hours.

German infantry moving up to attack positions.

Taylor Library

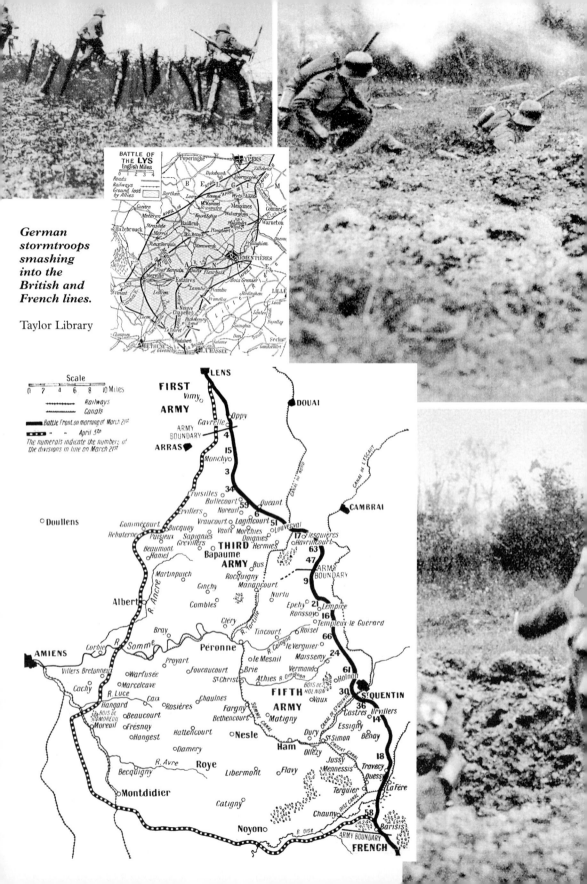

German stormtroops smashing into the British and French lines.

Taylor Library

BATTLE OF THE LYS

English Miles

Roads
Railways
Ground lost by Allies

BELGIUM

FRANCE

Scale

0 2 4 6 8 10 Miles

Railways
Canals
Battle Front on morning of March 21st
April 5th
The numerals indicate the numbers of
the divisions in line on March 21st

FIRST ARMY

LENS
Vimy
Oppy
DOUAI
Gavrelle
ARMY BOUNDARY
4
15
Monchy
ARRAS
3
34
Fuisilles
Bullecourt
Noreuil
Quéant
59
6
CAMBRAI
Ervillers
Doullens
Vraucourt
Lagnicourt
51
Gommecourt
Bucquoy
Vaulx
Morchies
Louverval
Hébuterne
Sapignies
Doignies
Hermies
Lesquières
17
Havrincourt
Beaumont
Puisieux
Grevillers
THIRD ARMY
Bapaume
Bus
63
Hamel
Martinpuich
Rocquigny
47
ARMY BOUNDARY
Ginchy
Manancourt
9
Albert
Combles
Nurlu
Epehy
21
Lempire
Ronssoy
16
Cléry
Templeux le Guerard
Bray
Tincourt
Roisel
66
Corbie
Péronne
R. Cologne
le Verguier
AMIENS
Proyart
le Mesnil
Maissemy
24
Villers Bretonneux
Foucaucourt
Brie
Vermand
61
Warfusée
St Christ
Athies
BOIS DE HOLNON
Holnon
Cachy
Marcelcave
Vaux
30
ST QUENTIN
Caix
Chaulnes
Fargny
Matigny
Castres
36
Urvillers
Hangard
Rosières
Bethencourt
Essigny
Benay
14
Beaucourt
Dury
St Simon
Moreuil
Fresnay
Hattencourt
Nesle
Ham
Jussy
18
Hangest
Damery
Ollezy
Travecy
Quessy
Becquigny
Roye
Libermont
Flavy
Mennessis
Terguier
La Fère
Montdidier
Catigny
Chauny
58
Barisis
Noyon
ARMY BOUNDARY
FRENCH

The German armies involved were the Seventeenth Army under Otto von Bülow, the Second Army under Georg von der Marwitz and the Eighteenth Army under Oskar von Hutier, with a corps from the Seventh Army supporting Hutier's attack. Although the British had learned the approximate time and location of the offensive, the weight of the attack and the preliminary bombardment was an unpleasant surprise. The Germans were also fortunate in that the morning of the attack was foggy, allowing the elite storm-troopers leading the attack to penetrate deep into the British positions undetected.

By the end of the first day, the Germans had broken through at several points on the front of the British Fifth Army, and after two days Fifth Army was in full retreat. As they fell back, many of the redoubts were left to be surrounded and overwhelmed by the following German infantry. The right wing of Third Army also retreated, to avoid being outflanked.

The German breakthrough had occurred just to the north of the boundary between the French and British armies, but after three days, the German advance began to falter as the infantry became exhausted and it became increasingly difficult to move artillery and supplies forward to support them. Also tales of near starving German troops gorging themselves on freshly captured British supplies and French wine became widespread.

Fresh British and Australian units were moved to the vital rail centre of Amiens and the defence began to stiffen. After fruitless attempts to capture Amiens, Ludendorff called off Operation Michael on 5 April 1918. The Allies lost nearly 255,000 men (British, British Empire, French and American). They also lost 1,300 artillery pieces and 200 tanks. All of this could be replaced, either from British factories or from American manpower. German troop losses were 239,000 men, largely the specialist storm-troopers who were irreplaceable. As a result of this, the 38th (Welsh) Division was one of a number of units to be moved into positions on the Somme, to attempt to stem the German advance, and bolster the decimated divisions there.

On 31 March 1918, the war diary of the 15th Welsh noted that the battalion left Pont De Nieppe at 13.00 hrs, and marched to Le Sart, near Merville. A note at the bottom of the page states 'Prior to entraining for unknown destination.'

The entire 38th (Welsh) Division, less the divisional artillery, was on the move again. The artillery in fact remained behind, and played a huge part in the defence of the Lys the following month, when a fresh German offensive, named Operation Georgette was launched there on 9 April 1918.

At 09.00 hrs on 1 March 1918 the 15th Welsh entrained at Merville, detraining at Mondicourt, East of Doullens at 17.00 hrs, leaving behind forever their fallen comrades who now lie buried within the huge military cemetery at Merville. They then marched south to Talmas, arriving at 03.30 hrs the following morning, and billeted there for the next few days. Just over five weeks later the important town of Merville was captured by the Germans, and remained in their hands until late August, 1918.

The entire 38th (Welsh) Division was now situated over an area some five miles north west of Albert, preparing to relieve the battered 47th and 2nd Divisions. On 5 April the 15th Welsh received orders to move, and marched to a position east of Herissart, where they bivouacked for the night. On the following afternoon the battalion marched to Toutencourt, and later in the day back to billets at Talmas. It seems either that the High Command couldn't decide where to place the 38th Division, or that they were playing some sort of game with the German Intelligence, but after three days in billets at Talmas, the 15th Welsh left there again on 10 April, moving to Warloy-Baillon, a village just west of Albert, and back on the old Somme battlefields of 1916.

Warloy-Baillon had been an important billeting and hospital centre throughout the war, and was relatively untouched by German shellfire, thus providing plenty of old farm buildings and houses in which the troops could rest and sleep. Within the village was a friendly estaminet, where the men could visit to buy egg and chips or the cheap *vin blanc* or *vin rouge* that was on offer.

On 11 April 1918 the 15th Welsh moved into brigade reserve, relieving the 5th Royal Berkshires, and moved into the trenches near Martinsart.

In the days following the move to the Somme, the dangerous situation facing the Allies on the Western Front had raised massive concerns in the High Command. On 11 April 1918 Sir Douglas Haig issued his famous 'Backs to the wall' order to his troops, which was read out to the men of the 15th Welsh while they were sat enjoying a game of cards. Their response was somewhat more laid back than was the response of troops who had been caught up in the terrible fighting during the retreat back from Bapaume, who felt loathing at such a statement from a man camped safely behind the lines.

The ruins of Merville in 1918 after it was captured by the Germans.

TO ALL RANKS OF THE BRITISH ARMY IN FRANCE AND FLANDERS

Three weeks ago to-day the enemy began his terrific attacks against us on a fifty-mile front. His objects are to separate us from the French, to take the Channel Ports and destroy the British Army.

In spite of throwing already 106 Divisions into the battle and enduring the most reckless sacrifice of human life, he has as yet made little progress towards his goals.

We owe this to the determined fighting and self-sacrifice of our troops. Words fail me to express the admiration which I feel for the splendid resistance offered by all ranks of our Army under the most trying circumstances.

Many amongst us now are tired. To those I would say that Victory will belong to the side which holds out the longest. The French Army is moving rapidly and in great force to our support.

There is no other course open to us but to fight it out. Every position must be held to the last man: there must be no retirement. With our backs to the wall and believing in the justice of our cause each one of us must fight on to the end. The safety of our homes and the Freedom of mankind alike depend upon the conduct of each one of us at this critical moment.

(Signed) D. Haig F.M.
Commander-in-Chief
British Armies in France
General Headquarters
Tuesday, April 11th, 1918

The lackadaisical recollections of Private Shanahan on this stirring speech show the laid back side to the characters of the Welshmen:

> It was when the German advances were making such progress that Field Marshall Haig issued his famous back to the wall, do or die letter. About this time, we were in support and in the dugout lit up by a couple of candles, a few men were playing brag or solo. I was sat alongside watching, when the sack over the entrance was drawn aside and our platoon officer entered. There was hardly room to stand erect so as to salute and the officer did not insist. Indeed, I think he sat down and proceeded to read the back to the wall letter. Of course by now it has become famous, like the declaration of human rights. He read it out as directed, folded it up, and said, "Well, that's it", when one of the players, anxious to resume playing, called out "Hearts is trumps boys". I don't suppose he was paying the least attention – world shaking events or the real possibility of defeat never crossed his mind. What do they call it- sang froid, no need to get excited, it would probably all come out in the wash.

On 15 April 1918 the battalion relieved the 13th Welsh in the front line, between Bouzincourt and Aveluy, north of the Somme capital of Albert. Albert was by now a far cry from the town that the Welshmen knew in 1916, and was also now in German hands, although British snipers sometimes worked in the town.

The trenches taken over by the Welshmen were in a terrible state of repair, some dating from 1914, some from the 1916 battles, and the remainder hastily dug in 1918. Casualties were now beginning to be suffered again. Captain Gerald Lancaster was wounded on 16 April, and every day men were evacuated from the line with wounds caused by shelling and gas, to be treated at the various Aid Stations in the area.

On 25 April 1918, the 15th Welsh was relieved by the 14th Welsh, and moved back into brigade reserve. The following morning saw them relieved by the 17th Battalion, Australian Imperial Force, and the weary men moved into billets at Contay, where they spent the night before moving to a tented camp at Toutencourt Wood the following morning. The battalion remained here until 2 May 1918.

In the meantime 113 Brigade had recaptured Aveluy Wood from the Germans, and 115 Brigade had then taken up positions there, relieving 113 Brigade on 25 April. Early on 3 May 1918, the 15th Welsh relieved the 17th Lancashire Fusiliers within Aveluy Wood. This was to be their 'home' for the coming months.

> Our forward positions were in the wood, in which there were plenty of trenches which were the remains of positions manned by troops during

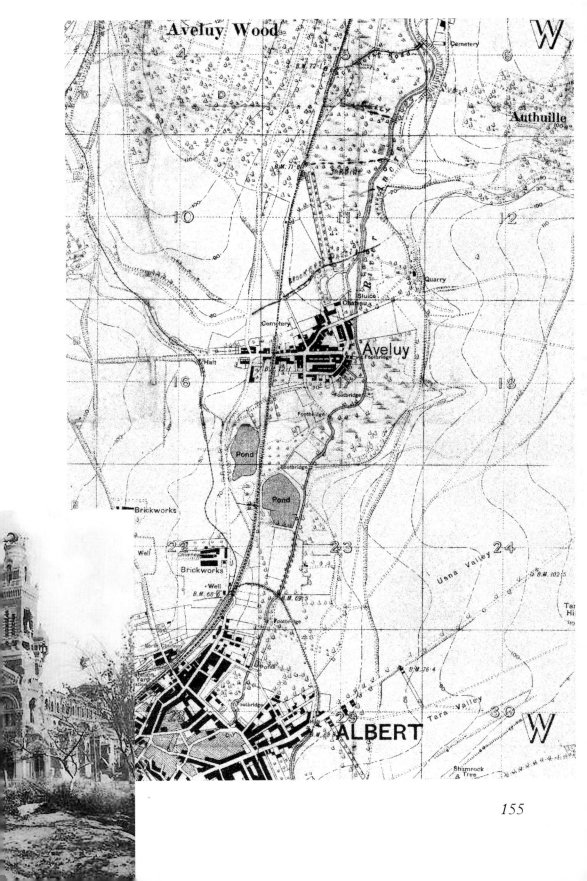

Aveluy Wood

Authuille

Aveluy

Brickworks

Pond

Pond

Brickworks

Usna Valley

ALBERT

Tara Valley

155

the Somme offensive. But the woods became part of the back area, and for months from the previous August or so, must have been a pleasant retreat from the noise of war. The trenches remained a little worse true, but even when the wood once again became part of the front, when we took over from another battalion, some parts were in good condition with dugouts in the side of the trench. These were not dug deep down in the ground, but even so there was room to lay down and sleep, even though there was only about three feet or so on top…

We could find our way to our posts blindfolded and on arriving, the relief was soon over. There was no ceremony – we simply dropped into position and the old lot got out and away. There were no fond farewells. The NCO posted sentries and those off duty soon were doing the usual, that is, sleep. Our turn in the wood soon passed and once again it was back to the chalk pits or Toutencourt. We would prefer always to go no further back than the chalk pits. They were a mile behind, and when we were there, work was out. Back at Toutencourt, someone would have us on some scheme or working party whereas at the chalk pits it was a life of ease.

Shanahan

Aveluy Church after the village's capture by the Germans in March 1918.

Four casualties were suffered during the relief, three men wounded and one killed. The dead man was Private Joseph Henry Davies of Manchester. Harry, as he was fondly known to his parents William and Elizabeth Davies, was buried at Harponville Communal Cemetery. The apt inscription at the base of his grave reads, 'Soldier lay thy weapons down, quit the sword and take the crown'. There is also a memorial to him on the grave of his parents at Manchester Southern Cemetery.

On 10 May 1918, the 15th Welsh, together with one company and two platoons of the 14th Welsh, and two companies of the 19th Welsh, moved forward to consolidate positions in the south west Corner of Aveluy Wood. The advance was to be preceded by a creeping artillery barrage, following meticulously drawn up plans and timing schedules. The plans had been prepared thoroughly by 114 Brigade, with night patrols on the days building up to the attack reconnoitring the positions, and the placing of forward equipment ready for the attackers.

At 08.52 hrs on the morning of 10 May 1918 the attacking force received orders to move, and at 09.00 hrs the artillery barrage opened up and the men moved forward into Aveluy Wood. The advancing men quickly became aware of shells falling to their north, in the British area, and it was soon realised that the barrage was falling short, holding up the advance and causing heavy 'friendly-fire' injuries amongst the Welshmen.

The Headquarters staff, wondering what was happening, sent Second Lieutenant L J Thomas forward to check on the advance, and he returned a while later with the position of the attackers, and the unwanted news that the barrage was falling short – right on top of the Welshmen.

At 11.00 hrs a message was sent by Captain Sampson, stating that the attack had failed due to the barrage, and the Commanding Officer of the 15th Welsh, Lieutenant-Colonel Parkinson, Captain Bucknall, the Brigade Major of 114 Infantry Brigade, and the Artillery Liason Officer moved to the front themselves to check on the situation. When they saw the graveness of the situation, the officers realised that there was no option but to re-occupy the original front line positions, and withdraw. Orders were sent to the artillery to restart the barrage at 16.00 hrs, and for the attack to continue, but thankfully the attack was eventually called off, and later that night the 14th Welsh moved into the line and relieved the 15th Welsh who moved back to brigade reserve.

Further investigations into the failure of the attack found that some companies of the 15th Welsh had gained their objectives, but the failure of the artillery barrage had condemned the attack to failure, with the Royal Artillery admitting the blame themselves in a later report.

Some batteries have been supplied with Ordnance with arcs and rulers which are fixed onto battery boards with drawing pins. The arcs are graduated into ? degree divisions, and there is no further mark on the arc except '1/2 degrees' is marked on the edge. The Major of the battery in question had fixed the arc on the board with drawing pins with handles and the handles of one of the pins was folded over the '1/2'... The Battery therefore opened fire on a line well in rear of our front line and measurements show that it would catch the third wave of the infantry at the time when the advance to the second objective was due... Finally, may I, on behalf of the whole of the Artillery of the V Corps, express my deep regret that mistakes on our part have caused so many casualties to the 114th Infantry Brigade, and should have undoubtedly prevented them from succeeding in the operation in which they were engaged.

Signed Brigadier-General R. P. Benson, General Officer Commanding Royal Artillery, V Corps.

15th Welsh War Diary, National Archives

The attack had cost the 15th Welsh a lot of good men. Twenty men died that day, and a further three died of their wounds over the coming days. Among the dead, the 15th Welsh alone had lost Captain Thomas Glyn Lloyd, and two of its Second Lieutenants, Elmore Wright George and Charles Llewellyn James and D I Rees (who was taken prisoner by the Germans). On top of this, the war diary reported 103 men wounded and a further two men missing. It had been a tragic mistake by the Royal Artillery which had cost the 15th Welsh dearly. Lieutenant John Radmilovic was wounded and died at home in Cardiff.

Captain Thomas Glyn Lloyd was the second son of the Venerable Thomas Lloyd, the Archdeacon of St. Asaph and the Vicar of Rhyl; the original training place of the 15th Welsh. He had been educated at Rossall School, and won a classical scholarship at Clare College, Oxford. In 1915 Thomas had been commissioned into the Welsh Regiment, and served with the 15th Welsh in France from July, 1916. He was promoted Captain in August 1917, and served with the battalion until his death on the tragic morning of 10 May 1918. Thomas is buried at Martinsart British Cemetery.

One of the other casualties was Private Trevor Davies of Resolven, a coal mining village near Neath. Trevor was just nineteen years old and is also buried at Martinsart British Cemetery.

Private Trevor Davies

Lance Corporal John Frederick Parry.

Another casualty of the abortive raid of 10 May was the twenty-eight year old Lance Corporal John Frederick Parry. John was a native of Llanwrig, Montgomeryshire, and the son of David and Elizabeth Parry, of Plas Curig, Towyn-on-Sea. John's parents ran the Brynawel Hotel in Aberystwyth prior to the war, and it was at Aberystwyth that John enlisted, joining the 15th Welsh. He was hit in the thigh by machine gun fire during the initial advance on the morning of 10 May, shattering his fibula. A Chaplain with the 38th Division, Reverend J Parry-Brookes, wrote to John's parents to tell them that he had spoken to John while he was being carried from the battlefield by two stretcher bearers, and that he was very cheerful. Sadly John died just hours later of his wounds while being treated at the military hospital at Doullens. The hospital Chaplain, R N Burns, wrote to John's parents to inform them of their son's death, and that he had suffered very little. John is buried at Doullens Communal Cemetery Extension, No. 2.

On 14 May 1918, after three days rest, the 15th Welsh moved back into the line, relieving the 14th Welsh in Aveluy Wood. The move cost

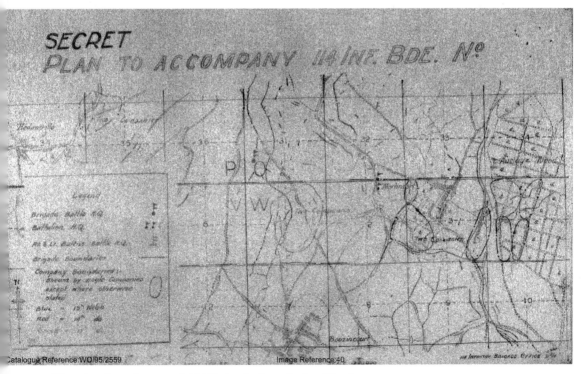

Plan for the advance of 114 Brigade into Aveluy Wood.

Plan of the objectives for 10 May 1918.

the 15th Welsh more men; Private William Edwards of Hay in Herefordshire, and Lance Corporal Donald McDonald of Polmont in Stirlingshire. Both men are buried side by side at Harponville Communal Cemetery.

Five other ranks were wounded that day, two of whom died of wounds two days later at the 56th Casualty Clearing Station at Gezaincourt. Private Frederick Ernest Maylam of Hastings, and Private Charles Robert Simkins of Roath are both buried next to each other at Bagneux British Cemetery at Gezaincourt.

This was to become another period of relative stability on the Somme, indeed on the whole of the Western Front now for the coming weeks. The 15th Welsh settled back into the routine of life in the front line, interspersed with time in brigade and divisional relief over the remainder of May, June and July 1918, spending time at Aveluy Wood, Toutencourt, Hedauville and Bouzincourt. Eleven more deaths in the battalion were suffered during this time, with injuries to the men on a regular basis, mainly from sporadic German shellfire.

By June, the 15th Welsh were in the Martinsart- Engelbelmer sector, on the north edge of Aveluy Wood, and remained in the area until 19 July 1918, when the entire 38th (Welsh) Division moved into reserve in the Herissart sector, with the 15th Welsh at Toutencourt Wood. The division remained in the area until 6 August, resting for the planned forthcoming offensive on the Somme.

For the coming weeks, the men enjoyed a taste of relative freedom. William Shanahan wrote:

> We had plenty of time to spare at Toutencourt and the evenings were mostly spent in the estaminets with which the village was well supplied. There was a choice of three intoxicants; white and red wine which we called vin blanc and vin rouge, and then there was champagne, a one and a half pint bottle for about five francs, say 4/3d. What year's vintage or in whose vineyard the grapes were grown never interested us, for as far as we were concerned it fizzed and sparkled and you felt good. At 4/3d or so it was cheap, and for those whose inclination leaned toward getting tipsy quick, champagne was their drink. Most chaps however stuck to the vin rouge or vin blanc. It tasted like vinegar and was as astringent as iodine, but that's all there was.
>
> The bar would be crowded, full of smoke and the wine seemed not to affect one as long as you remained in the room. But out in the open it soon got to work on you and depending how you could take it, you sang all the way home, songs about roses around the door - always, it seemed, songs with a nostalgic overtone. Those to whom the beer was proving strong were helped along and put to bed. Not much finesse was needed

*here - lay him down in the tent and put a few blankets over him, then
he would right until the morning.*

*Those villagers engaged in the drinks business must have made quite
a fortune. At Toutencourt, along with hundreds of others near the areas
where troops were constantly in occupation – I mean where they spent
their four days out of the trenches and when they were invariably paid
– our money soon found its way into madam's pocket. The officers on the
other hand went further afield, so their money found its way into the
hotels further in the rear.*

And he added,

*The country from Toutencourt towards and almost up to Thiepval
was a long rolling plain, the ideal corn growing area which indeed it
was. One could have soldiered on here forever. In this area at the end of
July, the fields were waist high with growing corn which was ripening
fast. The fields were large and there were no hedges. It was a fine sight
to those who appreciated it, large areas of corn swaying gently in the
breeze. As the enemy got no further, all this corn would have been
gathered into the barns by the end of August.*

Chapter 11

The Great Advance – The Battle Of Albert

THE BATTLE-WEARY MEN of the 38th (Welsh) Division enjoyed their time at rest in the Herissart sector, and divisional recreation positively flourished. Based at Toutencourt, various inter-battalion competitions took place during this spell, with a divisional sports meeting, horse show and race meeting being held, as well as the obligatory training.

On 6 August 1918 the 38th Division moved back to the Front. The 15th Welsh relieved the 10th Sherwood Foresters in support in the Aveluy sector, and remained here until 12 August, when they moved into the front line, relieving the 14th Welsh. The two battalions again exchanged places on 16 August, with the 15th Welsh moving back into reserve at Engelbelmer.

No.3 Platoon of the 15th Welsh at Toutencourt 1918.   Mary Curtis

This same pattern of support, front line, then reserve had been more or less followed throughout the battalion's time at war. William Shanahan wrote in his memoirs:

From the wood at about seven o'clock in the evening, the battalion would leave by companies to march up to Aveluy Wood which would be about four miles. Although there were no hills to speak of, the country around was one of gentle slopes with fair size woods. One would not think so but an army could easily be unobserved in the folds of the hills. So, by choosing their route, troops could move up some way, and halt until dusk when they would complete the journey.

We were on the whole fortunate in that we were not shelled on the way up and the reliefs were completed without damage. Some troops were detailed for front line duties. Six men and one NCO continued forward to some portion of trench were they would stay for twenty-four hours, being relieved the following evening. Often we would have preferred to remain up forward and not to be relieved, for working parties were the lot of all in the rear. Someone had been very busy digging reserve trenches in the rear of our positions, for complete systems were duplicated and in good order – should our front positions be overrun, new positions were ready to be occupied.

By now, a decisive Allied offensive had been launched against the Germans on the south side of the River Somme, near Villers-Brettoneux. This offensive was known as the Battle of Amiens, or as the German General Erich Ludendorff called it 'The Black Day of the German Army'.

The Australian Corps, together with units of the British Army and Cavalry, with the Canadian Corps to the south, had launched an offensive at dawn on 8 August 1918, centred along the old Roman road which still runs from Amiens to St. Quentin.

The British III Corps attacked north of the River Somme, the Australian Corps to the south of the River, and the Canadian Corps to the south of the Australians. Supported by tanks, the infantry made excellent progress, and the German lines were smashed. The Allies had made an advance of over 4,000 yards by 07.30 hrs that morning. This success proved to be the turning point of the war.

The success of this advance prompted plans for a further offensive on the site of the old Somme battlefields of 1916, central of which was based the 38th (Welsh) Division, and with it the 15th Battalion, the Welsh Regiment. Preparations for the attack were continued throughout the month and on 21 August 1918 the Battle of Albert commenced. The 15th Welsh were still at Engelbelmer, and on 22 August the battalion

British pioneers retaming the River Ancre Valley in 1918. Taylor Library

moved into the line west of Mesnil.

Their objectives were simple. To force a crossing of the River Ancre near St. Pierre Divion and to capture the German held positions at Common Lane and Chickweed Trench, near Hamel. This area would then be opened up to enable the safe crossing of reinforcements and supplies over the flooded Ancre Valley, and enable the advance to press on up the Thiepval Ridge, a position that just two years earlier had taken several months and countless lives to capture.

This first crossing was to be no mean feat. The flooded River Ancre had had its banks smashed by years of shelling, and the river now sprawled across its valley, sometimes 200 to 300 yards wide. This wide expanse was a quagmire of foul, sticky mud which just two years previously had been hotly contested by the Royal Naval Division during their successful attack on Beaucourt-sur-L'Ancre.

Nevertheless, on the night of 22/23 August, A and B Company of the 15th Welsh were sent out to cross the Ancre near Hamel, under the command of Captain Gerald William Lancaster and Lieutenant Glyn Williams. Under cover of darkness, the two companies waded through the murky waters of the Ancre, the war diary reporting that they were sometimes up to chest deep in muddy water and under continuous

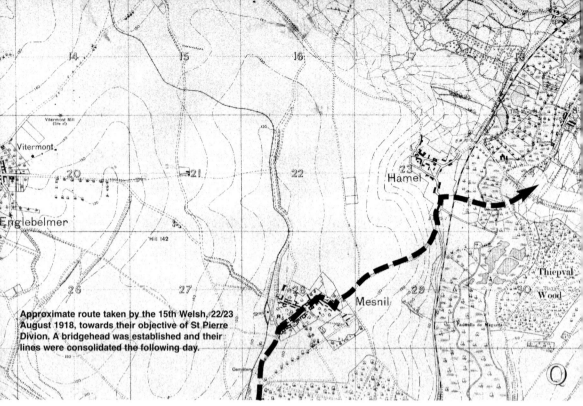

Approximate route taken by the 15th Welsh, 22/23 August 1918, towards their objective of St Pierre Divion. A bridgehead was established and their lines were consolidated the following day.

Trench map showing the area around St Pierre Divion, successfully crossed and captured by the 15th Welsh 22/23 August 1918.

machine gun and rifle fire. Conditions were horrendous, but the small teams reached the east bank, and captured their objectives at St. Pierre Divion, taking twenty five German prisoners and five machine guns in the process.

The initial attack was a success, with the war diary for the day showing that two men were killed, sixteen other ranks wounded and one man was missing after forcing the crossing. The amount of men lost was small indeed for such an important and valuable operation, which was to ultimately lead to the winning of the war.

One of the men to have been killed during the crossing was Sergeant Edward Thomas Spencer, of Edgemond, near Newport, Shropshire. Edward was killed on the night of 22 August as the initial crossing was taking place. His body was recovered from the battlefield, and buried at Mill Road Cemetery, Thiepval. He is the only man of the 15th Welsh to be buried there.

This successful advance by the two companies of the 15th Welsh was the key part of the initial assault, which had far-reaching results. From now on the British were on the offensive, and the 15th Welsh was to play

Sergeant Edwa
Thomas Spenc

an important part in this, sadly at the cost of many more young men's lives.

The Welshmen held onto their positions throughout the night, and faced a German counter-attack later that day, losing another six men killed, but they stubbornly clung on to their precarious foothold on the eastern bank of the Ancre. On the following day, 24 August, the 123rd Field Company, Royal Engineers hastily erected wooden walkways across the Ancre, thus allowing the remaining units of the 38th Division to safely cross the Ancre.

The remainder of the 15th Welsh crossed the Ancre that same day, reforming on the east side. The next move now was uphill against positions which two years previously had taken countless thousands of men's lives to capture, but unconcerned, the battalion fought on, rapidly pushing their way uphill from St. Pierre Divion toward the German positions on Thiepval Ridge.

The attack was a complete success, and Thiepval ultimately proved no obstacle for the battle hardened Welshmen. Over 1,000 prisoners were taken in the capture of the ridge, along with machine guns, trench mortars and huge amounts of stores, and after re-organising, the men of the 15th Welsh pushed on the attack and advanced towards Pozieres Ridge, reaching the village that afternoon.

From the former German positions on the Thiepval Ridge, viewing the uphill gradient and marshy ground over which two companies of the 15th Welsh advanced. The Ancre River is hidden behind the line of trees.

The direction of the advance of the
15th Welsh from St. Pierre Division

The soldiers themselves were amazed at the speed of their advance, with William Shanahan writing:

> I believe it was not the High Command's idea that we should advance so far ahead. I thought only a tidying up of the front line was intended, perhaps the local heights of Thiepval Ridge – a straightening of the line here and there, and things nice and tidy over the winter. As if to appear to confirm the rumours as to whether it was a general advance or not, the battalion was ordered to leave our heavy gear, great coats and valises, behind in our dugouts.

It seems as if the British Commanders had accomplished more than they had dared hope for, but Shanahan, now a Lance Corporal, had missed the crossing of the Ancre due to feeling unwell after having been slightly affected by gas from a German gas shell the previous night. He had been ordered then to stay in the sunken road which runs from Martinsart to Mesnil, and to guard the kit that had been left there by his comrades. When they didn't return as planned, he decided to catch them up, and made his way across the Ancre from Aveluy, and up over Thiepval Ridge towards the sounds of the fighting in the distance.

> My orders were to remain until the battalion returned and collect all the equipment left when they went forward that night. If I had obeyed instructions I should have been there for years, an old man wandering up and down the road, continually expecting the return of the battalion and forgotten by everyone, for who would have remembered having left me in the sunken road. I would have been posted as missing, and finally when the Germans once again were in France, they would have found me still in the sunken road looking like Rip Van Winkle and surrounded by fallen in dugouts and masses of webbing – the equipment

disintegrated, the brass buckles by now a dull green but still all guarded most diligently.

Well comes the morning, and I remember what a beautiful morning it was. I had slept the night in luxurious quarters. I had moved into the officers' dugout and there were cots and a coal stove in the middle. There I was, all alone, and when I awoke and climbed alongside the road, I could see far ahead and the quietness was strange. I could not hear a sound for the war had by now moved on, the attack having started in early morn when I was fast asleep. I cannot remember having breakfast but that only would be a piece of cheese and tea, but I do remember seeing in the distance, coming in my direction, a single soldier.

Of the thousands around previously, only he was to be seen and he would not have walked so nonchalantly across there the previous day. I called across and when he came near it was a chap I knew by name, Ernest Davies. He lived at Llanelli and was a Catholic and I think was in the same battalion, but in a different company. He was going home on leave. He lived with his parents at Brynallt Terrace, near the hospital. As I had several ounces of tobacco with me, I asked him if he would take it home to my father, which he did, but I never met him after that and I believe he was killed in action on his return.

Before he left, I had news from him as to how the war was progressing up front and guessed our chaps were never to return to the sunken road. Saying so long to him, we both parted – him on leave and I up forward to catch up and rejoin my company. The distance from Engelbelmer to our new positions on Thiepval Ridge would be about three or four miles, and I judged the battalion had got no further. How strange it was to walk over fields and along roads where, only the previous day, to walk about there would be inviting sudden death or to be badly wounded. But now, there was I on a fine August morning enjoying myself.

I should not have been concerned if I did not find the battalion for a few days and would have been content to be left to wander about unattached. However, it was now becoming a back area, infected with Military Police and nosy Brigade Majors who would look with suspicion upon soldiers alone. If I was carrying a duck board or screw picket, or pushing a wheel barrow, no one would have asked, but otherwise it was dangerous to be about by oneself; so the nearer one got to the fighting area the safer it was for the individual soldier.

William caught up with his comrades at Thiepval Ridge:

I passed through the village of Mesnil, crossed the partially submerged wooden bridge, then up to the slope the other side. There on the crest of Thiepval Ridge, in trenches recently occupied by the German troops, was the 15th Welsh Battalion, and D Company were the occupants of the section I had dropped into.

Throughout the remainder of 24 August 1918, the battalion pushed their way solidly towards Pozieres, and late in the afternoon the flattened village was safely back in British hands.

The capture of Pozieres Ridge had cost the lives of over 23,000 Australian troops during August 1916, yet just two years later both Pozieres and Thiepval Ridges had been taken with the loss of one officer and three other ranks killed, and twenty-seven men wounded from the 15th Welsh. The 38th Division on the whole had lost five officers and 113 other ranks killed. Modern methods of warfare had helped, but the

German Army was by now suffering badly from tired and poorly motivated troops. The triumphant Welshmen celebrated the fact by assembling for an informal group photograph at the edge of the ruined village.

The only officer killed with the 15th Welsh during this stage of the battle was Second Lieutenant Robert Charles Evans, a Solicitor, of Heulfry, Ruthin. Prior to the war, Robert had practised law at Bangor-Isycoed near Wrexham. Robert was murdered by a German prisoner captured at Pozieres, who had a concealed pistol on him. Needless to say the German didn't get another victim, he was shot dead almost instantly. Robert is the only Carmarthen Pal buried at Pozieres British Cemetery.

[His son, born just months after Robert's death, Robert Charles Evans (Junior), served as an Army Officer with the Royal Army Medical Corps in Burma during the Second World War, following in his late fathers footsteps. Robert Charles Evans, was part of the team of British climbers, along with Sir Edmund Hillary, who successfully climbed Mount Everest in 1953. He was later knighted as a result of this, and went on to be Principal of the University of Wales at Bangor, and President of the Alpine Club.]

Early in the morning of 25 August 1918, the 15th Welsh left Pozieres and advanced towards Bazentin-Le-Petit. At 04.30 hrs they moved in the direction of High Wood and Bazentin. Very little opposition was to be found so far, but here the battalion found itself held up by enemy fire, and was

Headquarters staff of the 15th Welsh after the successful capture of Pozieres 24 August 1918. Note the medal ribbons of the Military Cross on the two Officers to right of centre, and the ribbon of the Distinguished Conduct Medal on the chest of the man on the extreme right. Sadly none of these men are identified. IWM Q8214

The devastated road from Albert to Bapaume. Library and Archives Canada/PA-000884

forced to withdraw to a line 500 yards South of the Albert to Bapaume Road, 1,300 yards from Bazentin, where they joined the remainder of 114 Brigade. The going had been relatively easy so far.

How different was our advance to the advances of 1916, called the Battle of the Somme. Then, one quarter of a million or more men were lost by Britain alone and the gain barely a few miles of chewed up earth dotted with millions of shell holes. When the rain came, these shell holes soon filled and caused the death of many men in the night out on patrol or in working parties. They slipped in, and being loaded with equipment, were too tired to struggle. The sides would have been steep and crumbling and the men did sink quickly and were drowned. The wounded met their death in this way too. But now, August 1918, we were in back areas which had not suffered much damage. There were trench systems all over the place, half filled by now and overgrown with grass. Although nature had by now about five months to clothe the earth with grass, the whole place still looked desolate as all the trees had been cut down so it was easier to make progress. Despite a brush now and again with the enemy, we were soon up near Bapaume, the Germans retiring before us. The apple orchards had been cut down and delayed action mines placed in houses, bridges or at crossroads so no one knew when your billet and you would be blown sky high as indeed was the Bapaume town hall, which blew up some weeks later with great loss of life. Shanahan

By now the Germans had formed a defensive line running from Mametz Wood, through Bazentin-le-Petit to High Wood, so on 25 August 1918, all three brigades of the division pushed forwards across the high ground between Mametz Wood and High Wood. Weakened lines of Germans were swept aside at Mametz Wood by 113 Brigade, and 115 Brigade took Bazentin-le-Petit. The 14th and 15th Welsh captured the heights of Martinpuich, but were stopped at High Wood by a formidable German defence, and so the advance stopped temporarily. This resulted in 114 Brigade spending a difficult night in the shadows of High Wood, with several German counter-attacks having to be fought off during the night, but on the following morning, at 14.00 hrs on 26 August 1918 the 15th Welsh was ordered to advance and occupy the trenches on the Bazentin to Martinpuich Road.

Meanwhile, 113 Brigade pushed on at their side, and suffered heavy casualties in driving towards the western side of Longueval, when German troops hidden within the shattered remnants of Delville Wood counter-attacked. The men of 115 Brigade meanwhile advanced across the north side of Longueval, after enveloping the Germans within High Wood, where they consolidated their positions overnight, and 114 Brigade moved through them to take up the assault.

By now, the 15th Welsh had lost seventeen men killed, and over seventy men wounded or missing since the rapid capture of Thiepval and Pozieres. The only Carmarthenshire man killed from the total was the twenty-eight year old Private William Roberts of Burry Port. Many of these men's graves could not be identified after the war, and they are commemorated on the Vis-en-Artois Memorial, as is Private Roberts, whose grave was lost as a result of the constant artillery fire.

The battalion rested through the night, ready to renew the attack at daybreak. At 05.15 hrs on 27 August, a massive artillery barrage opened on the German positions, and the 15th Welsh attacked again, driving through a hail of bullets towards the German lines. After some heavy fighting, the Germans were finally driven out of their positions, allowing the battalion to establish themselves on a line from Flers in the direction of the west corner of Delville Wood, joining up with the 17th Division on the left of Flers, and the 14th Welsh on the right.

Later that night, the battered men of the 15th Welsh were relieved by the 10th South Wales Borderers and moved into reserve at High Wood. The roll call that night showed that three officers had been wounded, six other ranks killed and nineteen other ranks wounded or missing.

One of the casualties of the successful fighting of 27 August was Private Stanley Axford, of 83, Eureka Place, Ebbw Vale. Stanley had worked at Ebbw Vale as a grocer's assistant, and had attested on 18 September 1917 at Cardiff. He joined the 52nd Graduated Battalion of the Welsh Regiment on 25 January 1918 and then transferred to the 15th Welsh in France on 5 April 1918, joining them in the field on the 16 April.

Stanley was just nineteen years old when he was killed at Delville Wood on 27 August 1918, and was buried at the small Welsh Cemetery near High Wood. It was almost four years to the day when his bereaved parents finally found out the location of their son's grave, but by then the Imperial War Graves Commission had began work on consolidating the scattered burials and smaller war cemeteries into more manageable, larger cemeteries, and so Stanley's grave was moved to Caterpillar Valley Cemetery, near Longueval, where he lies today.

The Battle of Albert was now over. The German line had been well and truly broken, and the ground which the German had so bloodily won earlier in the year was being given up with much less of a fight. The next phase of the '100 day Offensive' was about to begin, but greater trials were to follow for the men of the Carmarthen Pals.

A captured German position during the Battle of Albert in August 1918. Taylor Library

Chapter 12

The Great Advance – The Battle Of Bapaume

ON 28 AUGUST 1918 the 15th Welsh was again relieved, and moved back into divisional reserve. Casualties up to this point, during the opening Battle of Albert, had been thirty-eight men killed, or died of wounds. Many more had been wounded. Later that night, the battalion moved into positions east of Delville Wood, and at 05.00 hrs on 29 August took up positions north east of Ginchy, where they remained in brigade support. The remainder of 114 Brigade, the 13th and 14th Welsh, had been tasked with the capture of Morval Village. That day, the 38th Division captured Ginchy Ridge, a position which had taken a month of fighting to capture in 1916. The fighting at Morval continued throughout the night, and throughout the following days.

During the capture of Ginchy Ridge, Second Lieutenant William Bowen had been wounded. William was the son of Henry and Mary Bowen, of 9, Milton Terrace, Mount Pleasant, Swansea. He had worked as a clerk with the Great Western Railway, at Swansea, and had enlisted in the Pembroke Imperial Yeomanry at the outbreak of war. William was then commissioned into the 3rd Welsh, before becoming attached to the 15th Welsh in France. He died of his wounds on 30 August 1918, and is buried at Fienvillers British Cemetery.

A letter sent to William's father at Swansea by another officer was published in the *South Wales Daily Post*, and read:

> *A better or a braver officer I never met, nor one so adored by his men. On the day he received his fatal wound he was in command of the company, as I was temporarily doing other duties but his men tell me that he was leading them without a thought of personal danger. I feel that I have lost one of my dearest friends, as well as a most loyal and faithful officer. I know it will comfort you to know that the battalion has covered itself with glory in this recent fighting and made for itself a great name – a name with which will always be associated by his surviving brother officers the name of that most gallant officer, your son. His name will never be forgotten by us as long as we remember this great and terrible war in which it is our proud privilege to take part.*

Memorial plaque to William Bowen.

Morval was being defended to the last man by the Germans, and on 31

August the 15th Welsh moved into positions facing Morval, at Church Post and the Quarry, from where they joined the last ditch attempt to take the village, on 1 September 1918. After heavy fighting 114 Brigade managed to take the shattered remains of Morval at about 17.45 hrs on 1 September. The other brigades of the 38th Division, 113 and 115, successfully captured the neighbouring village of Sailly-Saillisel, thus pushing the British line forward again. Seventeen men had been killed during the capture of Morval, and another forty men were either wounded or missing.

Five of the Carmarthenshire contingent of the 15th Welsh were amongst the dead. Private John Evan Jones of Llanelli; Private William Martin, was a holder of the Military Medal, and was from Carmarthen; Private William Thomas Arthur was another from Carmarthen itself; Private Harold Vivian Jones was from Llanelli, and Private William Jones was from Llanrug. The small military cemetery in Morval contains the graves of the men of the 38th Division who liberated it from the Germans in 1918. Six of these men were of the 15th Welsh, and two of these were men from Carmarthen Town, Privates William Martin and William Arthur.

The 15th Welsh, as indeed had the remaining units of the 38th Division, had suffered heavy casualties during the first few weeks of the advance [Including Lieutenant-Colonel Parkinson on 31 August], and as a result batches of reinforcements were drafted in to take up the

The ruins of Morval Church after the battle.

Reinforcements for the Welsh at Prees Heath Camp, 1918. The mixture is self-evident from undersized, to teenagers, to men in their late forties.

places of the dead and wounded. Many of these men were young soldiers, averaging eighteen years old, but some were men who had previously been deemed as being too old for active service, and were in their forties. The seasoned soldier, William Shanahan recalled:

> *There were replacements to make up our losses, mostly very young men who had received the minimum of training before being hurried out. We sat in groups of six or more and I was busy instructing them in care and maintenance of Lewis guns. As a preliminary, I enquired if they already had received some tuition regarding the Lewis gun. No, not one of them knew a thing about them but I guessed they had heard gossip at the camps in England of the dangerous tasks associated with machine gun crews, so no one wanted to have, if possible, anything to do with machine guns. The poor chaps had heard so much they all feigned ignorance. No indeed, they knew nothing about machine guns, but a few deliberate mis-instructions on my part and some could not contain their knowledge any longer and started to correct their teacher. Oh yes indeed, they did know something about guns after all. But the talk was always of how dangerous it was to have anything to do with guns or to be a bayonet man in a bombing party.*

And rather more uncharitably he went on to write that:

Some of them [had been] *sergeants or corporals, drill instructors at Pembroke, and it seemed the authorities were now scraping the bottom of the barrel. Several men had spent years at the depot as instructors of different military drills such as rifle practise or care of firearms. These must have gone soft and one sergeant had developed quite a corporation with good living. There they were, having been scraped from the barrel. The poor chaps lives were indeed hard, for the transition from an easy life at the depot to one long hard chore must have been painful.*

Nevertheless the war carried on, and at 10.00 hrs on 3 September, the battalion moved back to occupy trenches near the railway, and at 11.30 hrs moved forward again to Mortho Copse, west of Sailly-Saillisel. At 14.30 hrs 114 Brigade advanced, with the 15th Welsh in support, and gained yet more ground from the Germans. The 15th Welsh remained in reserve during this advance, and on 6 September was relieved, moving into divisional reserve.

The Battle of Bapaume was officially over, and the Allies were now pushing hard towards the positions of the Hindenburg Line. The Hindenburg Line was a vast system of defences, constructed by the Germans during the winter of 1916–17, stretching nearly 100 miles from Lens in the north, to the River Aisne near Soissons in the south.

The decision to build the line was made jointly by Field-Marshal Paul von Hindenburg and General Erich Ludendorff, who had taken over command of Germany's war effort in August 1916, during the final stages of the First Battle of the Somme. The Hindenburg Line was built across a salient in the German front, so that by withdrawing to these fortifications the German army was actually shortening its front. The total length of the front was reduced by thirty miles and enabled the Germans to release thirteen divisions for service in reserve. The line was subdivided into five areas, named from north to south: Wotan Stellung, Siegfried Stellung, Alberich Stellung, Brunhilde Stellung and Kriemhilde Stellung.

This impressive looking array of trenches had been methodically worked out by the Germans. Coupled with the scientifically worked out field of fire of the machine guns and defending artillery, and the belts of thick barbed wire, this was one of the strongest defensive positions the world had ever seen.

Beneath the entire length of the Hindenburg Line was an impressive network of tunnels and deep dugouts, designed to safely shelter the many thousands of German troops required to man the defences. It was indeed going to be a tough nut to crack, but as had been showed during the Battle of Cambrai in November 1917, it was not an impossible task.

Chapter 13

Advance To Victory

THE NEXT MAJOR TASK facing the 38th Division was the crossing of the Canal du Nord. Basically it was just a forward defensive position for the main Hindenburg Line, but in reality it was almost as difficult an obstacle to cross. The canal runs from the Oise River to the Dunkirk-Scheldt Canal, and in places has almost sheer sides leading down to the canal itself.

The Division moved into positions near Etricourt-Manancourt, and found that all of the bridges over the canal had been destroyed by the Germans, and that the Germans held the eastern side of the canal bank in great strength. During the next forty-eight hours the Germans smothered the area with gas shells, making the task in front of the Division seem almost impossible.

The story of the crossing of the Canal du Nord is told in detail in the 38th Divisional History, which is transcribed here. The 15th Welsh remained in reserve, but one of their Officers, now attached to the 14th Welsh, was to play a major role in the crossing:

> The enemy had machine guns on the bank but not covering the actual water, noticing this, Major Hobbs rushed a platoon down to an

A stretch of the mighty Hindenburg Line near Bullecourt.

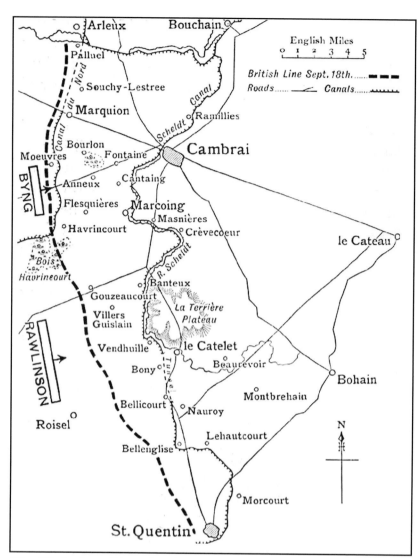

The Hindenburg Line, showing the positions of the attacking British Armies of Generals Byng and Rawlinson.

old trench on the near bank, from which a ditch led down towards the debris of the Etricourt road bridge; here the platoon engaged the attention of the nearest machine guns and one section crawled down the ditch across the fallen bridge and up the far bank; crawling on their stomachs this section advanced to within charging distance of the nearest machine gun, then leapt up and bayoneted the gunners; they were quickly joined by the remainder of the platoon and a bridgehead was formed which enabled the remainder of the company (under Capt. Beech, M.C.) to cross.

*Similar action took place at Manancourt where a company of the
14th Welsh Regiment. led by Major J. A. Daniels, D.S.O., M.C., of the
15th Welsh (attached to the 14th) crossed, and each of these battalions
had thus one company across by 11.30 hrs a.m.; these companies
cleared the eastern bank of the enemy and then pushed forward to cover
the crossing of the remainder of the Brigade, which was effected with the
help of the 123rd Field Company, R.E., by 5 p.m. This Field Company
worked continuously throughout the afternoon and night and the
following day; they were under shell fire the whole time, and had to
perform the whole of the work in gas masks; and sustained thirty
casualties; it was owing to their efforts that our relief by the 1st Division
the following night and their subsequent advance was made possible.*

*During the day (September 4th) the remainder of the Divisional
Artillery advanced in close support and came into action on the forward
slopes south of Mesnil; in order to do this they also had to move across
the open from Sailly-Saillisel in full view from the enemy's position
about Equancourt; that such a movement was possible without
prohibitive casualties is probably due to the action of the 17th Division
on our left, which was engaging part of the enemy's attention at the time.
A section of D Machine Gun Company crossed this ground at the gallop
this day in order to reinforce the remainder of the machine guns which
had either moved forward by night or had been carried forward by
hand.*

*All guns and vehicles approaching our forward troops had to move
through Sailly-Saillisel as being the only road; the site of this village was
under continual shell fire and it speaks well for the march discipline of
artillery and transport that nothing in the nature of a block ever
occurred in the traffic.*

By 11.30 hrs of 4 September 1918 the canal defences had been
breached, and the first major obstacle to the Hindenburg Line outer
defences had been crossed. Major Daniels had earned himself the
Distinguished Service Order for his gallantry and leadership, to add to
his Military Cross.

In two weeks of continuous fighting the 38th Division had driven the
Germans back fifteen miles, at the loss of over 3,000 men. It had
captured almost 2,000 Germans, six guns and numerous machine guns,
and was due for a well earned rest.

The crossing of the Canal du Nord had been straightforward for the
15th Welsh, as they had not been directly involved in the forcing of the
canal defences, but used as reinforcements after the crossing. Now the
new recruits came face to face with the horrors of war:

A British soldier who had been lying at the canal edge had, during the night, crawled into the water and was now half in and half out of the water. His facial injuries were terrible and he could not have possibly survived. His whole face, from the lower lip to above his eye, had been completely shot away, just as if it had been scooped out. There he lay all the cold night. He must have been unconscious the whole time and there was nothing we could do. I knew nothing in the world could save him, even if attention was close at hand. I had seen him first towards the evening for I had crossed the blown up, shattered bridge before it got dark. It was then I first saw him, for he was out of the water and alive. He must have been alive then for in spite of his injuries he had crawled or rolled over and died lying partly in the water.

On the top of the canal edge and only a dozen feet away, five or six wounded men were lying in a shell hole. They had been there all night, poor chaps. If we had known, our gun team would have done something for them. However later in the day we were withdrawn to Bapaume, not a great way to our rear, so I think the first aid men found them before night fell.

My gun team stayed the night in a trench some two feet deep and bricked. It was, I believe, some part of the canal's drainage system. It was here, some time before darkness, a young fellow of 18 or 19 came along and told me as the NCO in charge that he was wounded. Where he came from or how he crossed the canal I didn't know. He seemed OK to me, so I asked him where he was wounded. He replied, "My foot", slipped off his boot and showed me the back of his heel where a bullet had passed through the fleshy part, emerging near the instep. All I could see was a slight blue dot just as an indelible pencil had marked a dot there, but there was no blood. He wanted to know what he should do. We told him and he was soon some distance away, or I hope he was, for soon after the area around was under German gunfire.   Shanahan

In the period between the capture of Morval until the relief of the 15th Welsh on 6 September, sixteen more men were killed, two of whom were Pembrokeshire men, and two from Carmarthenshire. One of the Pembrokeshire men killed during this period, on 5 September 1918, was the twenty-nine year old Private Frederick Lloyd Phillips of Maenclochog. Frederick died of wounds at the Base Hospital at Rouen, and is buried there, at St. Sever Communal Cemetery Extension.

From 6 September until 11 September 1918 the 15th Welsh were held in reserve at Le Transloy. On 11 September they relieved the 10th Lancashire Fusiliers in reserve at Equancourt, with Captain J. Williams, MC in command due to the wounding of Lieutenant-Colonel Parkinson, DSO.

Private Frederick Lloyd Phillips

Bringing up the artillery across the Canal Du Nord in September 1918. Taylor Library

Canadian Engineers bridging the Canal Du Nord after its capture.
Library and Archives Canada/PA-003456

The 15th Welsh remained in divisional reserve at Delville Wood for the next few days, with the only casualty mentioned in the war diary occurring when the former Welsh Guardsman Second Lieutenant Burman, MM was accidentally wounded.

The war diary fails to make mention of the death of the twenty-eight year old Private James Prytherch of Llandovery. James had been born on 23 May 1890 at Blaenydu, in the parish of Llandingat in north Carmarthenshire. He was born into a proud Welsh family, his father Rees and Elizabeth had put down on their 1901 Census return that they could only speak Welsh, and not English. The family later moved to Nantllan in the small village of Myddfai, just south of the market town of Llandovery, where they were to remain. James must have become a victim of long range shellfire on 9 September, as the 15th Welsh was still in reserve then, and away from the ardours of the front line. He has no known grave, and so is commemorated on the Vis-en-Artois Memorial to the missing.

Captain Gerald William Lancaster, MC.

Also to die of wounds during these few days were three more private soldiers: Albert William Prance was from Solva, a small fishing village in north Pembrokeshire; Private Frederick Pritchard was from Sowdley, near Clun in Shropshire, and Private Henry Hiscocks was from Pencoed. Henry John Hiscocks was twenty-four years old, and was the son of Henry Hiscocks, of West House, Pencoed. He is buried at Bagneux British Cemetery, near the village of Gezaincourt.

Corporal Robert Matthews of Aberdare also died the day before the 15th Welsh moved back into the line, but the biggest blow to the battalion was the death of the gallant Captain Gerald William Lancaster, MC. Gerald Lancaster was the hero of the crossing of the Ancre on 24 August 1918, for which action he had been awarded his Military Cross. He was the son of William Henry and Annie Lancaster of Nottingham, and had been educated at Shrewsbury School. Gerald had worked as a mining engineer prior to the war, and had been commissioned in September 1914 into the 3rd Battalion, Monmouth Regiment. Gerald had been wounded twice before. He is buried at Terlincthun British Cemetery, Wimille. Gerald was twenty-nine years old.

Gerald William Lancaster's grave at Terlincthun.

On 15 September 1918, Lieutenant-Colonel Parkinson, DSO turned over the command of the battalion again to Major (temporary Lieutenant-Colonel) Ernest Helme, DSO. Helme was a seasoned campaigner, with a tough reputation, and had been attached from the Glamorgan Yeomanry. William Shanahan remembered an incident after Helme had taken command of the 15th Welsh:

On a hot early morning, two of us stood outside looking at two horsemen galloping like mad in the distance, raising clouds of dust and inviting shell fire. The Colonel of the regiment, a chap named Helme, rode a white stallion named Prince Pertab, a gift we were told from an Indian rajah, when he acted as an aide at the Delhi Durbar in the early part of the 1900s. He was looking thunder struck and however he managed it, he did stop them. When they finally came up to the Colonel, he waded into the two young gunners and ordered them off their horses, and indeed walk the horses they did until they both vanished in the distance. I'll bet they then galloped and wished the Colonel to an awful end.

The following day, 16 September 1918, the 15th Welsh was east of Dessart Wood, and that night they relieved the 13th Royal Welsh Fusiliers in support of the remainder of the 38th Division. The divisional area was now coming under heavy shellfire from the German artillery, and mixed with the destructive high explosive shells were the ever present gas shells, wounding four more men in B Company of the 15th Welsh.

At around 03.00 hrs on the morning of 17 September, a heavy thunderstorm swept over the area occupied by the 38th Division. The sodden men sheltered within their trenches, and were again hit by a German artillery bombardment later in the morning, thankfully causing

German prisoners taken during the Great Allied Offensive of 1918. Taylor Library

no casualties. At 09.30 hrs the Company Commanders met to discuss the plans for the following day. The men of the 15th Welsh were to take part in another assault on the Germans, this time over ground that had been fought over during the German withdrawal to the Hindenburg Line in the Spring of 1917.

The day was spent in preparation for the assault, and at 23.00 hrs on the night of 17 September the men moved into their assembly positions, with Battalion HQ moving to Heather Support. These lines were old German defensive trenches from the year previous, and afforded good shelter for the waiting men. By 01.30 hrs on the morning of 18 September, the men of the 15th Welsh had reached their assembly positions. This was the opening day of the Battle of Epehy, and the assault to be made by the 38th Division was against the outpost positions of the Hindenburg Line near Gouzeaucourt.

The 38th Division attacked from the left, from positions south-east of Gouzeaucourt. Zero hour was at 05.20, and the 15th Welsh took up their positions on the right of 114 Brigade, with their objective to

Aerial photograph of Gouzeaucourt, probably early 1917.

Gouzeaucourt

Advance of the 15th Welsh
18 September 1918

capture the German line running south-west of Gouzeaucourt, which can be seen in the photograph. Detailed plans for the attack of 114 Brigade made it clear that the 15th Welsh were to capture African and Heather Trenches (the Green Line), and then to press on and take the trenches south-west of Gouzeaucourt.

The companies of the 15th Welsh moved forward to their attack positions under the cover of darkness. The weather was wet and the ground was being saturated by German gas shells, meaning that the men had to march for the final mile to their assembly positions wearing their gas respirators. It was not a pleasant beginning to the assault.

Temporary Lieutenant-Colonel Helme was in command of the 15th Welsh; A Company under Captain Landman was on the right; B Company under Lieutenant D J Hughes was to the centre; C Company under Lieutenant J Roberts was to the left, and D Company under Second Lieutenant J W Jones was in reserve.

At Zero Hour, a creeping artillery barrage was opened up, and the first objectives were soon captured. The companies moved on to their final positions, following the artillery barrage, and by 06.00 hrs sketchy news had reached Battalion Headquarters of the progress being made. By now the wounded had started returning.

Captain Landman had been wounded, and so Lieutenant Philip Gillespie Bainbrigge took over command of A Company. On his return to the aid station at Battalion Headquarters, Landman informed of the capture of the Brown Line, with little resistance from the Germans. At 07.10 hrs Lieutenant Roberts of C Company was carried back to the Aid Post wounded. He reported on the battalion being half-way towards their objectives. A further report received from Lieutenant Mellis of the 38th Battalion Machine Gun Corps reported the successful capture and consolidation of the Green Line. The objectives had been captured, but at a heavy cost to the 15th Welsh. Sadly the promising Lieutenant Philip Gillespie Bainbrigge had been killed, as had Second Lieutenant Frederick John Louis David. Lieutenant W J Hughes, Lieutenant Roberts and Captain Landman had been wounded. It was still only 08.00 hrs.

A German counter-attack had also been beaten off by then, and the British units to the left and right had also made their objectives, pushing ever closer to the Hindenburg Line. By 19.30 hrs orders came in for the 38th Division to advance again, with the 15th Welsh in Support, and at 21.00 hrs the attack restarted. By the end of the day, the 15th Welsh had lost fifteen men killed, and three officers and 105 other ranks wounded.

The dead Lieutenant Philip Gillespie Bainbrigge had been an acquaintance of the famous war poet Wilfred Owen, and a close friend of Captain Charles Kenneth Scott Moncrieff MC, the famed Scottish writer and translator. Philip had been born in London the son of a Vicar in 1891, and was educated at Eton and Trinity College, Cambridge. He was Master at Shrewsbury School from September 1913 until March 1917, and trained with the Inns of Court Officer Training Corps from May 1917. Philip was commissioned in November 1917 as a 2nd Lieutenant in the 4th Battalion, Lancashire Fusiliers, and was then posted to the 15th Welsh in France from February 1918. Philip was a war poet; his one war poem appeared in *Slide Rule*, published in 1954, the autobiography of Nevil Shute, a former pupil of his. His play *Achilles in Scyros* is quoted in *Love in Earnest*.

Philip had met up with Wilfred Owen at the Clifton Hotel in Scarborough in February 1918, just before his move to join the 15th Welsh, and a month before Owen's return to the front. He is buried at Five Points Cemetery, Lechelle.

> If I should die, be not concerned to know
>   The manner of my ending, if I fell
> Leading a forlorn charge against the foe,
>   Strangled by gas, or shattered by a shell.
> Nor seek to see me in this death-in-life
>   Mid shirks and curse, oaths and blood and sweat,
> Cold in the darkness, on the edge of strife,
>   Bored and afraid, irresolute, and wet.

P. G. Bainbrigge

The attack near Gauche Wood was a success. Lieutenant William Allison White of the attached 38th Battalion, Machine Gun Corps was awarded the Victoria Cross for his part in the attack of the 38th Division, being credited with the capture of two German machine guns and their crews single-handed. He then turned one of the captured German machine guns onto the German counter-attack, helping to repulse them. The citation in the *London Gazette* for his award read:

> For most conspicuous bravery and initiative in attack.
>
> When the advance of the infantry was being delayed by an enemy machine gun, he rushed the gun position single-handed, shot the three gunners, and captured the gun. Later, in similar circumstances, he attacked a gun accompanied by two men, but both of the latter were immediately shot down. He went on alone to the gun position and bayoneted or shot the team of five men and captured the gun. On a third occasion, when the advance was held up by hostile fire from an enemy position, he collected a small party and rushed the position, inflicting heavy losses on the garrison.

Subsequently, in consolidating the position by the skilful use of captured enemy and his own machine guns, he inflicted severe casualties on the enemy. His example of fearless and unhesitating devotion to duty under circumstances of great personal danger greatly inspired the neighbouring troops, and his action had a marked effect on the operations.

Fighting continued here for the rest of the day, and also during the following day of 19 September. The attack of 114 Brigade had been successful in gaining their objectives south of Gouzeaucourt and late on 19 September 1918 the 15th Welsh was relieved by the 10th Lancashire Fusiliers, moving back into reserve.

Another seven men had been killed in action on 19 September, with further casualties coming in the following days, of men dying of wounds. The 15th Welsh Battalion war diary gives a list of officers who took part in the attack:

Major E Helme	Commanding Officer
Lieutenant C Burrington	Acting Adjutant
2nd Lieutenant G H Minshull	Intelligence
2nd Lieutenant Abel Jones	Signals
Captain Landman	O.C. A Company (wounded 18th)
2nd Lieutenant G E Lowe	O.C. A Company (from 6 a.m. 18th)
2nd Lieutenant T W Jones	O.C. B Company
Lieutenant Birny	B Company (O.C. C Coy from 8 p.m. 18th)
Lieutenant F Roberts	O.C. C Company (wounded 18th)
2nd Lieutenant David	Killed 18/9/1918
Lieutenant D J Hughes	O.C. D Company (wounded 18th)
2nd Lieutenant Whalley	D Company (O.C. D Coy from a.m. 18th)
2nd Lieutenant P G Bainbrigge	D Company (killed 18/9/1918)
Lieutenant E L Patterson	Medical Officer
Captain D Davies	C.F.

One of the other rank casualties that day was the 24 year old Private Godfrey Le Seelleur. Godfrey had been born in West Ham, and was the son of Mrs Eleanor Le Seelleur, of 20, Beaconsfield Road, Leyton, London. He had originally enlisted at Leyton into the 1/7th Battalion, the Essex Regiment on 31 October 1914 and had first seen action during the fighting at Gallipoli, landing there on 24 July 1915.

Godfrey was posted to the 15th Welsh early in 1918, and fought with the battalion on the Somme throughout the summer of 1918, before being killed on 19 September 1918. Sadly, he is another of the battalion to have no known grave. For the next six painful years, his mother and

British dead, killed in the September fighting near Epehy. Taylor Library

sister remained in correspondence with the then Imperial War Graves Commission, trying to locate the burial place of their loved one. The news wasn't going to be good though, as their final letter from the Imperial War Graves Commission, dated 26 February 1926 stated that the battlefields had been thoroughly searched, and that isolated burials had been re-buried in the newly created war cemeteries scattered throughout the Western Front. Godfrey's grave had not been located, and so today he is commemorated on the Vis-en-Artois Memorial.

For the following days, the 15th Welsh rested in reserve at a position north of Equancourt. On 24 September they moved to positions at Lechelles, a small village slightly north of Equancourt, and west of Havrincourt Wood, where some of the men of 114 Brigade were awarded decorations for their part in the crossing of the Canal du Nord. A good representation of men from 15th Welsh received medals for this action.

The men enjoyed another short rest period here, before moving on 28 September to positions at Fins Ridge Wood in

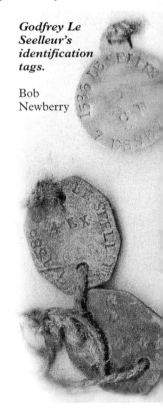

Godfrey Le Seelleur's identification tags.

Bob Newberry

190

brigade reserve, where the following day they were hit by a barrage of German yellow cross gas, causing three more casualties to the battalion.

During this short period out of the line, the 15th Welsh received further drafts of reinforcements, and rebuilt to something like full strength, ready for the next part of the great offensive, on the Hindenburg Line itself.

The 15th Welsh, as indeed was the whole of their Army Corps, with the Fourth Army on their right, was now up against the mighty Hindenburg Line. Patrols sent out to reconnoitre the strength of the defences had come back with information that it had not been exaggerated; indeed it was a formidable defensive position which would not be taken lightly, if at all.

The plan for the assault on the line was that the British Fourth Army would attack south of Bony, and that the American 2nd Corps, which by then was attached, would sweep northwards, while part of the Fourth Army secured the crossings at Vendhuile. By 28 September 1918 the whole of the 38th Division was in positions near Sorel le Grand and Heudicourt, and were now under orders to be ready to join the attack. They had been issued with orders for three different courses of action:

1) To either to relieve the American Troops and continue their northward advance.
2) To relieve the 4th Army troops at Vendhuile.
3) To assist in a frontal attack on the Hindenburg Line.

In preparation for whichever course of action was to be taken, the 38th Division moved into positions at Sorel le Grand and Hendicourt, where they awaited their orders.

The American 2nd Corps launched their attack towards Bony on 29 September, initially capturing both Bony and Bellicourt, two vital villages sat over the main Hindenburg Line. They had displayed great gallantry during their assault, but the inexperienced American troops had pushed on without mopping up the German dugouts, and found themselves isolated. The relieving Australian troops had to advance without an artillery barrage, as there was too much risk of annihilating the trapped Americans, and they lost heavily in their advance, finally taking until 1 October to recapture the ground.

The 38th (Welsh) Division had in the meantime been on stand by in reserve. On 4 October, the division was ordered in, and 115 Brigade reached Bony and relieved the 50th

Private
Godfrey Le Seelleur.
Bob Newberry

The 15th Welsh were in Reserve in Square P25, around the Village of Lechelles on the map above, during the end of September 1918

Division who had taken the offensive over from the Australians. The mighty Hindenburg Line had now been broken, and the casualties for the 15th Welsh had been very light, with just two men dying prior to the next stage of the offensive.

The Germans now began to withdraw to the Masnieres-Beaurevoir Line, which was a secondary defensive system behind the Hindenburg Line, and plans were drawn up for a fresh assault on these positions. In the meantime, elements of the Royal Engineers worked hard to clear jumping off points for this next phase of the offensive, through thick barbed wire entanglements, and over deep trenches.

192

The jumping off line ran north and south through the ruins of the village of Aubencheul, west of Villers-Outreaux. Both 115 and 113 Brigades were on this line, with 114 Brigade in reserve. The task for the 38th (Welsh) Division was simple; to advance over 5,000 yards through a strongly fortified position.

The plan was for both 113 and 115 Brigades to make the initial assault on the night of 7 October 1918, clear Mortho Wood, and hold the ground taken. In the morning of 8 October, 114 Brigade was to advance. The 13th Welsh were on the right, with the 15th Welsh on the left, with orders to pass each side of Malincourt. The 14th Welsh, with four tanks, were detailed to mop up the German defenders of Mortho Wood, and the attack was to push on, with the 15th Welsh tasked with gaining and holding the high ground at Gard Wood.

At 07.00 hrs 114 Brigade reached their assemble positions on the eastern edge of Villers Outreaux, and at 08.20 hrs a fresh creeping barrage started ahead of them. The attack began successfully for 114 Brigade. Unfortunately 115 Brigade had taken the wrong line, and was held up by strong German fire. This caused timing troubles for 113 Brigade, and in turn for 114 Brigade, which were to prove costly.

As a result of the delay caused by 115 Brigade, it was decided to

German guns wrecked by British artillery fire.   Taylor Library

After the fighting has passed on, battlefield waste.

delay the assault of 114 Brigade. However the orders were sent out too late, as they were already on the march, and so the order didn't reach them. As a result, it was dawn when 114 Brigade arrived between Villers Outreaux and Mortho Wood to find itself involved in desperate fighting in support of 113 Brigade. The 15th Welsh approached Mortho Wood cautiously. The men followed a light railway into the northern section of the wood, followed by the 14th Welsh, but found the defences too strongly held and fortified, but luckily two tanks arrived, and helped break the first defensive lines.

A breakthrough by the 2nd Royal Welsh Fusiliers further south, aided by some tanks, eased the situation of 113 Brigade, and the advance continued.

After some bloody fighting in Mortho Wood, 114 Brigade fought its way along the Villers Outreaux to Lesdain Road, but came under heavy fire from the fortified Angles Chateau just east of Mont Ecouvez, which was rushed and cleared out by 'A' Company of the 15th Welsh under Lieutenant W.J. Richards.

All this was just to reach the jumping off positions for the next stage of the attack, and at 11.30 hrs a creeping artillery barrage opened up. Again 114 Brigade advanced, and by the afternoon the final objective of the Premont to Esnes road was reached by 13.30 hrs. The Brigade held this position throughout the night, with the 15th Welsh suffering heavily from machine-gun fire from Mill Wood, an area un-cleared by 21st Division, and the following morning was relieved by elements of the 33rd Division.

The 15th Welsh had paid a heavy price for this successful offensive. Forty-four men had been killed in action on 8 October, and another three died of wounds on 9 October 1918. Six more men died of wounds on the following days as a result of this latest offensive, making a total of fifty-three men.

Among the dead were three second lieutenants, John Humphrey Jones, Tom Watson Jones and William David Owen. Of the Carmarthenshire contingent there were five dead. Private John Glanford Davies of Carmarthen is buried at Prospect Hill Cemetery, Gouy; Private Llewellyn Davies of Pencarreg is buried at Rocquigny-Equancourt Road British Cemetery, Manancourt; Private Robert Davies of Llanelli is buried at Moulin-De-Pierre British Cemetery; Private Albert Toft, another Llanelli man, is buried at Moulin-De-Pierre British Cemetery, and Private Idris Tudor Rees of Llanarthney is buried at Beaulencourt British Cemetery, Ligny-Thilloy.

Maze of barbed wire entanglements on the Hindenburg Line near Bony.

In fact most of the men killed that day now lie in the now peaceful war cemetery at Moulin-De-Pierre. The cemetery is mainly full of men of the 38th Welsh Division, most of whom died during the assault of 7/8 October 1918.

One of the dead men had only recently gained the Military Medal for his part in the assault of Gard Wood, Private Joshua Fielding, another of the Lancashire contingent. He had enlisted just after his eighteenth birthday, on 23 July 1917 giving his occupation as a newsagent, and his address as Fernlea, Carlton Road, Smallshaw, Hurst.

Joshua joined the 15th Welsh in France on 7 April 1918. He was just nineteen years old when he died gallantly during the fighting near Villers Outreaux, and is buried at Moulin-De-Pierre British Cemetery. Joshua had been awarded the Military Medal for his bravery during the fighting in the days prior to his death. The actual medal was eventually sent to his father Benjamin, in May, 1919.

Benjamin wrote back to the Army Medal Office enquiring as to the actions of his son which gained him the Military Medal, but sadly the details of these awards were not listed in the *London Gazette*, and the actions have since faded from memory.

The successful assault had cost the 38th Welsh Division a total of sixty-nine officers and 1,221 other ranks. It had been a hard day's work for the 15th Welsh, and now it was time for a well earned rest and the battalion moved into billets at Clary.

The work done by 114 Brigade had earned them special thanks for the commander of 38th (Welsh) Division, Major-General T.A. Cubitt:

> *Following a visit to the battlefield of the 8th inst., I desire to express to you and to all ranks under your command my unbounded admiration at the bravery and determination of the troops in surmounting the most difficult obstacles and in finally capturing the furthest objectives, despite an initial set-back, that was due to no fault of their own.*
>
> *And I specially wish to thank and congratulate personally the 14th and 15th Welsh for their brilliant determination, courage and most skilful fighting throughout the day. No praise can be too high for their performance.*

After four peaceful days at Clary the battalion took over billets from the 17th Royal Welsh Fusiliers at Troisvilles. They remained here until 19 October 1918 when they were ordered forward into support. A, B and C Companies were attached to the 13th and 14th Welsh, with D Company in reserve. The great defensive systems that the Germans had set their hopes on had been smashed by a series of brilliant manoeuvres. From now on it was going to be warfare in open country, a war of a type

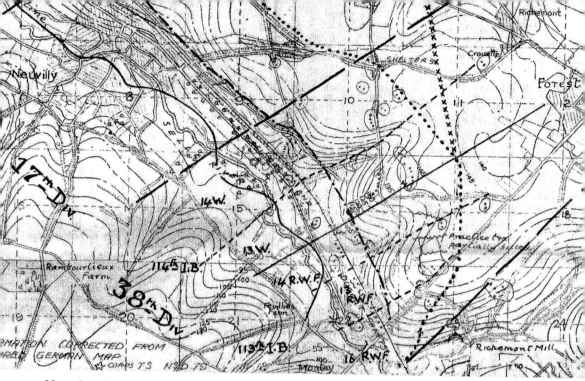

Map showing positions of the 17th and 38th Divisions during the Battle of the Selle.

that hadn't been seen for four long years.

> *We were now able to walk freely along the top of the trenches and not across a tortured half mile with no more than a narrow space in between the shell holes while our positions in the trench were being raided and bombed. The grass was green and, except for having gone wild and a rank growth a cow would not care for, the going was easy. The older men relished the difference. The later drafts joining us as replacements had never experienced any other conditions and their helplessness was pitiful. They had no idea how to take cover except that which came by instinct and natural reaction, whereas the older, experienced soldier knew of an hundred and one ways to take advantage of cover and to judge where it was safe to shelter, when to run and again where to stay put.*

Shanahan

This was the time of the advance to, and the subsequent Battle of the River Selle. The 33rd and 38th Divisions were working in tandem, leapfrogging each other and pushing up north-east in the direction of the Le Cateau to Cambrai Road, and up towards the Forest of Mormal, the area so proudly fought over by the original British Expeditionary Force in those far off days of August 1914. For the next few days it was the turn of the 33rd Division to carry the advance, and soon they had

197

pushed north of Le Cateau and moved towards the River Selle, forcing a crossing over the river on the 10th October. Operations carried on here for the next few days, with footbridges being erected and forward posts being established.

In the meantime, the elements of the 38th Division were being moved up closer to the line, and readied to relieve the 33rd Division on the night of the 13/14 October. As planned, on that night 115 Brigade relieved 100 Brigade of 33rd Division near Montay.

They remained at the front of the line for the coming days, with the 15th Welsh of 114 Brigade still in support. On the night of 18 October, the front held by the 38th Division was extended to include the Montay to Forest road, and 114 Brigade moved into the line, taking up positions on the left of 113 Brigade, with the 15th Welsh in reserve at Troisvilles.

The division was now in place, ready to press forward a fresh offensive against the German lines on the Selle, and at 02.00 hrs on 20 October, the preliminary barrage opened up. The rate of this barrage was to be 100 yards in four minutes, which was deemed ample time to allow the infantry to keep up, and for the two brigades to move forward, mopping up the pockets of German resistance as they went.

The plan for 114 Brigade was to attack with the 13th Welsh on the right and the 14th Welsh on the left. One company of the 15th Welsh was attached to the 13th and two to the 14th Welsh, the remainder in

A British Lewis Gun team during an advance, Autmun 1918. Taylor Library

brigade reserve. The objective was a line from Amerval to Montay. The River Selle itself ran in a valley, with the opposing bank strongly held by the Germans.

As a mirror of the successful crossing of the Ancre in August, the River Selle was forded by men of the 15th Welsh, under Captain J G Owen, MC, who led B Company across, and dug in on the north bank of the river, under heavy fire. The advance successfully consolidated positions on the German side of the Selle, and the 15th Welsh began to mop up German positions on the railway line and around the quarry. By evening the objectives had been reached, and over 200 Germans had been captured, along with four field guns, three trench mortars and forty machine guns.

A number of casualties were again suffered by the 15th Welsh. Second Lieutenant George Henry Minshull, MC was killed, along with six other ranks. George Minshull is buried at Montay-Neuvilly Road Cemetery, as is another casualty of the day, Private Robert Griffiths of Felinfoel.

The attack had been perfectly carried out, with relatively few casualties to the 38th Division. On 21 October, 115 Brigade relieved both 113 and 114 Brigades, and the men moved back to billets at Bertry, then on 23 October back to Troisvilles.

Again, Major-General Cubitt was proud of his men:

> *I am once again lost in admiration at the gallantry and determination of the troops of this Division in surmounting the obstacles with which they were confronted. You formed up in boggy ground, crossed a difficult river (for the fourth time since 21st August), attacked up a glacis swept by machine gun fire, stormed a precipitous railway embankment 40 to 50 feet high, and in pouring rain, very slippery and deep going , in the hours of darkness, established yourselves on the final objective punctually and to time.*

These were very proud words from the Commanding Officer. Life in Troisvilles was as good as it had been for a long time for the war weary men of the 38th Division. The local inhabitants had just been liberated from four long years of German rule, and the men were treated like kings. However there was still a way to go before the war was to be won.

During the next few days the 33rd Division pressed on with the advance towards the Forest of Mormal, and early on the morning of 26 October, the 33rd Division had captured Englefontaine, a village sat on the western edge of the Forest of Mormal. The 38th (Welsh) Division relieved them there, in readiness for the next stage of the advance.

On 29 October the 15th Welsh moved forward to the front line at Englefontaine, taking over positions held by the 2nd Royal Welsh

Fusiliers, with posts pushed out in advance positions. The Battle of the Selle was over and won. German defence and spirit was now crumbling fast, and behind the scenes an Armistice was being negotiated.

Company Sergeant Major Robert Fairclough of Farnworth played an important part in the fighting during these final days of the war. Robert had joined the Battalion at Rhyl as a sixteen year old, and had landed with the Battalion in France on 2 December 1915. In less than three years the young man had worked his way up to Acting Company Sergeant Major, and was a veteran of Mametz Wood and Passchendaele. He was to receive several commendations for his bravery during the last few weeks of the war, which resulted in him being awarded the Distinguished Conduct Medal on 11 March, 1920. Robert survived the war, but returned to hardship in Farnworth, where he worked as a railway fireman for several years. During World War Two Robert again stood against the Germans, working at a munitions factory in Bolton. He died in the late 1950s.

Company Sergeant Major Robert Fairclough, DCM.
Mrs Joan Jarvis

The 33rd and 38th Divisions had together forced their way up along the Forest of Mormal. This mighty forest had split the British Expeditionary Force in retreat during 1914. The 15th Welsh billeted at Englefontaine, were on the west side of this gloomy and foreboding forest. Casualties had slowed down, but were still a regular occurrence, with another thirteen men dead by the end of October 1918. Mormal was regarded as so large an obstacle that preparations were made for the next stage of the advance over the next few days, and the offensive for now was halted. The objective for the 38th Division was now the strategically important railhead of Maubege, and further delays were out of the question.

On 4 November the 15th Welsh moved forward for operations in the Forest of Mormal, and remained in reserve until 113 and 115 Brigades took their objectives. The forest itself was split by diagonal 'rides' and contained huge clearings where the Germans had been harvesting wood. The advance took place under an intensive creeping barrage, and the men were ordered to keep 300 yards behind the barrage, to minimise the risk of unnecessary casualties.

The men of 115 Brigade had the toughest role, but broke through the strongly held edge of the forest. Once inside, 113 Brigade leap-frogged them, and continued the advance into the Foret de Mormal.

This second objective was reached by around 10.30 hrs, and so 114 Brigade moved from their positions at Croix and Forest, reaching the original line by 08.30 hrs where they also entered the forest. After a pause for breakfast, 114 Brigade reached 113 Brigade within the dark confined of the forest, and took over the assault, with 15th Welsh on the right, 14th Welsh to the left, with 13th Welsh in support.

By now, the 15th Welsh was almost back to full strength, with thirty Officers and 855 Other Ranks noted, but almost half were left in reserve around forest. However, 114 Brigade moved through towards their objectives, reaching it by around 14.00 hrs. Patrols pushed further on, but no contact could be made with the enemy, who were crumbling fast.

Due to the good work done by 114 Brigade, the 38th (Welsh) Division had pushed on four miles further than the divisions to each side. On the morning of 5 November 1918, the 33rd Division relieved the tired men of 38th (Welsh) Division from within the forest, leaving 114 Brigade to aid them. On 8 November, the Germans began to withdraw, and so on 8 November 1918, 114 Brigade moved out from the Forest of Mormal.

> When the march was to end and how far we had to go, no one knew. We only knew that at the end of the day or night we might have a dixie of tea. What we would eat would be perhaps the unexpired portion of our ration, an army biscuit, no doubt very nutritious but hard as stone. To break it into smaller pieces, we used to pound it with the handle of our bayonet then chew away at it or soak the smaller pieces. Sometimes, as a luxury, there was served or dished out currant duff. This delicacy consisted of soaked army biscuits and currants made into a dough, rolled, and tied in a sandbag. It was boiled for hours and unwrapped and cut into thick rounds. It went down fine, even though it was rubbery and would have bounced two or three feet if dropped, but for all that it tasted good. Shanahan

Little did they know it at the time, but they were marching to billets in Ecuelin, east of Aulnoye, on the eastern side of the great forest. On their way to Ecuelin, the 15th Welsh advanced through the large town of Berlaimont. The men were getting battle weary by now, and had no idea of how close to the end of the war they were, as the Germans still fought doggedly.

> Soon we passed through a town, Berlaimont. It was a big railhead with prison cages which for months had held our men who had been taken prisoner but now they were empty. A huge dump of coal was smouldering away. However, this was not to be our objective and the night was spent in a wood on the outskirts of the village, Ecuelin by name, and quite a small place. However in the wood when day broke, men were coming down the roads, all injured and bandaged. So we were now ready to move forward and take over whatever it was the injured men had come up against, but strangely enough we somehow heard

rumours of an impending Armistice and sure enough the news was more than rumours. Soon we were marching to the rear and found billets in the village of Ecuelin where we stayed until the new year. Some poor fellows did not even make it to Armistice Day for many were killed up to an hour or less before the hostilities ceased. How sad to be killed when peace was so near. Shanahan

In fact it was here at Ecuelin that the men of the 15th Welsh saw out the end of the Great War, with the Armistice having being signed, and the declaration of peace being declared at 11.00 hrs on 11 November 1918. The 38th (Welsh) Division as a whole had captured forty-five German officers, 3,037 other ranks, 520 machine-guns, fifty trench mortars and forty-three heavy guns during the one hundred days offensive. It had paid a heavy price in manpower for these successes, having lost 407 officers and 8,274 other ranks during its three hard years at war on the Western Front.

The 38th (Welsh) Division remained based around Aulnoye after the Armistice, and received the honour of an inspection by King George V on 3 December. Here at Aulnoye the men settled down to training and recreation. Various schemes were dreamt up to try and stop the troops getting bored and disruptive, and a major part of this was organised sporting events. One of the first organised events was the 114 Infantry Brigade three mile road race, which was won in due course by the 15th Welsh. They were rewarded for their victory with a silver plated trophy, inscribed with the details of their success.

This cup was later to be presented to the Carmarthenshire

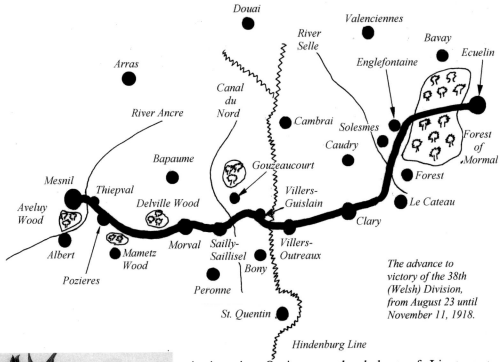

The advance to victory of the 38th (Welsh) Division, from August 23 until November 11, 1918.

Hindenburg Line

Antiquarian Society, at the behest of Lieutenant-Colonel Parkinson, along with a bugle belonging to the battalion. This bugle has been long since lost, but the trophy remains in the care of the Carmarthenshire Museum, situated at the Bishop's Palace at Abergwili.

The 38th (Welsh) Division was not picked to become part of the Army of Occupation after the war, but was to be demobilised, and so during December over 3,000 coal miners were allowed to go home, with much sadness on their part, as good friends had been made, under very trying circumstances, and there was a genuine feeling of regret at having to part from these friends who the men had trained, fought, lived and socialised with over the preceding months and years.

A diminished force now remained in France, and the Staff of 38th (Welsh) Division had come up with a good way of relieving the boredom. During December 1918 a 38th Divisional Rugby Team was set up, and an itinerary was being prepared, which would give the men some testing matches over the coming months.

The Christmas of 1918 came and went, and after Christmas the 38th (Welsh) Division moved into billets back on the Somme, spread around the villages of Querrieu, Allonville, Warloy and Glisy, East of Amiens, with the 15th Welsh billeted at Allonville.

Allonville was quite a small village and, like most on the Somme, consisted of the church and the large house or chateau of the local magnate, the usual pond and the street which seemed to be all barns with big double doors through which the hay wagons were driven and the hay forked out on both sides. Another door led out into a yard and to the rear of the barn, with stables and pig sties flanking both sides – the whole forming a compact nearly square area.

It was at this house that I often sat in the kitchen with a dozen or so mates drinking coffee from tiny cups. The stove, I think it was called a marmite, was a pot bellied affair with a hole in the centre of its belly and fed with whatever fuel was about. The back of the stove ran for a foot or two with the flue pipe at the rear and with small ovens, one with both sides. The heat, of course, was drawn to the flue and passed between the ovens, providing the necessary heat to cook. An iron bowl sat on the top of the stove like a cauldron and provided the ready made coffee. Madam would pop in some ground coffee, more water and there was your coffee, ready once more. The father sat at a bench on a raised platform in the room and performed the functions of the village cobbler. During the day he would be out very early in the fields, weeding, thinning, sowing or helping at a huge horse driven threshing machine. There also were machines driven by belt from steam engines. Shanahan

In the meantime, thousands of servicemen were still stationed in France awaiting release from the Army, and they had to be kept entertained. The already successful 15th Welsh cross country team went on to win the 38th Divisional race at Pont Noyelles on 19 January 1919, and the 38th Divisional Rugby Team went on tour to Paris.

53rd Welsh at Hyde Park, March 1919.

The first match was against an Australian Trench XV, which the Welsh drew nil-nil. This was a good warm-up for the men, but they lost to a French XV on 1 January 1919 by thirteen points to six, before coming back and beating Paris by nine points to six on 5 January 1919. The next two matches were against fellow teams from V Corps, in a tournament which the 38th Division won after two decisive victories; first by beating the 17th Division by fifty-six points to nil, and then by beating the 21st Division by thirty-two points to nil. The team went on to tour South Wales, beating Neath by fifteen points to three; Swansea by thirteen points to three; Llywynypia by thirteen points to nil, and then taking on a 'Rest of Wales XV' at St. Helens, where the 15th Welsh had originally formed in 1914, which was aptly drawn three points to all.

On 12 January 1919 Lieutenant-Colonel Parkinson DSO re-assumed command of the 15th Welsh from Lieutenant-Colonel Helme, DSO, who had relinquished his command on 10 January. Ernest Helme had assumed command on 15 September 1918, guiding the Battalion throughout the advance to the Mormal Forest.

During the month of February 1919, demobilisation of the 15th Welsh was well under way, and by 27 February the strength of the battalion was down to just eleven officers and fifty six men. Six officers and eighty-six men had left the battalion that day to be attached to the 1/6th Welsh in Germany, as part of the Army of Occupation. On 8 March, the remnants of the 15th Welsh moved to billets at Blangy-Tronville, where they remained until 17 May 1919 when they entrained at Longeau for Le Havre. The train departed at 19.35 hrs, and arrived at Le Havre at 10.10 hrs the following morning. The men then made the march to Harfleur Camp, where they awaited their move home, which came on 23 May 1919; final destination Newmarket.

The *London Gazette* of 7 October 1919 stated that Lieutenant-Colonel Thomas William Parkinson, DSO had relinquished Command of the 15th Welsh. He had commanded the Battalion more or less all the way through the war, since being given command on 10 November 1915, and reverted to his 1915 rank of Major with the York and Lancaster Regiment. Lieutenant-Colonel Thomas William Parkinson, DSO returned to serve with the York and Lancaster Regiment, and took up a post in command of the Depot at Pontefract, in which position he remained until 1921.

In 1924 Major Parkinson DSO took command of the 1st Battalion, York and Lancaster Regiment until retiring from his position in 1928. In 1927 Lieutenant-Colonel Parkinson founded the Regimental Association of the York and Lancaster Regiment, which still exists today.

He is recorded in 1958 as being made Deputy Lieutenant of Brecon, and was residing at Llanwysg, Crickhowell.

The time of the 38th (Welsh) Division, and indeed of the 15th Welsh was drawing to a close now. On 18 May 1919, the Prime Minister, David Lloyd George made a visit to the old Somme battlefields to see where his son had fought with the 38th Division, and met up with the Head Quarters Staff of the Division that day at Villers Brettoneux. The great orator was on his way to the Paris Peace Conference, and then to Versailles to attend meetings about the Peace Treaty, the terms of which were still in some doubt at the time, and spoke to the gathered Welshmen for the last time;

> These terms are written in the blood of fallen heroes. The Germans have been reckoning on this job for years, even working out the number of spikes per yard of barbed wire. We never dreamt of being in a position like this. In order to make it impossible to occur again we have had to make these terms severe. We must carry out the edict of providence and see to it that the people who inflicted his shall never be in a position to do so again.
>
> The Germans say they will not sign. Their newspapers say they will not sign. The politicians say the same, and we know that all politicians speak he truth. We say, "Gentlemen you must sign. If on don't do so in Versailles you shall do so in Berlin.
>
> But it is useless for four of us to go "on our own" to Berlin. If we four go we must have the Army behind us. We are not going to give way. The future of the world is dependent on this peace being imposed on Germany. If it is necessary for you to march to Berlin, if your leave is cancelled or your departure for England delayed, you will know that I alone am responsible, so you had better get your firing party out now. See that the seal is put on the document which you have helped to write, and we shall have peace reigning throughout the whole world.

The division was not to be needed again though. The terms of the treaty were agreed by the 'Big Four' of Lloyd George, Woodrow Wilson, George Clemenceau of France and Orlando of Italy, and signed off on 28 June 1919, with terms harsh enough to provoke the German people to rise again less than twenty years later.

The war diary of the 15th (Service) Battalion, the Welsh Regiment, for the period of the Great War was finished, and signed off at the end of May 1919. A proud history was for now at an end. The battalion was not to be formed again until the coming of the Second World War, and then it would be used purely as a home service battalion, on garrison duty within Britain.

The cadre of the battalion, consisting of only three officers and twelve other ranks, disembarked at Southampton on 23 May 1919, after three years and six months of service in France. They were received at a presentation ceremony in the town of Carmarthen by members of the Council, where, at the request of Lieutenant-Colonel Parkinson, the battalion handed over to the Carmarthenshire Antiquarian Society the Silver Cup won by themselves during the Cross Country championships, and the bugle.

Of those who went out to France as part of the original battalion in December 1915, the following returned with the Cadre: Lieutenant-Colonel T W Parkinson, DSO, Captain & Quartermaster J R G Morgan, MC, Regimental Quarter Master Sergeant S T Evans, MSS, Company Quartermaster S Roberts, Sergeant Millichap, Corporal Paget, Corporal T C Johns, Lance Corporal J O'Leary and seven other men whose identities remain sadly unknown. Some men had been chosen to join the occupying forces in Germany, and remained in the Army for a further spell, joining the 53rd Welsh. On 1 March 1919 the battalion was among a group of others which was reviewed at Hyde Park in London by King George V, before being sent out to Germany as part of the Army of Occupation.

Far from feeling ecstatic about the end of hostilities, and the thought of returning home, many of the men were to miss the camaraderie of

The pay book of 54270 Lance Corporal William David Shanahan.

being a soldier, and returned to civilian life to find that Britain was in the throes of a depression, which made work hard to find for many. The feelings of loss were written about in the final pages of the memoirs of William Shanahan:

Looking back, I would not have missed the experience. One realised the relative value of things and we soon put aside in order of importance what was, in the light of experience, to be of value to us. Again, what was thought important, we soon found to be not in the least important. It was a revelation of how men behave under such conditions- the comradeship and the willingness to help each other. There was always someone who would share whatever they had, generous yes. If only the same spirit had persisted in the years following, how different would have been the lot of many of the men. Having had their chance to learn a trade, but having been prevented by the war, they found on return to civil life that the splendid attitude of the men in France to one another had gone. Life became a fight to obtain work and it was either low wages or no work. Men had to go on the dole and exist on a bare state allowance, singing in groups, knocking on the door with cap in hand, selling note paper, pins or just plain begging. As I know quite well in many cases, those being begged from were worse off than the beggar.

For years I have nursed a desire to return to the scenes of my service in France, but never could find sufficient money. Now when we could visit, we are too old and it is sad to see your pals, whom you remember as you were yourself, young and full of beans, able to march fully loaded, to bear fatigue easily – it is sad now to meet them much older, some in poor health, and then to hear of their death. How vividly the mind then recalls experiences together – what close friends you were, how one would willingly risk his life to help you and now all is over. One by one the old soldiers pass on and soon the old soldiers will be the survivors of a later war, fought in 1939-45. So it goes on until that day when wars are no more.

Appendix I

Casualties of the 15th Welsh

From 25 August 1918 until the signing of the Armistice on 11 November 1918, the battalion, under the command of Lieutenant-Colonel Helme, DSO, took part in every engagement in which the 38th (Welsh) Division was involved, the most important of these being the capture of the Ancre, the capture of Morval, crossing of the Canal Du Nord, Gouzeaucourt, Villers Outreaux, Selle River crossing, and Mormal Forest.

Just during this final stage of the Great War, from the Battle of Albert on to final victory on 11 November 1918, its casualties amounted to forty officers and 900 other ranks killed and wounded. The 15th Welsh, the Carmarthen Pals, during the whole course of the war, had lost over 570 men dead by the signing of the Armistice, forty-four of whom were officers, with at least another seven men known from the battalion to die as a direct result of the war in the coming six months afterwards.

Over 1,121 men were listed as wounded in the *Carmarthen Journal* (1,420 in the Battalion War Diary), with a further forty-three men missing, some of whom are included in the figure of over 560 dead, as their fates were discovered after the war. Five men died in 1915, 122 in 1916, 162 men in 1917, 273 men in 1918 and four men in 1919, making a total of 568 men known to have died with the 15th Welsh, including those who died after the war had ended, and those who had moved to different units. Of these men, twenty-eight had died of sickness, 134 had died of wounds, and the remaining 400 plus had been killed in action. Over eighty of these men were from the Bolton area, almost one hundred from Carmarthenshire, and eighteen from Pembrokeshire. There were many men from Glamorgan, some from Shropshire and Cheshire, a few from Scotland and even one man from Canada. Over 160 of these men have no known graves, and are commemorated on the various war memorials on the Western Front. One man is on the Cambrai Memorial, two are on the Ploegsteert Memorial, five are on the Pozieres Memorial, sixty-four are on the Thiepval Memorial, twenty-three are on the Tyne Cot Memorial, forty-one are on the Vis-en-Artois Memorial and twenty-six men are commemorated on the Menin Gate Memorial at Ypres.

Burials are scattered throughout the Western Front and back in Britain. 150 men are either buried or commemorated in Belgium, 388 in France, one man in Germany and twenty-six in Britain (thirteen in England and thirteen in Wales). The average age of the men who died was twenty-five years old. The youngest casualty was just sixteen, and the eldest was forty-two.

The last man of the battalion to have died in France was Lance Corporal James Coffey, the Son of James and Emma Coffey, of 7, Clint Road, Edge Hill, Liverpool. He had enlisted on 12 June 1917 at Liverpool, where he worked as a postman. James had joined the battalion on the Somme on 5 April 1918, and was wounded just two days later, returning to duty a month later. James had been temporarily attached to the Royal Engineers on postal duties, and on the night of 18 February 1919 he was lighting an acetylene gas generator aboard the Cologne Mail Train when it exploded. A fragment of the exploding gas generator struck James in the head, and he died instantly. James was buried at Terlincthun British Cemetery, Wimille. The Court of Enquiry harshly deemed his injuries, and thus his subsequent death to have been self-inflicted.

Private Gordon Richard Cynlais Thomas was the second last man of the 15th Welsh to die as a result of the Great War, and the last Carmarthenshire man of the battalion to have been recognised as a casualty of war by the Commonwealth War Graves Commission. He was the son of David Thomas, of the Ship Inn, Llanelli, and was just twenty-two years old when he died on 15 March 1919.

Other men were to die in the years to follow, but are not recognised as war casualties in the official sense, but their wounds, both physical and mental, left deep scars which remained with the men for the rest of their lives.

Interestingly, out of the original number of officers who became part of the 15th Welsh at Rhyl, during the formation of the Battalion, several were to be killed in action whilst in the service of the Royal Flying Corps, or Royal Air Force as it was later to become. The Royal Flying Corps had originally been formed on 18 May 1912. At the outbreak of the Great War it was realised that aircraft would be an essential part of modern warfare, and so it was rapidly expanded in size. As a result, many adventure seeking young officers volunteered for service, and were transferred from the Army as a result, training as pilots or observers. The former 15th Welshmen to die with the Flying Services were; Lieutenant Reginald Burgess, Second Lieutenant Godfrey Benjamin Joseph Firbank, Lieutenant Gwyn Arthur Griffiths, and Lieutenant William Bertram Protheroe. Several officers also died with other Army Battalions [The details on these men are to be found in the Nominal Roll of Officers, in Appendix IV].

Lance Corporal James Coffey. Last man of the battalion to die in France.

The grave of Private Gordon Richard Cynlais Thomas Box Cemetery in Llanelli.

Some of the other ranks who died with other Battalions after initially serving with the 15th Welsh were:

Private Michael Cavanagh originally served with the 15th Welsh with the regimental number 19903. He was another of the Bolton men, the son of John and Sarah Cavanagh, of 11, Garden Street, Chorley, Lancs. Michael transferred to the 2nd Battalion, Leinster Regiment, and was killed in action at the Battle of Messines, on 9 June 1917. He has no known grave, and is commemorated on the Ypres (Menin Gate) Memorial. He was just nineteen years old.

Private Alfred Fogg was another Bolton man, the son of Richard and Martha Ellen Fogg, of 158, Deane Road, Bolton. Alfred originally served with the 15th Welsh with the regimental number 20977, but transferred to the 2nd Battalion, South Lancashire Regiment. Alfred was killed in action during the Battle of the Lys, on 10 April 1918. He was just twenty years old, and has no known grave, and so is commemorated on the Ploegsteert Memorial.

Private William Edward Pearson was another of the Bolton contingent, and was the son of James and Annie Pearson, of Halliwell, Bolton. He originally served with the 15th Welsh with the Regimental Number 20875, but transferred to the 2/4th Battalion, South Lancashire Regiment. William was twenty-six years old when he was wounded during the Battle of the Hindenburg Line, and he died as a result on 6 October 1918. He is buried at St. Sever Cemetery Extension, Rouen.

Private James Thomas Price was the son of William and Phoebe Price, of Treleddidfawr, St. David's, Pembrokeshire. He had originally served with the 15th Welsh with the number 20991, but later transferred to the 8th Battalion, South Lancashire Regiment. James was killed in action during the latter stages of the Battle of the Somme, on the south bank of the River Ancre on 1 October 1916. He was twenty-seven years old, and is commemorated on the Thiepval Memorial.

Private Henry John Rowlands, was from the Rhondda, and had originally enlisted there into the 10th Welsh. He must have been one of the original batch of men from the 10th Welsh that was sent to help form the 15th Welsh, with Henry being allotted the service number 22281. He later transferred into the 13th Battalion of the Tank Corps, and was killed in action during the first few weeks of the German Offensive on the Lys, on 25 April 1918. Henry is commemorated on the Tyne Cot Memorial.

This is not a complete list of the men who had transferred from the 15th Welsh, and died with other battalions, as it is almost impossible to trace these men without a nominal roll of the 15th Welsh, which as far as is known does not exist. Both for the main listing of men who died in service with the battalion and these men who died with other units, apologies if anyone is found to be missing, but every effort has been taking to try and make these details as accurate as humanly possible.

Appendix II

The Roll of Honour

Rank	Name	No.	Date of Death
Private	Absalom, Herbert	59245	20/08/1917
Private	Acock, Frank	202111	11/03/1918
Private	Allen, Arthur Laugharne	291399	23/03/1918
Private	Allen, Harry Montague	20965	11/07/1916
Lance Corporal	Allen, Wilfred	12538	21/09/1918
Private	Allen, William Henry	20100	11/07/1916
Private	Anderson, Richard John	20534	09/03/1916
Private	Andrews, Edward James	54810	27/07/1917
Private	Andrews, John Edward	285360	07/09/1917
Lance Corporal	Antell, Arthur	47485	24/02/1917
Major	Anthony, Percy		10/07/1916
Private	Arthur, William Thomas	54130	01/09/1918
Private	Ashman, George	33276	01/08/1917
Private	Ashton, George William	47659	28/07/1917
Private	Axford, Stanley	72983	27/08/1918
Private	Badnell, Arthur John	285395	11/03/1918
Lieutenant	Bainbrigge, Philip Gillespie		18/09/1918
Private	Baker, James	291733	19/09/1918
Private	Balderson, Robert	20292	19/03/1916
Private	Ball, Edward	54605	26/08/1918
Private	Ball, James	20074	10/07/1916
Private	Barnett, George Leonard	20346	18/09/1918
Private	Barnett, William John	35104	24/08/1918
Lance Corporal	Barrow, Arthur	23852	09/10/1918
Private	Barrow, George	37384	11/03/1918
Private	Bartlett, Robert James	59780	22/08/1917
Private	Beal, Cecil Charles Branston	44209	10/05/1918
Private	Beasant, Walter Henry	64527	08/10/1918
Sergeant	Bennett, Harry	23914	10/05/1918
Private	Bennett, William Edward	203580	24/08/1918
Private	Bickerstaff, Thomas Charles	19861	14/07/1916
Sergeant	Bickerstaffe, William	20201	08/06/1918
Private	Billington, Arthur George	37983	18/06/1917
Private	Bird, Harry	35087	11/07/1916
Sergeant	Bithell, Herbert Lewis	21028	18/03/1918
Private	Boardman, William	20345	28/07/1917
Private	Bond, Eric Henry	72820	08/10/1918
Private	Booth, Leonard	20289	11/07/1916
Private	Bowen, Ernest	200043	18/09/1918
Private	Bowen, George Winfred	201578	20/08/1917
Private	Bowen, Thomas John	35120	11/07/1916
2nd Lieutenant	Bowen, William		30/08/1918
Private	Bradbury, Thomas	285447	08/10/1918
Private	Brain, George Heal	20503	17/03/1916
Private	Breach, William Herbert	72817	27/08/1918

Corporal	Brightwell, Thomas	26521	18/09/1918
Lance Corporal	Brindle, James	20381	18/06/1918
Private	Brown, John James	20552	11/07/1916
Private	Brown, Pryce	19900	20/07/1916
Private	Brown, Samuel Edward	72821	01/09/1918
2nd Lieutenant	Burgess, Reginald		07/07/1916
Corporal	Burley, William Henry	32696	29/08/1918
Private	Burton, William	37313	08/10/1918
Sergeant	Bush, Ernest Frederick	19993	25/01/1916
Private	Byrne, James	53948	28/07/1917
Lance Corporal	Cadle, Herbert	20828	27/04/1918
Private	Capper, Leonard	290691	18/09/1918
Private	Carey, Patrick Michael	54604	07/05/1917
Private	Cavanagh, Michael	5717	09/06/1917
Private	Cay, William	59374	04/08/1917
Private	Chadwick, Albert	21067	10/07/1916
Private	Chadwick, James	20807	20/10/1916
Private	Chadwick, Thomas Benjamin	20832	31/07/1917
Captain	Chamberlain, John MC.		14/05/1917
Private	Chapman, James Ernest	20054	11/07/1916
Lance Corporal	Chapman, William Arthur	285401	23/08/1918
Lance Corporal	Church, Edward Charles	477530	20/08/1917
Private	Clarke, Ernest	55744	12/05/1918
Private	Clarke, Walter	72830	28/08/1918
Private	Clee, Thomas	285363	16/08/1917
Private	Clewes, William	20702	16/08/1916
Private	Close, William John	20500	01/08/1917
Lance Corporal	Coffey, James	72827	18/02/1919
Private	Cokley, Daniel	21086	11/07/1916
Private	Cole, James	73016	04/11/1918
Private	Coleman, James	20890	17/08/1917
Private	Coleman, Joseph	21058	11/07/1916
Private	Collins, John Bryant	35213	11/07/1916
Private	Combs, Phillip Alfred	54988	10/08/1918
Private	Connoly, John	24827	28/08/1918
Private	Coulton, Arthur	73007	08/10/1918
Private	Cridland, William	202999	12/03/1918
Private	Crook, William	73002	13/01/1919
Private	Crossley, Jesse	73009	26/08/1918
Private	Cunningham, Joseph	20692	28/02/1916
Private	Dash, Horace	20480	05/04/1917
2nd Lieutenant	David, Frederick John Louis		18/09/1918
Captain	David, Thomas William		27/07/1917
Private	Davies, Albert	44630	10/05/1918
Private	Davies, Arthur Raymond	53954	27/07/1917
Private	Davies, Ebenezer	45200	20/02/1917
Private	Davies, Evan John	20739	10/07/1916
Private	Davies, Evan Thomas	54551	10/05/1918
Private	Davies, Francis Joe	285450	08/09/1917
Private	Davies, Frank Victor	47247	19/09/1916
Private	Davies, Frederick	53950	02/08/1917
Private	Davies, John	20630	01/05/1917
Private	Davies, John Glanford	73738	08/10/1917
Private	Davies,Joseph Henry	285402	03/05/1918
Private	Davies, Llewellyn	30422	08/10/1918

C.Q.M.S.	Davies, Mansel	20091	10/02/1916
Private	Davies, Martin	28541	01/10/1918
Private	Davies, Nathaniel	20927	09/03/1916
Captain	Davies, Percy Hier		16/08/1917
Private	Davies, Reginald	25193	17/03/1916
Private	Davies, Robert	62306	08/10/1918
Private	Davies, Samuel John	20061	21/07/1916
Private	Davies, Thomas	65552	18/09/1918
Private	Davies, Thomas Haydn, MM	20732	30/01/1917
Corporal	Davies, Thomas John	21074	11/07/1916
Private	Davies, Tommy	266456	10/09/1917
Private	Davies, Trevor	266065	10/05/1918
Private	Davies, William	14490	04/09/1918
Private	Davies, William Henry	54489	04/09/1918
Private	Davies, William John	20575	06/08/1917
Private	Dawes, Ronald Guy	290694	23/08/1918
Private	Day, William	65543	04/09/1918
Private	Dayton, Stanley	25831	19/09/1918
Lance Corporal	Demaine, John	20626	15/02/1917
Private	Denton, Frank Charles	54969	22/08/1917
Private	Derrick, Herbert	21786	19/05/1916
Lance Corporal	Deyes, William Percival	290309	03/09/1918
Private	Dodd, John Henry	19909	09/03/1916
Private	Driver, Wilfred	54047	26/08/1918
Private	Dryland, John	53953	30/06/1917
Private	Duncan, Robert	59370	28/07/1917
Private	Dunford, George	54782	08/10/1918
Private	Dunn, James	20509	15/02/1917
Private	Dunsford, Henry John	55782	11/10/1918
Private	Dutfield, William Henry	75504	31/10/1918
Corporal	Dutton, Herbert Henry	201910	08/10/1918
Private	Eade, John William	53919	28/07/1917
Private	Earles, William Henry	54990	22/04/1918
Private	Edmunds, Samuel	22403	27/07/1917
Private	Edwards, Christopher	53894	04/11/1918
Lance Corporal	Edwards, David John	30213	30/04/1917
Private	Edwards, Evan	43033	10/05/1918
Private	Edwards, William	266612	14/05/1918
Sergeant	Evans, Benjamin	20115	11/07/1916
Private	Evans, David	17551	11/03/1918
Private	Evans, David Charles	54294	30/04/1917
Private	Evans, David Ellis	23312	19/06/1918
Private	Evans, David John	75286	23/10/1918
Second Lieutenant	Evans, Frederick William		28/10/1916
Private	Evans, George	20125	18/03/1916
Lance Sergeant	Evans, Griffith Albert	26738	08/06/1917
Private	Evans, Herbert	44198	11/07/1916
Private	Evans, John Emlyn	26736	11/01/1916
Private	Evans, Morgan Rees	53914	18/09/1918
Private	Evans, Phillip Charles	53957	30/07/1917
Private	Evans, Richard Henry Evan	20043	08/10/1918
2nd Lieutenant	Evans, Robert Charles		24/08/1918
Private	Evans, Samuel Henry	25083	21/07/1918
Private	Evans, William Bailey	39705	04/08/1917
Private	Evans, William Edward	23786	21/04/1918

Lance Corporal	Evens, Tola	242141	18/09/1918
Private	Eynon, Thomas	19992	13/03/1916
Private	Farrow, George	20665	08/02/1917
Private	Farrow, Herbert	20858	08/02/1917
Sergeant	Fielding, James	19891	11/07/1916
Private	Fielding, Joshua, MM	72851	08/10/1918
Second Lieutenant	Firbank, Godfrey Benjamin Joseph		11/09/1916
Private	Fisher, John	18810	05/08/1917
Private	Fletcher, Hugh	73025	28/08/1918
Private	Fogg, Alfred	43348	10/04/1918
Private	Foley, Patrick	59376	08/10/1918
Private	Foley, William Hambling	34994	20/03/1916
Private	Foots, James Todd	59375	31/07/1917
Lance Corporal	Forrest, Henry	21030	11/07/1916
Private	Foster, Sidney Gordon	54826	31/07/1917
Private	Francis, Albert	20211	14/06/1915
Corporal	Francis, Gwilym	20449	11/07/1916
Private	Froy, Jesse	47782	11/04/1917
Private	Fry, William Henry	25378	05/09/1918
Private	Garley, Arthur	47745	27/07/1917
Private	Garside, John	50522	22/04/1918
Private	Garside, William John	65186	13/04/1918
2nd Lieutenant	George, Elmore Wright		10/05/1918
Sergeant	German, Archie Ernest	53962	26/08/1918
Private	Gerrard, William	20993	11/07/1916
Private	Gibbon, Charles	65572	30/08/1918
Private	Gibbs, Harry	53961	04/08/1917
Private	Gibbs, William	38467	10/05/1918
Private	Gibson, William	21669	30/08/1918
Lance Sergeant	Gilchrist, Lindsay	59488	27/07/1917
Sgt Instructor	Goble, Alfred	16487	31/05/1917
Private	Grant, John	31193	10/07/1916
Private	Grassick, William Duthie	59380	22/08/1917
Private	Gray, Uriah	32640	09/10/1918
Private	Greenland, Thomas Henry	73162	04/09/1918
Private	Griffiths, David	20584	22/06/1915
Private	Griffiths, Edwin	59498	27/07/1917
Lieutenant	Griffiths, Gwyn Arthur		02/06/1917
Private	Griffiths, Ivor Samuel	20499	11/07/1916
Private	Griffiths, Robert	73685	20/10/1918
Private	Griffiths, Robert William	60723	05/09/1917
Private	Griffiths, Thomas John	20454	04/02/1917
Private	Griffiths, William Alexander	202750	04/10/1918
Private	Griffiths, William Henry	54577	28/07/1917
Private	Griffiths, Willie	53625	11/03/1918
2nd Lieutenant	Hall, John Reginald		10/07/1916
Private	Hall, Joseph Gilbert	53966	28/07/1917
Private	Hall, Joshua	20431	10/07/1916
Private	Hallett, James Edwin	54957	31/07/1918
Private	Hamer, Jack	72856	01/09/1918
Private	Hanlon, Joseph (Farrow)	20348	28/07/1917
Private	Harcombe, Bethnel	21769	10/07/1916
Sergeant	Harding, Charles William	26713	08/06/1917
Lance Corporal	Hardwidge, Henry	20649	11/07/1916
Corporal	Hardwidge, Thomas	26634	11/07/1916

Lance Corporal	Harries, William Esaiah	44228	22/08/1917
Lance Sergeant	Harris, John Hopkin	18506	11/07/1916
Sergeant	Harris, Thomas	18500	01/06/1916
Private	Harrop, Robert	285413	22/08/1917
Private	Hartnett, John Henry	25239	04/11/1918
Private	Haslam, Adam	20314	09/09/1916
Private	Hatherell, Herbert	59440	10/05/1918
Private	Hawkins, Henry Thomas	35044	11/07/1916
Private	Hay, Percy	54497	10/05/1918
Private	Head, Charles Manning	47756	27/07/1917
Lance Corporal	Hearn, Arthur	20418	11/07/1916
Private	Hebbs, Albert	59387	08/10/1918
Private	Heseltine, Henry	54224	23/08/1918
Private	Hewett, William Frederick	59385	28/07/1917
Corporal	Hey, Ernest	20044	11/07/1916
Private	Heywood, Harry	20821	26/08/1918
Private	Higgins, Albert Edward	56983	04/09/1918
Private	Hill, David John	62338	23/08/1918
Private	Hill, Herbert	291799	28/08/1918
Lance Corporal	Hill, John Thomas	20801	03/12/1916
Lance Corporal	Hillier, George	26714	17/03/1916
Private	Hilton, Edward	61205	08/10/1918
Private	Hirst, John	20791	11/07/1916
Private	Hiscocks, Henry John	45519	12/09/1918
Private	Hitchen, Robert	73044	21/09/1918
Private	Holland, Albert	53801	08/10/1918
Private	Holmes, Herbert	59382	27/12/1918
Private	Holmes, James	73033	22/08/1918
Private	Hopkins, Daniel	21629	28/07/1917
Private	Hopkins, David William	75181	08/10/1918
Corporal	Hopkins, William Owen	54286	09/11/1918
Private	Horne, Alfred	201621	28/07/1917
Private	Horseman, Ernest	26636	01/08/1917
Corporal	Howarth, Thomas	19920	01/08/1917
Private	Howells, David	20188	09/03/1916
C.S.M.	Howells, Harry	54246	05/06/1917
Private	Howells, William	20096	21/03/1916
Private	Huddleston, John Marchbank	60499	11/05/1918
Private	Hughes, David Thomas	20609	07/07/1916
Private	Hughes, Elias	20130	10/07/1916
2nd Lieutenant	Hughes, Thomas		08/10/1918
Private	Hughes, Thomas Ellis	73034	26/08/1918
Private	Hughes, William	20750	07/09/1917
Private	Hughes, William	25008	28/04/1918
Private	Hughes, William	54595	30/04/1917
Private	Hughes, William Selby	29189	16/08/1917
Private	Hughes, William Trevor	53967	04/05/1918
Private	Hull, George	51550	08/09/1917
Private	Hulm, John	72866	18/09/1918
Captain	Humphreys, Percy Lloyd		31/07/1917
Private	Humphreys, Richard	35141	11/07/1916
Private	Hunt, Edward Albert	290900	15/03/1918
Private	Hunt, John Henry Porter	21049	11/07/1916
Private	Huntingdon, Henry	285455	09/11/1918
Sergeant	Hurst, Albert	19923	28/07/1917

Private	Hutchinson, Frederick	73183	27/07/1918
Private	Hyde, James	75445	05/11/1918
Private	Iddenden, Frederick	59240	26/04/1918
Private	Ingham, Thomas	73187	23/08/1918
Private	Isaac, Sidney	19871	10/07/1916
Private	Isherwood, Herbert	20857	06/05/1918
Private	Jacob, Charles Henry	73339	29/09/1918
Private	James, Bert	75294	31/10/1918
2nd Lieutenant	James, Charles Llewellyn		10/05/1918
Private	James, David	35048	05/09/1918
2nd Lieutenant	James, Evan		27/07/1917
Lance Corporal	James, James	22127	11/07/1916
Private	James, John Hopkin	54289	01/08/1917
Private	James, Thomas	26816	26/09/1918
Private	James, Thomas John	73578	05/11/1918
Private	James, William	20755	11/01/1917
Private	Jenkins, Arthur Gower	20770	23/11/1917
Private	Jenkins, Bertie	35328	11/07/1916
Private	Jenkins, Ivor	76648	08/10/1918
Private	Jenkins, Ivor	77431	08/10/1918
Private	John, John James	60742	31/08/1917
Private	John, Stephen James	54267	01/08/1917
Private	John, Thomas Henry	38127	11/07/1916
Private	John, William David	20006	14/03/1917
Sergeant	John, William Thomas, DCM	20155	02/11/1918
Private	Johnson, John	20901	11/07/1916
Private	Jones, Bernus	44923	30/08/1918
2nd Lieutenant	Jones, Cecil Norman		09/11/1917
Private	Jones, David	20536	11/07/1916
Lance Corporal	Jones, David John	25650	22/08/1918
Sergeant	Jones, David Lewis	20124	14/03/1917
Private	Jones, Edgar	26909	31/07/1917
Private	Jones, Ernest Wynn Leonard	201840	04/09/1918
Private	Jones, Harold Vivian	54300	01/09/1918
Private	Jones, Harry	19927	09/02/1916
Private	Jones, Henry James	73050	30/08/1918
2nd Lieutenant	Jones, Henry Myrddin		13/11/1916
Private	Jones, Hopkin	24864	19/08/1917
Private	Jones, Howell	75237	08/10/1918
Private	Jones, Humphrey	32798	11/04/1918
Private	Jones, James	20026	10/07/1916
Corporal	Jones, John	20027	10/07/1916
Private	Jones, John	20819	09/03/1916
Private	Jones, John	44060	11/07/1916
Private	Jones, John Evan	40670	29/08/1918
Private	Jones, Jones, John Henry	20092	04/09/1917
2nd Lieutenant	Jones, John Humphrey		08/10/1918
Lance Corporal	Jones, Milwyn	54041	28/07/1917
Second Lieutenant	Jones, John Owen		06/06/1917
Private	Jones, Rees	75289	16/11/1918
Private	Jones, Thomas	20784	01/07/1916
Lance Corporal	Jones, Thomas Cosslett	35168	28/07/1916
Private	Jones, Thomas Lewis	75123	20/10/1918
2nd Lieutenant	Jones, Tom Watson		08/10/1918
Private	Jones, William	63092	01/09/1918

Private	Kelsall, Harry	53979	30/08/1918
Private	Kenny, William Joseph	73056	26/08/1918
Lance Corporal	Killeen, David	20772	15/02/1917
Private	Killelay, Harry	73059	27/08/1918
Private	King, Edmund Charles	23648	27/10/1918
Private	Kirby, John	72878	08/10/1918
Private	Kite, Charles Frank	59410	31/07/1917
Private	Knight, James William	54964	08/10/1918
Captain	Lancaster, Gerald William, MC		14/09/1918
Private	Langford, Benjamin	76659	08/10/1918
Private	Langford, William	285356	22/08/1917
Private	Leahy, James	40069	11/07/1916
Private	Leman, Montague William	201914	08/10/1918
Private	Leonard, William Thomas	59444	27/07/1917
Private	Leseelleur, Godfrey	54891	19/09/1918
Private	Lewis, Arnold Cecil Ewart	35027	09/03/1916
Private	Lewis, Arthur Leonard	16787	12/03/1918
Private	Lewis, Benjamin Thomas	20145	11/07/1916
Private	Lewis, David	54277	30/04/1917
Private	Lewis, David Rees	53981	10/05/1918
Private	Lewis, Henry	76673	08/10/1918
Private	Lewis, Ivor Idris	20853	01/08/1917
Sergeant	Lewis, Richard Ernest	18145	01/08/1917
Private	Little, William James	46337	24/08/1918
Private	Llewellyn, George David	38605	04/03/1917
Captain	Lloyd, Thomas Glyn		10/05/1918
Private	Lock, Ernest Reginald	62774	21/09/1918
Captain	Lord, Arthur		12/02/1917
2nd Lieutenant	Lowe, George Ernest, MC		28/10/1918
2nd Lieutenant	Lucas, Clifton Mallett		10/07/1916
Private	Lydeard, Maurice William	46053	22/08/1917
Private	Mackenzie, Walter Edward	50524	22/08/1917
Private	Magnall, Richard	291939	18/09/1918
Private	Male, David John	73749	18/10/1918
Private	Manhan, C. (A. J. Williams)	203429	04/09/1918
Private	Maple, Cecil Owen	20660	10/07/1916
Private	Marshall, David John	74177	01/11/1918
Private	Martin, George	25941	01/08/1917
Private	Martin, William, MM	20462	30/08/1918
Private	Mather, William	20699	11/07/1916
Private	Matthews, John	35126	11/07/1916
Corporal	Matthews, Robert	25026	15/09/1918
Private	Maylam, Frederick Ernest	54984	16/05/1918
Private	McCracken, Thomas	73204	26/08/1918
Lance Corporal	McDonald, Donald	47785	14/05/1918
Private	McDonald, Frederick	285466	26/08/1918
Private	McHugh, Martin	291223	19/09/1918
Private	McWilliams, William	73203	05/09/1918
Private	Mercer, Jacob	72891	08/10/1918
Private	Meyler, Levi	20144	27/05/1918
2nd Lieutenant	Minshull, George Henry, MC		20/10/1918
Private	Morgan, David	54295	17/03/1918
Lance Corporal	Morgan, David John	20793	27/07/1916
Private	Morgan, David Reginald	20581	09/05/1916
2nd Lieutenant	Morgan, George Elton		19/08/1917

Rank	Name	Number	Date
Private	Morgan, Gilbert Bowen	20621	04/09/1918
Private	Morgan, Thomas John	20975	14/07/1916
Corporal	Morris, William	20749	27/02/1917
Corporal	Mort, Richard	20258	11/07/1916
Private	Moses, Lewis John	20918	04/08/1916
Private	Mugglestone, Walter	20374	09/03/1916
Private	Mulville, William	60768	20/10/1918
Sergeant	Mumford, Eli	22487	20/03/1916
Private	Murphy, Ernest	43220	16/08/1916
Private	Naylor, Frank	291347	26/08/1918
Lance Corporal	Newell, James	20714	29/05/1919
Lieutenant	Newman, Leslie Charles		27/12/1917
Private	Norris, Charles	54961	08/09/1917
Private	Noyes, John Robert	35079	11/07/1916
Private	O' Connor, Thomas	32520	07/07/1916
Private	O' Connor, Thomas	241768	06/09/1918
Private	O' Shea, Daniel	285475	11/03/1918
Private	Osborne, George	20511	08/01/1916
Private	Outtridge, Edward Henry	51054	27/07/1917
Private	Owen, Albert Ernest	53918	30/04/1917
Private	Owen, Griffith	20086	31/07/1917
Private	Owen, Herbert Samuel James	19883	07/06/1917
Private	Owen, Robert Richard	285370	29/10/1917
Private	Owen, Thomas George	44035	05/08/1917
2nd Lieutenant	Owen, William David		11/10/1918
Private	Parker, Wiliam	285580	21/11/1918
Lance Corporal	Parry, John Frederick	32518	10/05/1918
Sergeant	Parry, Reginald Ernest	35055	28/08/1918
Private	Parsons, Charles	54972	01/08/1917
Private	Parsons, Robert William	266556	08/10/1918
Private	Paul, Richard	48193	10/05/1918
Private	Payne, Albert John	54812	08/09/1917
Private	Pearce, George Frederick	285428	26/06/1918
Private	Pearce, Joseph	21791	12/01/1916
Private	Pearce, Samuel Edward	51297	28/07/1917
Private	Pearson, William Edward	34123	06/10/1918
Private	Pegram, Arthur	54956	26/05/1917
Private	Pendry, Samuel	26646	08/10/1918
Corporal	Pennington, Arthur, MM	20358	26/08/1918
Private	Perry, Alfred Brice	73213	30/08/1918
Private	Peters, Albert	32589	08/10/1918
Private	Phillips, Frederick Lloyd	45045	05/09/1918
Major	Phillips, Christian Gibson		10/07/1916
Corporal	Pidgeon, Arthur	47482	18/09/1918
Private	Pike, William Edward	24432	11/03/1918
2nd Lieutenant	Pilling, William, MC.		22/10/1918
Corporal	Place, Robert	285393	14/06/1918
2nd Lieutenant	Postlethwaite, William		14/03/1918
Corporal	Potts, Archie	18734	31/07/1917
Private	Powell, David	76653	08/10/1918
Private	Prance, Albert William	54587	07/09/1918
Corporal	Pratt, William George	290620	22/08/1917
Private	Price, David	76650	13/10/1918
Private	Price, David John	60779	27/10/1918
Private	Price, James Thomas	34123	01/10/1916

Corporal	Price, John	16456	01/09/1918
Private	Price, John	21042	11/07/1916
Private	Price, Rees	73655	20/10/1918
Corporal	Pridmore, Lawrence	21093	10/07/1916
Private	Pritchard, Frederick	291652	11/09/1918
Private	Pritchard, Henry	75136	20/10/1918
Private	Pritchard, Philip (Richards)	19976	28/07/1917
Private	Proctor, Ernest	202306	26/08/1918
Private	Proctor, James	56318	08/10/1918
Lieutenant	Protheroe, William Bertram		12/06/1917
Private	Prytherch, James	54383	09/09/1918
Private	Puddephat, Leonard John	47739	01/09/1918
Corporal	Punter, Hubert Miles	18872	22/10/1918
Sergeant	Pye, John	27657	25/11/1917
2nd Lieutenant	Radmilovic, John		03/11/1918
Private	Ramsden, Joseph	20686	03/05/1916
Private	Rawcliffe, Thomas	59462	08/10/1918
Lance Corporal	Read, Frederick Charles	47734	30/04/1917
Corporal	Reed, Thomas Walter	38239	26/08/1918
Private	Rees, Idris Tudor	75290	09/10/1918
Lieutenant	Reese, William		02/02/1917
2nd Lieutenant	Reeves, Harry Charles		24/08/1916
Private	Regan, Edward	266902	22/08/1917
Private	Rement, Martin	24367	28/10/1918
Private	Rex, Charles	56386	08/10/1918
Private	Reynolds, Harry	49347	04/08/1917
Corporal	Richards, Ernest Harry, MM	54983	01/08/1917
Corporal	Richards, George Henry	58493	29/10/1918
Private	Richards, Henry Morgan		30/01/1917
Lieutenant	Richards, William John		12/10/1918
Lance Corporal	Richardson, Alexander	53927	15/10/1918
Private	Roach, George	25084	11/03/1918
Lieutenant	Roberts, Arthur Hosbury Starkey		04/11/1918
Sergeant	Roberts, Griffith John	38251	08/10/1918
Private	Roberts, Robert Ellis	202754	21/04/1918
Private	Roberts, Sam	21053	10/07/1916
2nd Lieutenant	Roberts, Victor George		27/07/1917
Private	Roberts, William	202701	26/08/1918
Private	Robinson, James	65253	19/09/1918
Corporal	Roblings, George	26790	15/02/1917
Private	Rogers, Thomas	20640	30/04/1917
Private	Ross, Joseph	59461	10/05/1918
Private	Rossiter, Robert	23628	08/09/1917
Private	Rowlands, Henry John	301963	25/04/1918
Private	Salisbury, Percy	285433	22/08/1917
Sergeant	Sandiford, Samuel	19942	11/07/1916
Private	Saunders, Francis John	47763	01/04/1917
Lieutenant	Sampson, Richard Harry		29/10/1918
Sergeant	Sawyer, Richard John, MM	22747	13/03/1918
Private	Seamons, William	54212	13/03/1918
Private	Seed, James	20443	01/03/1918
Private	Sellings, Horace Jasper	43285	16/08/1916
Private	Sexton, William Dennis	202758	27/10/1918
Private	Simkins, Charles Robert	290354	16/05/1918
Private	Smith, George Davidson	47736	28/05/1917

Private	Smith, James	14297	04/08/1917
Corporal	Smith, Peter Croasdale	20261	01/04/1918
Private	Smith, Stanley	20491	11/07/1916
Private	Smith, William Henry	23605	05/11/1918
Sergeant	Spencer, Edward Thomas	27682	22/08/1918
Private	Stagg, John Henry	35186	01/08/1917
Private	Stansfield, John	60542	31/10/1918
Private	Stephenson, Charles	20429	04/11/1915
Private	Stevens, Albert	23651	18/09/1918
Private	Stevens, Arthur	20276	11/07/1916
Private	Sullivan, Daniel	19987	11/07/1916
Private	Thatcher, Harold Sidney	44179	28/07/1917
Private	Thickins, Charles	21906	06/05/1916
Private	Thomas, David	44204	11/07/1916
Private	Thomas, David George	60794	06/09/1917
Private	Thomas, Dyfed Watcyn	53897	01/05/1917
Lance Corporal	Thomas, Gordon Richard	57799	15/03/1919
Sergeant	Thomas, Howard	26779	26/08/1918
Private	Thomas, Hugh William	54986	28/07/1917
Private	Thomas, James Joseph	22775	11/07/1916
Private	Thomas, John	40003	28/07/1917
Private	Thomas, Joseph Lewis	20659	01/08/1917
Private	Thomas, Ralph	266332	27/07/1917
Lance Corporal	Thomas, Thomas	21568	01/06/1916
Private	Thomas, Thomas Gwynfor	54597	21/08/1918
Private	Thomas, Thomas Henry	22073	31/07/1917
Private	Thomas, Walter	46898	08/10/1918
Private	Thomas, William Rhys	267172	23/04/1918
Private	Thorne, Alfred	35369	28/07/1917
Private	Thorne, William	34995	06/08/1917
Private	Thorne, William Frederick	75170	08/10/1918
Private	Thornley, James	20507	11/07/1916
Private	Tierney, John	20294	14/07/1916
Corporal	Tiffin, William Stordy	61096	18/09/1918
Private	Toft, Albert	285435	08/10/1918
Private	Tomkins, George	54284	30/04/1917
Private	Trimby, Charles	31177	05/03/1918
Private	Tucker, George	35176	11/07/1916
Private	Turner, Stanley Rudolph	285437	22/08/1917
Private	Vaissiere, George Charles	60403	01/08/1917
Private	Voyle, William John	19065	13/05/1918
Private	Waite, Walter	28991	19/09/1918
Private	Waite, William John	26803	14/12/1915
Private	Walker, Joseph	18791	08/10/1917
Private	Waller, Alfred	32004	11/07/1916
Private	Walmsley, Herbert	20834	11/07/1916
Private	Walsh, James	20960	11/07/1916
Corporal	Wannell, Walter William	34901	16/06/1918
Private	Ward, Andrew	20872	25/05/1916
Private	Ward, Frederick	16995	14/12/1915
Private	Ward, Joseph	285166	11/03/1918
Private	Waters, James	50950	27/10/1918
Private	Watkins, Lloyd	73714	04/11/1918
Private	Watson, Alfred Valiant	47766	30/04/1917
Private	Watson, Peter Henry	20886	03/01/1916

Private	Watson, Samuel	39200	23/08/1918
2nd Lieutenant	Watts, Albert Edward		22/04/1918
Private	Webster, Charles	73236	20/05/1918
Private	West, Donald	87630	01/08/1917
Private	Whalley, Alfred	20368	11/07/1916
Private	White, Gwilym	74010	19/09/1918
Private	White, Jack Clayton	20764	01/09/1917
Private	White, Thomas Christmas	37746	05/12/1917
Private	Whittle, Thomas	20961	17/08/1917
Private	Wilde, Herbert	20331	11/07/1916
Private	Wilkinson, Harry	20938	16/02/1916
Private	Wilkinson, William	59369	10/05/1918
Private	Williams, Albert	285750	01/09/1918
Private	Williams, Benjamin	200492	26/07/1917
Private	Williams, Charles Edward	43257	05/09/1918
Private	Williams, David	45771	18/09/1918
Private	Williams, David Henry	28643	31/08/1918
Private	Williams, Edward Llewellyn	20729	11/07/1916
Private	Williams, Harry	20321	10/07/1916
Sergeant	Williams, Job	38020	05/11/1918
Private	Williams, John	75209	08/10/1918
Private	Williams, John	75265	08/10/1918
Private	Williams, John Charles	201121	04/09/1918
Private	Williams, John Henry	34690	10/05/1918
Private	Williams, Rees Meredith	43792	26/07/1917
Private	Williams, Thomas Sydney	203543	10/05/1918
Signaller	Williams, William	54589	20/10/1918
Private	Williams, William David	72952	04/11/1918
Private	Williams, William John	21072	09/02/1916
Private	Wills, Albert George	21066	20/07/1917
Sergeant	Winstone, William Henry	20248	31/07/1917
Private	Withers, William Arthur	44163	20/09/1918
Private	Wood, Edgar	62682	08/10/1918
Lance Corporal	Woodcock, Charles	44935	10/05/1918
Private	Wooton, Thomas	77561	08/10/1918
Private	Wright, William	285372	27/10/1918
Private	Wyatt, Thomas William	40140	26/08/1918
Private	Young, Thomas	23165	15/03/1918

This is the list of known casualties of the battalion, taken from the database of the Commonwealth War Graves Commission, *Soldiers Died in the Great War*, *Officers Died in the Great War*, and from several newspaper archives and obituary notices.

Included in the list are the men who initially served with the 15th Welsh, but were subsequently transferred to other battalions, and were then killed in their service.

Appendix III

Awards to the Battalion

The Carmarthenshire Battalion won a fair share of military distinctions during its time at War, although it was not to gain the honour of a Victoria Cross winner from within its ranks.

According to an article in the *Welshman* at the end of 1919, three men won the Distinguished Service Order (DSO), one of whom won it twice; twenty-seven men won the Military Cross (MC), three of whom won it twice; twenty-two men won the Distinguished Conduct Medal (DCM); sixty-four men won the Military Medal (MM), three of whom won it twice; one man was awarded the Meritorious Service Medal (MSM). Four men were awarded foreign decorations, and sixteen men were Mentioned in Despatches (MID) during the course of the war. These numbers are slightly inaccurate, as some awards were Gazetted after the article was published. Also some former 15th Welshmen gained awards whilst serving with other units.

These men, where known, are remembered on the following pages. Also listed are the members of the Battalion who gained awards while with other units, and awards gained after the war.

The Order of the British Empire (MBE)

Lieutenant (Acting Major) John Williams, MBE, MC & Bar.
John had won the Military Cross twice while serving with the 15th Welsh during the war. After the Armistice he remained with the Army, and took part in Operation Archangel, when the British sent a force to aid the White Russian forces in their fight against Communism in 1919. John was awarded the MBE. (Military) in the *London Gazette* of 3 March 1920 on the recommendation of the General Officer Commanding-in-Chief, Allied Forces, in recognition of valuable services rendered in connection with Military Operations in Archangel, North Russia. (dated 11.11.19.). He also gained the award of the Russian Order of St. Stanislas, 2nd Class with swords, for Russia.

Lieutenant Oscar Bedford Daly, MBE, MID.
Oscar was awarded the MBE (Military) for his work on the 38th Divisional Staff, after being posted from the 15th Welsh, and was Mentioned in Despatches.

The Distinguished Service Order (DSO)

Captain Dennis Kemp Bourne, DSO, MID.
Dennis was awarded his Distinguished Service Order after being transferred into the 9th Welsh. His Citation, Gazetted on 16 November 1917 read: 'For conspicuous gallantry and devotion to duty. He took command of his Battalion and led them with conspicuous ability and fearlessness to the attack on an enemy position, and captured and held it under very heavy machine gun fire. His leadership and initiative while in command of the Battalion were of the greatest value during a most critical period.'

Acting Major Francis Richard Dale, DSO, MC.

Francis had originally been commissioned into the Royal Welsh Fusiliers, and had been posted to the 15th Welsh. He was awarded his Military Cross while with them, and then transferred back to the Royal Welsh Fusiliers where he gained his DSO. The award was gazetted on 1 April 1919, while he was attached to the 16th Battalion, Royal Welsh Fusiliers. His Citation, Gazetted on 1 April 1919 read: 'For conspicuous gallantry and devotion in command of his battalion at the crossing of the River Selle, near Le Cateau, on the 20th October, 1918. The operation was extremely difficult, but, after daring reconnaissances, his orders, combined with his splendid leadership and example, were responsible for the complete success of the operation. On two occasions later he led his battalion through heavy barrages and intricate country, with the greatest courage, gaining the objectives, and capturing four .77 guns.'

Acting Major James Arthur Daniel, DSO, MC & MID.

His DSO was awarded to him while he was temporarily attached to the 14th Welsh. It was Gazetted on 10 January 1919 and read: 'For conspicuous gallantry during an attack. He organised a patrol and advanced covering party, who established a bridgehead and covered the crossing over the river of the remainder of the battalion, enabling them to start the attack punctually. He subsequently dealt with some enemy machine guns, and brought on the rear companies to the final objective. It was largely due to his personal influence and power of command that the advance was so successful.'

Lieutenant-Colonel Harry Gardiner, DSO.

Harry gained his DSO after being promoted from the 15th Welsh and attached to the Duke of Wellington's (West Riding) Regiment. His citation, dated 29 October 1915, read: 'For conspicuous gallantry and determination during operations at Suvla Bay, Gallipoli peninsula, on 8th August, 1915. He continued to lead his men forward after being twice wounded, and only gave up after being wounded a third time.'

Lieutenant-Colonel Ernest Helme, DSO & Bar.

Ernest Helme won the DSO twice. The Citation for his first DSO, dated 2 December 1918 read: 'For conspicuous gallantry and ability. He organised and carried out the crossing of a river by his battalion with great foresight and skill, and during the subsequent advance and operations lasting several days his example of personal courage, and his powers of organisation and command enabled his men successfully to accomplish all the tasks they were called on to perform.'
Ernest won his second DSO soon after, thus gaining a Bar to his original DSO. The Citation, dated 30 July 1919 read:
'For gallant and skilful leading of his battalion near Villers Outreaux on October 8th, 1918. Owing to another brigade having been checked in their attack on the front enemy trenches his battalion had to delay their advance for some time while suffering heavily from artillery barrage. By his personal efforts, skill and determination the battalion, which had been thrown into some confusion, was rallied and assembled for the further advance, eventually reaching a further final objective. It was almost entirely due to his gallant leading that the advance was enabled to continue after the check experienced.'

Lieutenant-Colonel Thomas William Parkinson, DSO.

Thomas was Gazetted on 14 January 1916 with his DSO for 'Service in the Field', just months after his being promoted to Lieutenant-Colonel, Commanding 15th Welsh. Sadly there is no citation to be found.

The Military Cross

Lieutenant William Proctor Bell Ashton, MC.

His Citation, Gazetted on 10 January 1919 read: 'For conspicuous gallantry and devotion to duty. He found himself, a few hours after joining the battalion, the only surviving officer in his company in an assault on an enemy position. When the company was checked by hidden wire and very heavy fire of all kinds, he rallied and led them forward, going on in advance and fearlessly exposing himself while he cut the wire. By his courage and fine leadership he extricated his company from a perilous position.'

Captain Percy Ronald Ayers, MC. (Adjutant)
His MC was Gazetted on 28 December 1917. Percy was commissioned from the Devon Regiment on 10 June 1916. No Citation can be found, but the award would have been for Ypres. He retired from the army a Lieutenant-Colonel on 23 October 1947 after having served with the 4th Welch, Territorial Army during the inter-war period and World War Two.

Lieutenant Gordon Estcourt Berry, MC. (Attached from Brecknock Battalion, South Wales Borderers)
His Citation, Gazetted on 4 October 1919 read: 'For conspicuous gallantry and able leadership. On 4th Nov., 1918, in Mormal Wood, his company had been ordered to push forward and capture La Pature before dark. He led his platoon forward, and, after a fight at the entrance of the village, in which some thirty enemy were killed and wounded, drove the enemy out of the village and captured the entire objective.'

Captain Cuthbert Bevington, MC. (Attached from 4th Welsh)
His Citation, Gazetted on 31 January 1919 read: 'For conspicuous gallantry and devotion to duty on 8th October, 1918, when acting adjutant in charge of battalion headquarters at Mortho Wood. About 60 of the enemy suddenly appeared; he at once attacked them with what men he had, killing some and capturing the rest with two machine guns. Later in the day he helped to reorganise the battalion after heavy fighting, and enabled it to continue the advance.' He left the Battalion on 11 April 1919 and returned to the 4th Welsh, TF.

Lieutenant Montague George Bostock, MC. (Attached from Honorable Artillery Company)
His Citation, Gazetted on 31 January 1919 read: 'For conspicuous gallantry and devotion to duty north of Villers Outreaux on 9th October, 1918. While in command of the advanced guard of the battalion his party came under heavy fire from the front and flank. He organised two sections which attacked and captured two machine guns, killing the crew. Later in an attack on six machine guns he was severely wounded, but carried on until he collapsed.'

Captain John Chamberlain, MC. (Formerly S.W.B. Attached 14th Welsh)
Gazetted 1 June 1917. No Citation can be found.

Captain Francis Richard Dale, DSO, MC. (Attached from Royal Welsh Fusiliers),
His Citation, Gazetted on 2 December 1918 read: 'For conspicuous gallantry and able leadership in command of reinforcements during an attack. When the right battalion was counter-attacked and in difficulties, he led forward a company to its assistance, and finding the O.C. had been wounded he took command of a difficult situation and reinforced threatened points skilfully. Through his efforts the situation was restored and the right battalion was able, under his command, to continue operations until relieved.'

Major James Alfred Daniel, DSO, MC, MID.
His Citation, Gazetted on 24 July 1917 read: 'For conspicuous gallantry and devotion to duty. He commanded a raiding party with great success. To his careful training beforehand and gallant leading during the raid much of the success is due.' James became second in command of the 1/6th Welsh after the end of the war, spending ten months in Germany as part of the Army of Occupation.

Lieutenant G.A. Demay, MC, C.S., RAMC (Attached)
No Citation can be found but his award was mentioned in *The Welshman* newspaper.

Lieutenant John Evans, MC.
His Citation, Gazetted on 28 August 1916 read: 'For conspicuous gallantry during operations. He held on to a portion of a wood with great determination- for several hours till relieved by another regiment.'

Captain William John Foster, MC.
His Citation, dated 11 January 1918 read: 'For conspicuous gallantry and devotion to duty. When ordered to reinforce another battalion, he found it much depleted, and, as senior officer present, he took command, reorganised the defence, and held his ground under very heavy hostile fire, although seriously wounded by shell fire, personally supervising the work of his men.'

Lieutenant Benjamin George Fox, MC.

His Citation, Gazetted on 10 January 1919 read: 'For conspicuous gallantry in command of a company. He fought his way across a river and through heavy machine-gun barrage to his objective. Though wounded he remained with his men until he had placed them in a position where it was possible for them to consolidate. He behaved splendidly, and in the course of this operation captured eleven prisoners and two machine guns, and killed the teams of the latter.'

Second Lieutenant Clifford Donald Gimblett, MC.

His Citation, dated 9 December 1919 read: 'On 8th October, 1918, at Chateau Dangles, he took over command of his company after his company commander had been wounded, and led them on with great gallantry and dash, and captured an enemy field battery. Later, at Walincourt Mill, he led the remainder of his company and captured an 8-inch howitzer, and throughout the day displayed fine leadership and initiative.'

Lieutenant Robert Albert Griffiths, MC.

His Citation, Gazetted on 31 January 1919 read: 'This officer, on 24th August, 1918, at Thiepval, when one of his Lewis gun sections had all become casualties, took the gun himself, and, advancing, firing from the hip, killed sixteen Germans in two machine-gun posts, both of which he captured. Though he was wounded during the operation, he continued leading his platoon until he collapsed through loss of blood. His courage and determination were magnificent.'

Second Lieutenant Harold John Hayward, MC.

His Citation, dated 29 November 1918 read: 'He led his platoon in a raid on a system of tunnels with great vigour and initiative, and after heavy hand-to-hand fighting succeeded in capturing two machine-gun positions at the exits of the tunnels. In attacking a third position he was wounded, but he continued to fight and direct his men, and extricated them in safety. His courage and able leader-ship in a difficult situation were admirable, and his example greatly inspired his men.'

Captain Francis Henry Jordan, MC & Bar.

Francis Jordan was awarded the Military Cross, twice during the course of the war. His first MC was Gazetted on 26 September 1917, the citation published on 9 January 1918 read: "For conspicuous gallantry and devotion to duty. He led his platoon with remarkable ability during a reconnaissance of the enemy's trenches, obtaining information which was most valuable in subsequent operations. In the attack which followed he displayed the greatest gallantry and coolness, largely contributing towards the success of the operation."

His Second MC, earning him a Bar to the original, was Gazetted on 29 November 1918 and read: 'For conspicuous gallantry and initiative in an attack. He led his men with great skill and determination, and captured all has objectives, together with a whole company of the enemy. Though, wounded, he remained with his men until he had established them in their position.'

Captain Gerald William Lancaster, MC. (Died of Wounds), (Attached from 3rd Monmouth Regiment),

His Citation, Gazetted on 2 December 1918 read: 'He was specially selected to command one and a-half companies, to reconnoitre across a river, and. secure crossings. The duty was of a difficult and dangerous nature, but he carried it out with complete success, capturing five machine guns and some prisoners, and inflicting losses on the enemy. The battalion crossed in safety two days after. He was subsequently wounded for the third time, but he continued to lead and encourage his men at a critical moment, until he collapsed from loss of blood. His gallantry and fine leadership have been conspicuous on more than one occasion.'

Captain Thomas Landman, MC and Bar.

Thomas Landman won the MC and Bar. His first Military Cross when he was a Lieutenant. The Citation in the London Gazette, dated 26 May 1917 read: 'For conspicuous gallantry and devotion to duty when in command of a raiding party. Although severely wounded he continued to lead his men, and succeeded in carrying out the task allotted to him. He has previously done fine work.'

His Second MC, earning him a Bar to his MC, was Gazetted on 10 January 1919 and read: 'For conspicuous gallantry and ability to command. On taking his company to the support of another battalion he found the latter withdrawing in some confusion. The night was very dark and the conditions most trying, as the men had been exposed to heavy shelling for some hours. Thanks to his cool courage and determination, however, the battalion, which had lost its commanding officer, was rallied and led back to its evacuated position, which he succeeded in holding against repeated enemy counterattacks.'

Lieutenant George Ernest Lowe, MC. (Killed),
His Citation, Gazetted on 1 February 1919 read: 'On 18th September, 1918, at Gouzeaucourt, after all other officers had been killed or wounded by heavy shell and machine-gun fire, he led the company with great gallantry and dash in the final assault on the objective. When held up by machine-gun fire from a strong enemy position he made a reconnaissance and then led two bombing parties round the flank under cover of his Lewis guns and captured the position, killing about 100 of the enemy and capturing two anti-tank guns with ammunition. He held this position with only seventeen men until the arrival of another battalion, against a counter-attack by some 200 of the enemy. His courage and determined leadership were admirable.'

Captain John Currie McDonald, MC.
His Citation, Gazetted on 8 January 1918 read: 'For conspicuous gallantry and devotion to duty. During an attack he displayed powers of leadership of a very high order, and led his men to their objectives with great skill and determination.'

Lieutenant George Henry Minshull, MC. (Killed),
His Citation, Gazetted on 11 January 1919 read: 'For conspicuous gallantry and devotion to duty. When no reliable information could be obtained from the front line, all the runners having become casualties, this officer volunteered to go forward and report on the situation. For six hours he was exposed to incessant machine-gun barrage, crawling not only to his own battalion, but along the front of the whole brigade. On the way he found and collected many disabled wounded and stragglers, directing them to their companies. He eventually got back to battalion headquarters with full information, after setting a remarkable example of courage and endurance.'

Lieutenant (Acting Captain) Hopkin Trevor Morgan, M.C.
Hopkin had served with the 15th Welsh after being commissioned into the 5th Welsh. He was awarded the Military Cross while re-attached to the 1st Battalion, Wiltshire Regiment. His Citation, dated 29 November 1918 read: 'This officer did fine work in the capacity of adjutant during active operations. He frequently went forward under very heavy fire and cleared up the situation, and at various stages during the advance was of great assistance in directing the battalion under heavy fire until the objective was gained. He showed great courage and devotion to duty.'

Lieutenant Isaac Stanley Morgan, MC.
Listed in the Carmarthen Journal as J. P. Morgan, this is probably the correct man. His Citation, Gazetted on 24 July 1917 read: 'For conspicuous gallantry and devotion to duty. He commanded a platoon in a successful raid on the enemy lines. He was wounded during the operation, but continued to control his men until they withdrew from the enemy trenches. He set a splendid example throughout.'

Lieutenant Jenkin Rees Gwyn Morgan, MC. (Quartermaster).
His Citation, Gazetted on 11 January 1919 read: 'For conspicuous gallantry and devotion to duty. He brought the transport through a concentrated barrage on the track to battalion headquarters and then ran the rations to the front line across ground exposed to machine-gun fire and shelling. His action not only secured the supply of rations to his own battalion, but, owing to their weakness from casualties, they were able to supply rations also for the battalion on the flank, which would otherwise have been without food for twenty-four hours.'

Lieutenant J. P. Morgan, MC.
This Officer was listed in the Welshman in 1919. There is no more information available.

Second Lieutenant Andrew Geraint Joseph Owen, MC.
There is no citation for this award, but it was listed in the *London Gazette* of 28 December 1917.

Captain Frank Cyril Palmer, MC.
His Citation, Gazetted on 9 December 1919 read: 'For gallantry and good leadership on 4th November, 1918, whilst the battalion was advancing through Englefontaine to the assault his company came under enemy barrage. He displayed great initiative in cutting the heavy wire fencing and diverting his men to the flank, rejoining the main body, in time to advance up to time from the assembly position and capture and consolidate his objective.'

Lieutenant E. L. Patterson, MC. (U.S. Army Medical Corps).
No Citation can be found, but his award was mentioned in *The Welshman* newspaper, and also in *The History of the Welsh Regiment, Part II.*

Second Lieutenant William Pilling, MC. (Royal Welsh Fusiliers).
William served in the ranks with the 15th Welsh, before being commissioned into the Royal Welsh Fusiliers, winning the MC towards the end of the war. His Citation, Gazetted on 11 October 1918, read: 'For conspicuous gallantry during a battalion raid, when he showed very excellent leadership. He reorganised a section which had met with determined resistance and led them in person, capturing five prisoners and killing several of the enemy. By his coolness and grasp of the situation he inspired confidence in all.'

Second Lieutenant Frederick John Radford, MC, MM.
His Citation, Gazetted 16 September, 1918 read: "For conspicuous gallantry and devotion to duty. When the enemy attempted to break through his company front he was unceasing in encouraging and inspiring his men to resist all attacks. He untiringly walked across the front in the open, despite hostile machine-gun fire, and held on to his position until ordered to withdraw. Later, he carried out several reconnaissances."

Lieutenant Frank Roberts, MC.
His Citation, Gazetted on 11 January 1919 read: 'For conspicuous gallantry and fine leadership in an attack. With only sixteen men and no officer left he consolidated the position gained, and by judicious use of his Lewis guns he deceived the enemy as to his numbers and held on to his position for 24 hours without support on his flank, under heavy shell fire, inflicting considerable casualties on the enemy both with his own guns and with machine guns captured the day before. He did splendid work.'

Captain John Delahaye Sampson, MC.
Gazetted 31 May 1918, no citation can be traced. John Sampson remained in the Territorial Army after the war, but sadly lost his commission when his solicitors business in Oldbury collapsed.

Second Lieutenant Horace Enfield Simmons, DFC, MC & Bar.
His Citation, dated 25 March 1917 read: 'For conspicuous gallantry and devotion to duty during a raid on the enemy's trenches. He displayed great courage and skill in fixing a torpedo in position in the enemy's wire. He has at all times set a fine example.'
Horace later transferred to the Royal Air Force, and it was while serving with their 'A' Detachment in Russia that he gained a Bar to his Military Cross. His Citation, dated 30 March 1920 read: 'At Cherni War, on 27th August, 1919, Lt. Simmons, flying a D.H.9, carried out work usually assigned to Scout machines. Descending to water level, he attacked a large fleet of enemy vessels, being hotly received by enemy fire from every description of guns. This daring attack created the utmost confusion amongst the Bolshevik troops, who suffered heavy casualties. Lt. Simmons has always displayed courage and ability of a high order during the operations in South Russia.'

Captain Wilfred Newell Soden, MC, MD, RAMC. (Attached)
Gazetted 29 December 1916. No Citation can be traced.

Second Lieutenant David Robert Thomas. MC.
His Citation, dated 29 July, 1919 read: 'On October 20th, 1918, his company was in assembly position on the River Selle. Heavy machine-gun fire opened on the company, but he set a fine example of coolness, and directly the barrage lifted led them on to the railway embankment, and accounted for some fifty enemy and six machine guns, killing some of the enemy with his revolver. Owing to his marked gallantry and initiative, the whole of the railway cutting on the front of the battalion was denuded of the enemy.'

Second Lieutenant Lewis John Thomas, MC.
His Citation, Gazetted on 11 January 1919, read: 'For conspicuous gallantry and initiative in an assault. He led his company with the greatest dash and accounted for nine machine guns .and their teams. Singlehanded, when on one occasion separated from his company, he effected the

capture of fifteen of the enemy, whom he farced to surrender while he covered the entrance of the dug-out. He showed splendid courage and determination.'

Lieutenant T. J. Thomas, MC, RWF. (Attended 113th L.T.M.B.)
His Citation, Gazetted on 3 October 1919 read: 'For conspicuous gallantry and ability in the attack on Mortho Wood, near Auben-Cheul-au-Bois. On the 8th October, 1918, he carried out a reconnaissance for a position for his light trench-mortar battery, under heavy hostile shelling. Later, under severe shelling, he maintained his battery in action, during which he was wounded. His conduct throughout the operations up to that date was mainly instrumental in enabling the light trench mortars to take a more than ordinarily active and useful part.'

Captain Harold Wilcoxon, MC & Two Bars. (Attended 13th Welsh).
Harold originally served with the 15th Welsh before transferring to the 13th Welsh. He went on to win the Military Cross and Two Bars. The Citation for his first award, dated 26 July 1917 read: 'For conspicuous gallantry and devotion to duty. He led his company in a raid on the enemy trenches with marked ability. In the preliminary reconnaissance he worked for many nights in No Man's Land.'
His second award, earning him a Bar to his Military Cross, dated 2 December 1918, read: 'For conspicuous gallantry and devotion to duty during an attack. He led his company in face of heavy fire, and secured his objective together with many prisoners and machine guns, besides killing a large number of the enemy. He set a magnificent example to his men, and inspired their confidence by his fearless leadership.'
His third award, earning him a Second Bar to his Military Cross, dated 4 October 1919, read: 'For marked gallantry and able leadership in the advance through Foret de Mormal on 4th and 5th Nov. 1918. Having gained his objective in the Green line, he was ordered to advance with his company some 4,500 yards. He successfully reached and consolidated his objective, taking about 50 prisoners. He then pushed out fighting patrols and made good the ground up to the railway west of Berlaimont, thus clearing the way for another division to pass through.'

Captain John Williams, MBE, MC & Bar.
Listed in the Carmarthen Journal as James, this is the correct man. John was awarded the Military Cross twice during the course of the war. The Citation for his first award, dated 24 July 1917 read: 'For conspicuous gallantry and devotion to duty. He led his platoon with great courage and ability. His able training beforehand was of the greatest value to the success of the enterprise.'
His second award, earning him a Bar to his Military Cross, was Gazetted on 11 January 1919, and read: 'For conspicuous gallantry in an assault on a village. When his commanding officer was wounded he led the battalion with such effect that the enemy were enveloped before they could concentrate their machine-gun fire on the attacking waves. After the objective was taken he headed the party which mopped up the machine-gun posts in the rear who were hindering consolidation with their fire. He displayed fine courage and leadership.'

Lieutenant John Glyn Williams, MC.
His Citation, dated 10 January 1919 read: 'In spite of an incessant bombardment of gas shells and machine-gun fire, with sniping from the rear, and though suffering from the effects of gas himself, he inspired his men with his own spirit of gallantry and determination, and though no rations or water could be got up to them for forty-eight hours the position was held and repeated counterattacks by the enemy were beaten off. He set a splendid example throughout a trying period.'

The Distinguished Conduct Medal

Although not gaining the honour of any of its men having won the Victoria Cross during the war, the 15th Welsh was graced with some acts of outstanding Gallantry, as befits the awarding of the twenty-two Distinguished Conduct Medals to men of the Battalion. The DCM is regarded as being just one notch below the Victoria Cross, and was sometimes just the stroke of a pen away from being so. Below are Citations, from the *London Gazette*, of these known awards of the DCM to the Battalion, with the date of the Gazette in brackets.

285550 Serjeant Frank Axon (Stockport)
When the consolidation of his company was being harassed by machine—gun fire from a flank, he collected some bombs, and, working skilfully round, he bombed the guns with great effect, and captured them and ten prisoners, whom he brought back with the guns. His gallantry and initiative were worthy of great praise. (15.11.18)

40055 Private Fred Bennetta (Bolton)
For conspicuous gallantry and devotion to duty. During a critical period of forty eight hours these runners maintained uninterrupted communication between company and battalion headquarters, continually passing through heavy artillery and machine-gun barrage. They also carried rations when practically all the ration party were wiped out. Their courage and devotion to duty were an example to all. (5.12.18)

40035 Corporal Thomas Bradshaw (Bolton)
For conspicuous gallantry and devotion to duty during reconnaissance of enemy trenches. He led his section forward in the face of heavy rifle and machine gun fire, and bombed two enemy dug-outs, killing the occupants. He was the only one of his section who returned. A few days later he was stunned by a shell during the attack, but on regaining consciousness rejoined his Company, and continued to lead his section with great pluck and determination. (26.1.18)

47750 Private Arthur Brandon (Luton)
For conspicuous gallantry and devotion to duty. During a critical period of forty-eight hours these runners maintained uninterrupted communication between company and battalion headquarters, continually passing through heavy artillery and machine-gun barrage. They also carried rations when practically all the ration party were wiped out. Their courage and devotion to duty were an example to all. (5.12.18)

54601 Private David Davies (Aberdare)
For conspicuous gallantry and devotion to duty. He made his way through an enemy barrage to the front line to obtain information as to the situation. Though wounded on the way out he returned with the required information. He did very gallant work. (26.1.18)

21690 Corporal Hiram Davies (Maesteg)
When the advance was checked by the fire of three machine guns he at once organised and led a bombing party, which he skilfully manoeuvred to within short distance of the nest of machine guns. Shortly afterwards the advance progressed without opposition. His determined and gallant behaviour was worthy of very high praise. (15.11.18)

54631 Private Thomas J. Davies (Merthyr Tydfil)
For conspicuous gallantry and devotion to duty. This man has done continuous good work as stretcher bearer since his battalion came overseas, particularly during fighting. (21.10.18)

47481 Serjeant Christopher J. Dee (Cardiff)
For conspicuous gallantry during an attack. He handled the company with brilliant vigour and initiative, and held the men together under heavy fire in consolidating his objective, pending the arrival of a company commander. Later, he exposed himself fearlessly in bringing in and tending wounded. He showed fine courage and devotion to duty. (5.12.18)

26721 Serjeant Edward Evans (Clun, Salop)
For fearless courage on 8th October 1918, near Chateau Angles. His platoon was attacking the chateau under very heavy fire. He rushed forward accompanied by two men and captured one officer and forty other ranks. His action at a most critical moment enabled not only his own battalion, but troops on the left flank, to work forward to the assembly positions, and throughout the twenty-four hours hard fighting his leadership, dash and fine courage were conspicuous. (10.1.20)

20959 Serjeant (Acting Company Serjeant Major) Robert Fairclough (Farnsworth, Bolton)
For great courage and initiative throughout the recent operations. In the fighting round Englefontaine, on 31st October 1918, he led a patrol, and drove out a party of the enemy from a

house and advanced the line some 500 yards. Again, on 5th November, in Mormal Forest he, as acting company Serjeant-major, was greatly responsible for keeping his company well together. On 1st November he volunteered and went out in search of a missing officer, exposing himself to great risk within a few yards of an enemy sniper's post. (11.3.20)

54981 Serjeant Stewart Grover (Portslade)

For conspicuous gallantry and devotion to duty. As platoon sergeant he has done consistent good work, particularly on the occasion of a raid, and also during an attack. His reliable conduct, coolness, and power of leadership have been most marked. (17.4.18)

54804 Serjeant (Acting Company Serjeant Major) Albert Edward Hines (Poplar)

For most conspicuous gallantry and dash. At Chateau Angles, north of Villers Outreaux, on 8th October 1918, he organised a bombing party against a machine-gun post, and led them forward under a hail of machine-gun fire: he himself leaped on to the parapet and shot the team and put three guns out of action. He then reorganised his company and led them forward again until he fell severely wounded. He showed fine courage and devotion to duty. (2.12.19)

55426 Corporal T.W. Holding (Newton Abbot)

He led his section against a machine gun that was causing severe casualties to our men. He killed the team and captured the gun. When his platoon commander became a casualty, he took command and led the men with great dash during four days' hard fighting. He set a splendid example throughout the operations. (15.11.18)

20155 Serjeant William T. John (Llanelly)

On 20th October 1918, his platoon commander was killed whilst swimming the Selle. He at once took command, and on emerging from the river re-organised his platoon under heavy machine-gun fire, and led them forward, capturing a machine gun and crew, and turning the gun on the enemy. He then pushed forward again and captured two small enemy trench howitzers. He showed gallant leadership and did excellent work. (2.12.19)

19864 Company Serjeant Major David A. Jones, MM. (Cardigan)

For conspicuous gallantry and devotion to duty during a preliminary reconnaissance. When an officer was severely wounded close to a hostile post, seeing that the patrol was in difficulties, he at once went to them, and carried the officer back himself, under heavy hostile rifle and machine-gun fire. His coolness and courage were most marked. (3.10.18)

21893 Private Evan J. Jones (Penrhiwceiber, Glam)

During four days' heavy fighting this man who was company runner, went backwards and forwards in full view of the enemy under severe fire from snipers and machine guns and never failed to deliver his messages to the battalion commander and inform him of the situation at the advanced position. He was eventually wounded. He set a fine example of staunch devotion to duty under peculiarly trying and dangerous conditions. (15.11.18)

35071 Private Thomas John Lock (Senghenydd)

He manoeuvred his Lewis gun into position against an enemy machine gun that was holding up our advance, and engaged it with great effect, putting fourteen of the enemy out of action and capturing the gun. He was wounded later in a similar enterprise. During several days hard fighting he set a splendid example of courage and determination to the men with him. (15.11.18)

47589 Private James T. McCarthey (Bromley)

For conspicuous gallantry during an attack. When his platoon was checked by machine-gun fire, which was causing heavy casualties, he single-handed got round the rear of the post and was responsible for the capture of it and fifty men. He displayed great courage and initiative. (5.12.18)

36243 Corporal George Morgan (Henllys)

For conspicuous gallantry and devotion to duty in handling his troops and rallying his men. When the enemy worked round his flank he stuck to his ground and offered material resistance. His value to his officers was infinite. He was wounded, but made efforts to continue resistance until ordered to the aid post. (3.9.18)

23760 Private Griffith Morgan (Rhymney)

For most conspicuous gallantry and initiative during the action on 20th October 1918, across the River Selle, near Montay. His company was ordered to mop up the railway embankment which was very strongly held with enemy machine guns. On one occasion he rushed forward alone, bombed an enemy post, killing three and wounding one of the enemy. He then ran on shooting into the enemy with his rifle, and eventually returned with 20 prisoners and a machine gun. Throughout he set a splendid example of courage to all. (2.12.19)

19994 Company Serjeant Major William G. Probert (Rhyl)
For conspicuous gallantry and devotion to duty. For eighteen months this warrant officer has carried out his duties as company sergeant-major in a most able and conscientious manner, and frequently shown himself cool and courageous. (21.10.18)

19251 Serjeant David Rees (Maesteg)
For conspicuous gallantry and devotion to duty. During four days heavy fighting he was always in the forefront, leading his men in a very gallant manner and steadying and encouraging them by his splendid example of coolness and composure under the heaviest fire. He took a prominent part in the capture of a machine gun and its whole team. (15.11.18)

57224 Corporal John E. Rees (Cardiff)
For conspicuous gallantry and devotion to duty. He led his section with great dash and gallantry against an enemy machine gun that was causing heavy casualties. He killed the team and captured the gun, thus greatly assisting the advance. (15.11.18)

9358 Serjeant D. Roberts-Morgan (Awarded with RWF-later 15th Welsh)
For conspicuous courage and ability when, as a Platoon Serjeant, he organised bombing parties against the enemy in dugouts who would not surrender.' (1.9.16)

22394 Serjeant Alfred Speake (Trealaw) 15th Bn.
For conspicuous gallantry and devotion to duty. During the operations he showed conspicuous gallantry and ability as a platoon Serjeant and as acting company Serjeant-major. On one occasion, when all his officers had become casualties, he took command of the company, and was of invaluable assistance to the new company commander. (17.4.18)

59456 Company Serjeant Major Richard G. Stevenson (Alexandria)
For conspicuous gallantry and devotion to duty. At Chateau Angles, north of Villers Outreaux, on 8th October 1918, under heavy machine-gun and artillery fire, he was invaluable in reorganising the battalion, which had been fighting hand to hand for four hours on its way to assembly position. He was quite fearless, and did much by his personal action to restore the situation in readiness in readiness for a further advance. (2. 12. 19)

55394 Private Henry Strike (Hayle)
For conspicuous gallantry and devotion to duty. During an attack his company came under heavy machine-gun fire from the flank. Arming himself with grenades he proceeded to search for the gun, and having located it, he worked round and attacked it from the rear, and killed or captured the whole team and took the gun. His courage and initiative were worthy of great praise. (15.11.18)

56800 Serjeant Walter C. Tarling (Cardiff)
On 20th October 1918, on the River Selle, where bridges had been destroyed, he plunged into the river and led his company across in the teeth of heavy machine-gun fire. He was in the water the whole time helping men to cross, and only one Lewis gun was lost in the transit. He then reorganised the company on the bank, and advanced to and occupied the objective. He showed great gallantry and coolness, and rendered excellent service. (2.12.19)

20485 Lance Corporal Moses Thomas (Llanelly)
For conspicuous gallantry in action. When his entire section was wiped out by concentrated shrapnel and machine-gun fire he continued alone to fire his Lewis gun and covered the withdrawal of his company. Later, during an attack, he killed sixteen of the enemy, firing his Lewis gun from the hip, thereby capturing two machine guns. He showed splendid courage and determination. (5.12.18)

35155 Private Charles J. Wallace (Gilfach, Glam)
At Thiepval, on 24th August 1918, two platoons became detached during the advance from the rest of the company. As the enemy were in vast preponderance of numbers the situation was

critical. After various attempts he succeeded in single-handed fighting his way through the enemy's nests of dug-outs at dawn to these two platoons, where he succeeded in establishing in touch with the rest of the company, with the result that resistance on the enemy part was immediately reduced and the capture of the village immediately affected. He showed fine courage and determination. (3.9.19)

30697 Lance Serjeant I. Williams (Bridgend)
For conspicuous gallantry and devotion to duty. He has done consistent good work as a section leader, and particularly on patrol. He invariably displayed great courage and coolness under fire. (17.4.18)

The Military Medal

Awards of the Military Medal are notoriously difficult to trace. Out of the reported sixty-four winners of the Military Medal to men of the 15th Welsh, three men won it twice (the MM and Bar). Below are some of the men who can presently be identified as having been awarded the Military Medal with the battalion.

Number	Rank	Name	From	Gazetted
20521	L/Corporal	F Bamber		25/05/1917
25928	Private	F Bebb		28/09/1917
44424	L/Corporal	G Bowden	Cwm	17/06/1919
40035	Corporal	T Bradshaw	Bolton	22/10/1917
882	2nd Lieutenant	G W Burman	(With W.G.)	
21051	C.Q.M.S.	H Burnhill		16/11/1916
54601	Private	D Davies	Aberdare	28/09/1917
20527	Sergeant	D J Davies	Aberdare	17/06/1919
22732	Private	J J Davies	Llanddewi Brefi	16/11/1916
20501	L/Corporal	R J Davies	Llanelli	02/11/1917
20732	Private	T H Davies		14/12/1916
54631	Private	T J Davies		07/10/1918
73019	Private	W E Davies	Ruabon	11/02/1919
	Private	A Edwards	(Medals in Regimental Museum)	
20662	Corporal	D A Evans		16/11/1916
20153	Private	W H Evans		06/07/1917
72851	Private	J Fielding	Hurst	11/02/1919
20434	Sergeant	W P Fitzgerald		06/07/1917
20887	Sergeant	C A Freeman	Pontardulais	17/06/1919
20554	Private	W R Gidman	Ramsbottom	11/02/1919
55288	Sergeant	D Grant	Six Mile Bottom	11/02/1919
20206	Sergeant	W H Griffiths	Llanelli	14/05/1919
26752	Private	G Herbert	Chepstow	15/05/1919
25267	Private	E J Higgins	Bedlinog	11/02/1919
19988	Corporal	J W Hirst	Bolton	26/03/1917
20306	Corporal	T Holland	Preston	11/02/1919
54762	Private	C G Housden	Saffron Walden	11/02/1919
19921	Sergeant	D Howarth		25/05/1917
20871	L/Corporal	I Jenkins	Neath	13/09/1918
202695	Private	J B Jenkins	Treffgarne	11/02/1919
26752	Private	E John	Ferndale	14/05/1919
19864	Sergeant	D A Jones	Cardigan	08/06/1916
19864	Sergeant	D A Jones	(Bar to MM)	09/07/1917
20666	Private	F H Jones		06/07/1917
200239	Corporal	G Jones	Llanelli	11/02/1919
19980	L/Corporal	T Jones		06/07/1917
73058	Private	W Kay	Burnley	14/05/1919

20800	Sergeant	T Makin	Bolton	17/06/1919
20462	Private	W Martin	Carmarthen	11/02/1919
19971	L/Corporal	T G Matthias		07/06/1917
38132	Corporal	D McAuliffe	Cardiff	25/09/1917
23698	Sergeant	W McKie	Cardiff	11/02/1919
23760	Private	G Morgan	Rhymney	12/03/1919
20311	Sergeant	T Morgan	Aberavon	28/09/1917
20549	Sergeant	B R Morris	Haverfordwest	11/02/1919
10487	Sergeant	E Morse	Manorbier	11/02/1919
20143	L/Corporal	J A Owen	Loughor	14/05/1919
18481	Serjeant	E Parry	Gelli, Rhondda	28/09/1917
20358	Corporal	A. Pennington		28/09/1917
59800	Private	C A Philpotts	Griffithstown	11/02/1919
56642	Corporal	F J Radford	(With RWF)	16/09/1918
20182	Private	T J Rees	Llandebie	28/09/1917
54983	Corporal	E H Richards		06/07/1917
20419	Sergeant	J H Richardson	Llanelli	11/02/1919
9358	Captain	D Roberts-Morgan	(With RWF)	
22747	Sergeant	RJ Sawyer	Mardy	09/07/1917
40058	Serjeant	J Schofield		01/09/1916
40058	Serjeant	J Schofield	(Bar to MM)	25/05/1917
20778	Sergeant	S H Stephenson	Nelson	17/06/1919
26794	Corporal	D Thomas	Tylorstown	28/09/1917
26794	Corporal	D Thomas	(Bar to M.M.)	01/07/1919
35155	Private	C J Wallace	Gilfach	31/12/1918
19954	Sergeant	W Welsby	Bolton	14/05/1919
23736	L/Corporal	T Whitelock	Ystrad	02/11/1917
38020	Sergeant	J Williams	Caerphilly	11/02/1919
20663	Sergeant	J Williams	Carmarthen	11/02/1919

Serjeant 19864 David A Jones gained his first Military Medal for his bravery during the Battalion's time in French Flanders, before their move to the Somme. The Bar to his Military Medal was earned while he was acting Company Serjeant Major with the 15th Welsh at Ypres. The Cardigan man went on to gain the Distinguished Conduct Medal in 1918, becoming the most decorated of the 'other ranks' in the 15th Welsh.

The second man of the battalion to earn a Bar to his Military Medal was 40058 Serjeant James Schofield. He had gained his first award during the fighting at Mametz Wood, and was awarded a Bar to the medal after his part during the 31 May 1917 raid on the Morteldje Estaminet.

Corporal 26794 David Thomas of Tylorstown was awarded his first Military Medal for Ypres. His Bar was probably awarded for the one hundred days offensive after the Battle of Albert.

19971 Lance Corporal
T G Matthias.

The Meritorious Service Medal

Only two members of the 15th Welsh gained the honour of being awarded the Meritorious Service Medal for their service with the Battalion during the war. A third man, Regimental Serjeant Major Isaac Jones, was awarded his while attached to the 16th (Training Works) Battalion, South Lancashire Regiment.

20080, Quarter Master Sergeant Thomas Evans, from Calais.
His award was Gazetted on 18 January 1919. Thomas arrived in France on 4 December 1915, and also gained the 1914/15 Star, War and Victory Medals.

61792 (19995), Regimental Sergeant Major Isaac Jones, from Ammanford.
His award was Gazetted on 3 June 1919. Isaac had arrived in France with the Battalion in December 1915 and was Mentioned in Despatches for his work at Mametz Wood. He had previously been awarded the Queen's South Africa Medal with three Clasps, as well as the 1914/15 Star, War Medal, Victory Medal with Oakleaf, and the Army Long Service and Good Conduct Medal. His MSM was awarded for 'valuable services rendered in connection with the war'.

23715, Sergeant Joseph Edward Powell, from Cardiff.
His award was mentioned in the Peace Gazette of 3 June 1919. Joseph arrived in France on 4 December 1915 and also gained the 1914/15 Star, War and Victory Medal.

Mention in Despatches

Sixteen men of the Battalion were reportedly Mentioned in Despatches during the war, which resulted in them being awarded a bronze oak-leaf emblem to wear on their Victory Medal. Below are some of the men that have been traced, again some being MID with other units;

Captain Dennis Kemp Bourne, DSO, was Mentioned in Despatches in the *London Gazette* of 21 December 1917.

59234, Private Wallace J. Brightman, was Mentioned in Sir Douglas Haig's Despatch of 16 March 1919, Gazetted on 9 July 1919.

Lieutenant Oscar Bedford Daly, was Mentioned in Despatches while attached to the 38th Divisional Staff.

Major James Alfred Daniel, DSO, MC, who was Mentioned in Despatches twice, Gazetted on 6 December 1916, and on 28 December 1918.

285387, Serjeant Samuel Daniels, was Mentioned in Sir Douglas Haig's Despatch of 16 March 1919, Gazetted on 9 July 1919.

Second Lieutenant Alfred George Gallop, was Mentioned in Despatches on 1 January 1916, probably for Ypres.

Major Ernest Helme, DSO, who was Mentioned in Despatches twice, Gazetted on 20 December 1918 and on 5 July 1919.

Lieutenant Thomas Hywel Johns, was Mentioned in Despatches while attached to the 6th South Wales Borderers, on 21 December 1917.

Second Lieutenant Abel Jones, was Mentioned in Sir Douglas Haig's Despatch of 16 March 1919, Gazetted on 9 July 1919.

Second Lieutenant Henry Myrddin Jones. His Mention in Despatches was shown on his Medal Card.

Regimental Sergeant Major Isaac Jones, of Ammanford. His Mention was Gazetted on 2 January 1917, and was probably for his actions in steadying the battalion at Mametz Wood after they had suffered serious casualties amongst the officers of the battalion.

Captain Arthur Claude Lancaster. Arthur was Mentioned in Despatches twice during the course of the war, the first for the Pilckem Ridge, and was awarded a Belgian Decoration.

Captain Thomas Landman, MC & Bar. Thomas was Mentioned in Despatches for a trench raid at Boesinghe, as well as receiving the MC & Bar.

Second Lieutenant Thomas M. Matthews, who was Gazetted on 28 December 1918.

Second Lieutenant George Elton Morgan. George was Mentioned in Despatches for Ypres.

Captain Hopkin Trevor Morgan, MC. Hopkin was Mentioned in Despatches for the Pilckem Ridge, Gazetted on 21 December 1917.

22750, Sergeant James John Roberts, of Laugharne. The date of his Gazette cannot be traced, but a local newspaper report of 5 January 1917 reported his award.

Major Jenkin Rees Gwynn Morgan, MC. Jenkin was Mentioned in Despatches for Ypres, in 1917.

20984, Corporal Teddy T. Rogers, of Llanelli was Mentioned in Sir Douglas Haig's Despatch of 16 March 1919, Gazetted on 9 July 1919.

Second Lieutenant Cyril Idris Williams of Camrose, Pembrokeshire.

Second Lieutenant Henry Myrddin Jones, of Neath was Mentioned in Despatches after being Commissioned into the 10th Royal Welsh Fusiliers.

Lieutenant-Colonel Thomas William Parkinson, DSO. Thomas was Mentioned in Despatches in January 1916 and January 1917.

Major Aneurin Rhydderch. Aneurin was Mentioned in Despatches several times during the course of the war.

Lieutenant Evan Silk. Evan was Mentioned in Despatches once.

Lieutenant George Tutt. George was Mentioned in Despatches twice; on 4 January 1917 and on 21 December 1917.

2376 Lance Corporal Thomas Whitelock, M.M., was Mentioned in Despatches and commissioned into the 109th Infantry, Indian Army.

Lieutenant Arthur Gregory Williams, was Mentioned in Sir Douglas Haig's Despatch of 16 March 1919, Gazetted on 9 July 1919. He had been promoted to Captain with the 114th Light Trench Mortar Battery.

Foreign Decorations

Four men of the Battalion were recorded as being awarded with decorations from foreign governments during the course of the War. Again, these are notoriously difficult to trace. Some gained awards after the war for service in North Russia:

20988, Private William John Jones of Ammanford. Was awarded the Belgian Croix-de-Guerre on 12 July 1918.

Captain Arthur Claude Lancaster. Was decorated twice with Foreign Awards; The Chevalier of the Belgian Order of Leopold was awarded and detailed in the *London Gazette* of 24 September, 1917. The Belgian Croix-de-Guerre was also conferred upon Arthur, and detailed in the *London Gazette* of 11 March 1918.

20800 Sergeant Thomas Makin, of Farnworth, Lancashire. Was awarded the Belgian Croix-de-Guerre on 12 July 1918. He was also the holder of the Military Medal.

20419 Sergeant John Henry Richardson of Llanelli. Was Awarded the French Medaille Militaire, Gazetted on 30 January 1919.

Lieutenant Horace Enfield Simmons, DFC, MC & Bar. As well as being awarded the Military Cross twice, and the Distinguished Flying Cross, Horace was awarded the Order of St Vladimir, the Order of St Stanislas 3rd Class with Swords and Bow, and the Russian Cross of St George, for service in North Russia.

Major John Williams, MBE, MC, & Bar. John was awarded the MC and Bar during the course of the war. As well as gaining the MBE. (Military) for his services during the later Operation Archangel, John was awarded the Russian Order of St Stanislas, 2nd Class with Swords. His medals are held by the Regimental Museum in Cardiff.

Appendix IV

Nominal Roll of Officers, 1914–1919

Sadly there is no trace of a Nominal Roll for the 15th Welsh, although by using information from several sources (including the official Army Lists, *London Gazette* records, Commonwealth War Graves Commission records, the Battalion War Diary and also David Warren's excellent and as yet un-published Roll of Officers of the Welsh Regiment), it is possible to produce a Nominal Roll of officers of the battalion. There are quite possibly a few omissions and errors, but every effort has been made to eliminate as many of these as possible.

The officers are listed below, with their final ranks attained- for simplicity 'Temporary' commissions or appointments are not shown- and brief biographical details where available. [Note: some of these men later served with other units, while some were attached to the 15th Welsh from other units].

Adams, Sydney, Lieutenant. Sydney was commissioned Second Lieutenant into the 15th Welsh on 28 November, 1917 after serving as Warrant Officer Class 2, No.26605, in the Welsh Regiment. In November 1918 he was attached to the 1st King's Shropshire Light Infantry. He survived the war, and received the British War and Victory Medals.

Anthony, Percivale, Captain. 'Percy' was born into the family which owned the Hereford Times. He was educated at Dulwich College, where he became a renowned cricketer and played in the Dulwich Eleven in 1895 and three following years. Later he played for Herefordshire, in 1900 heading the batting averages with 47.14. He had also appeared for Worcestershire 2nd XI and the Wanderers, of Johannesburg. Percy served in the South African War with the Welsh Regiment. He was commissioned Captain in the 15th Welsh on 27 November 1914, and promoted Major 27 April 1916. Percy was killed in action at Mametz Wood 10 July 1916 aged twenty-six, and is commemorated on the Thiepval Memorial. His medals, the 1914/15 Star, British War and Victory Medals, were issued to his step-mother Mrs Anthony, of 'St Rode', Chesham Bois Common, Bucks.

Appleton, Anthony Charles Frank, Lieutenant. Anthony was commissioned Second Lieutenant into the 20th Welsh on 27 January 1916, and was attached to the 15th Welsh. He was promoted Lieutenant 27 July 1917, remaining with the 15th Welsh until the end of the war. He relinquished his commission on completion of service 1 September 1921. Anthony was awarded the British War Victory Medals, which were sent care of: TF Appleton Esq, 'Hilldene', Palace Road, Llandaff, Cardiff.

Ashton, William Proctor Bell, MC, Lieutenant. William was commissioned into the 4th Welsh (TF) on 26 June 1918. He was posted to the 15th Welsh, joining them on their advance to victory on the Somme. William found himself thrown straight in at the deep end, and in his first action showed such courage and initiative to merit the awarding of the Military Cross, [as listed in the Honours and Awards Chapter]. William survived the war, and was appointed to be Instructor of Musketry, 3rd Class, with the Royal Army Ordnance Corps, with the rank of Lieutenant, 1 September, 1923. He received the Military Cross, British War Medal and Victory Medal, which were sent to him at 66, High Street, Blackwood, Monmouth.

Ayers, Percy Ronald, MC, Captain. Percy was born in Great Yarmouth, Norfolk. His army career commenced in February 1913, when he enlisted as a Private in the Devon Regiment. Percy served on the Western Front until mid 1916, by which time he had been promoted Sergeant. On 10 June 1916 Percy was commissioned Second Lieutenant in the Welsh Regiment, and posted almost immediately to the 15th Welsh, fighting with them at Mametz Wood. On 3 January 1917 Percy was promoted Acting Captain, subsequently serving as Adjutant of the 15th, serving with them throughout the remainder of the war. Percy was awarded the Military Cross, [as listed in the Honours and Awards Chapter]. He remained in the army after the war, serving with the 2nd Welsh at Chatham and Dublin. He then served as Adjutant to the 4th Welsh at Llanelli, and as Captain with the 1st Welch until 1933, when he joined 2nd Welch in India. During World War II he raised and commanded 19th Welch and was later Commandant of the POW Camp. He was one of the last Officers of the Great War to die, while visiting family in Sydney on 1 July 1993. He was ninety-eight years old. For his service in the Great War Percy received the Military Cross, 1914 Star & bar, British War Medal and Victory Medal. The given addresses for Percy were 'Depot', 15th Bn Welsh Regiment HQ Cardiff. & Care of London City & Midland Bank, Winchester.

Bainbrigge, Philip Gillespie, Second Lieutenant. Philip was the Son of Prebendary and Mrs Bainbrigge, of London. He had attended Shrewsbury School, followed by Eton as a King's Scholar and Trinity, Cambridge with a scholarship taking a First Class in both parts of the Classical Tripos, obtaining his degree in 1914. He then joined the Staff at Shrewsbury School, until March 1917, and after training with the Inns of Court OTC, he was gazetted into the Welsh Regiment, but gained a transfer to the Lancashire Fusiliers. Philip was wounded during the Battle of Epehy on 18 September 1918, dying that same day. His Company Commander had become wounded, and Philip had taken command of his Company. He 'led on his men who thoroughly trusted him, captured the objective and then during consolidation, in anticipation of counter attack, courageously led a patrol to reconnoitre a sunken road suspected of holding the enemy in force to his front.' Philip was twenty-seven years old and is buried at Five Points Cemetery, Lechelle. He was awarded the British War and Victory Medals, which were sent to his Mother, Mrs PJ Bainbrigge, at 52, Northumberland Street, Edinburgh.

Bennett, David Pryce, Lieutenant. David was commissioned Second Lieutenant into the 15th Welsh on 26 September 1917. He remained with the battalion for the remainder of the war, and survived.

Berry, Gordon Estcourt, MC, Lieutenant. Gordon originally enlisted as Private, service number 534952 with the 15th London Regiment. He was commissioned into the South Wales Borderers, but was posted to the 15th Welsh. Gordon was awarded the Military Cross, [as listed in the Honours and Awards Chapter] Gordon relinquished his commission with the South Wales Borderers in 1921.

Bevington, Cuthbert, MC, Captain. Cuthbert was commissioned on 1 March 1917 into the 4th Welsh (TF). He was attached to the 15th Welsh, and was promoted Lieutenant on 1 September, 1918, and Acting Captain two weeks later. Cuthbert gained the Military Cross during the fighting at Mortho Wood, [as listed in the Honours and Awards Chapter]. Cuthbert was also awarded the British War and Victory Medals, which were posted to him at 7, Victoria Street, Blaina, Monmouth. He relinquished his commission on 30 September 1921, and was granted the rank of Captain.

Bostock, Montague George, MC, Captain. Montague originally served as Private, Service number 3888, with the Honorable Artillery Company. He was commissioned Second Lieutenant into the Welsh Regiment on 30 January 1916. He served with the 16th Welsh, before being posted to the 13th Welsh when the 16th Welsh was disbanded at the beginning of 1918. He was posted to the 15th Welsh from the Reinforcement Camp at Rouen on 1 September, 1918, and joined them during their drive towards the Hindenburg Line. Montague was soon to gain the award of the Military Cross, [as listed in the Honours and Awards Chapter]. Montague relinquished his commission on completion of service on 4 June 1919. As well as his Military Cross he was awarded the 1914/15 Star, British War Medal and Victory Medal, which were sent to him at 72, Elsham Road, Kensington, W14.

Bourne, Dennis Kemp, DSO, Captain. Dennis was commissioned Second Lieutenant into the Welsh Regiment on 11 March, 1915. He originally served with the 15th Welsh, but transferred to the 9th Welsh, and landed in France with them on 4 October 1915. By 17 September, 1917 Dennis had been made Adjutant of the 9th Welsh and promoted Acting Captain. He soon gained the honour of winning the Distinguished Service Order, [as listed in the Honours and Awards Chapter]. He was also 'Mentioned in Despatches'. Dennis was admitted to the 6th British Red Cross Hospital on 25 March 1918 suffering from a gunshot wound to the right elbow. After returning to England for treatment he was moved to a Staff posting, but after the Armistice was accepted as a Volunteer for Army of Occupation Duty and was posted to the 53rd Welsh. In addition to his Distinguished Service Order, Dennis received the 1914/15 Star, British War Medal and Victory Medal with MID emblem. They were posted to him at Herald Chambers, 48, Carl Street, Coventry.

Bowen, William, Second Lieutenant. William was the son of Henry and Mary Bowen of Swansea. He had worked as a clerk with the Great Western Railway at Swansea before enlisting into the Pembroke Yeomanry, reaching the rank of Serjeant, with the service number 5067. He transferred to the 13th Welsh before being commissioned Second Lieutenant into the 3rd Welsh on Welsh 26 June, 1917. William was then posted to the 15th Welsh in France. He died of wounds during the fighting on the Canal du Nord on 30 August 1918. An extract from his obituary from the South Wales Daily Post read: 'A better or a braver officer I never met, nor one so adored by his men. On the day he received his fatal wound he was in command of the company, as I was temporarily doing other duties but his men tell me that he was leading them without a thought of personal danger. I feel that I have lost one of my dearest friends, as well as a most loyal and faithful officer. I know it will comfort you to know that the battalion has covered itself with glory in this recent fighting and made for itself a great name - a name with which will always be associated by his surviving brother officers the name of that most gallant officer, your son. His name will never be forgotten by us as long as we remember this great and terrible war in which it is our proud privilege to take part.' For his service in the war he was awarded the British War and Victory Medals, which were claimed by father, H Bowen Esq., of 6, Milton Terrace, Mount Pleasant, Swansea.

Boyle, George Leslie, MBE, TD, Captain. George was commissioned Second Lieutenant into the 14th (Swansea) Battalion, Welsh Regiment, and by 5 May 1915 had made his way up to Captain and Adjutant with them. He was then posted to the 15th Welsh for a time, before moving back to the 14th Welsh on 8 November 1918. George remained in the Army, Commanding the Cambridge & County School Contingent, OTC. He also served with the Home Guard during the Second World War, earning him the MBE (Military), as well as the Territorial Force Decoration. For his Great War Service he was awarded the 1914/15 Star, British War and Victory Medals, which were sent to him at 13, Eltisley Avenue, Cambridge.

Brain, Jonathan Henry Patrick, Captain. Jonathan was born 17 March 1896, and was a member of the famous 'Brains Brewery' family of Cardiff. He was commissioned Second Lieutenant into the 3rd Welsh from Winchester School OTC, and served with them in France from March 1915. He was posted to the 15th Welsh on 10 December 1915, before becoming attached to the Royal Flying Corps from July 1915 where he was promoted to Captain, before being transferred to the Highland Light Infantry. He relinquished his Commission from the 3rd Welsh on 1 April 1920, retaining the rank of Captain. For his service during the Great War, Jonathan was awarded the 1914/15 Star, British War and Victory Medals, which were posted to him at Cwrt-yr-Ala, near Cardiff, South Wales. After the war Jonathan played first class cricket for Glamorgan, making his debut as wicket keeper in 1920. He also owned several successful racehorses and had his own wandering XI of friends and acquaintances who played an annual series of fixtures against the top club sides in South Wales. Jonathan died at Dinas Powis on 11 December 1945.

Burgess, Reginald, Lieutenant. Reginald was commissioned Second Lieutenant into the 15th Welsh on 4 January 1915. He transferred to the 38th Division Army Cyclist Corps on 15 May 1915 and moved to France on 3 December 1915. Reginald then volunteered for service with the Royal Flying Corps, and served as an Observer with 22 Squadron. On the opening day of the Somme Offensive, Reginald was acting as Observer to Pilot Lieutenant J H. Firstbrook, on a photo

reconnaissance mission over Clery-Longueval, when their aeroplane, FE2b, Serial 6365, was shot down over the German lines. Both men were taken prisoner, but Reginald was badly wounded in the crash, dying as a result on 7 July 1916. He is buried at Douchy Les Ayette British Cemetery. He was awarded the 1914/15 Star, British War and Victory Medals, which were claimed by his father Mr W Burgess, of 'Moat House', Narberth, Pembs.

Burman, George William, MM, Second Lieutenant. George originally served as Guardsman, number 882, in the Welsh Guards, and moved to France in August 1915. After being awarded the Military Medal for the Somme in October 1916, George was commissioned Second Lieutenant into the 13th Welsh. He was posted to the 15th Welsh in August 1918 and served with them until being wounded during the Great Advance on 18 September 1918. George was listed in 1927 on the Army List Supplement as 'Lt. (MM) Class I, RARO. Voluntarily on the Reserve list.' He was awarded the Military Medal, 1914/15 Star, British War and Victory Medals for his service, which were sent to him at 5, Station Approach, Penarth, Glam.

Chamberlain, John, MC, Captain. John was a successful businessman, born on 22 December 1881, the younger son of Arthur Chamberlain JP of Moor Green Hall, Moor Green Lane, Moseley, Birmingham. He enlisted in the 6th Battalion Royal Warwickshire Regiment on 9 September 1914 and was commissioned as a Second Lieutenant in the 3rd Battalion South Wales Borderers on 6 October 1914. John requested a posting to France, and so joined the 1st Welsh, serving with them at Second Ypres in April 1915 where he was shot in the stomach. After recovering he was promoted Captain, and joined the 15th Welsh in October 1915, serving with them until after the fighting at Mametz Wood. John then took the Senior Officers' Command School Course at Aldershot in the first two months of 1917. He returned to the front in April as Second in Command of the 14th Welsh, and was in temporary command when he was killed by a stray shell at Boesinghe in the Ypres salient on 14 May 1917, and is buried at Ferme-Olivier Cemetery. The award of the MC appeared in the *London Gazette* of 4 June 1917 [see Appendices; Awards to the Battalion]. On hearing of his death, his brigade commander, Brigadier-General T O Marden, wrote;

"He was in every sense a pal of mine...The country can ill afford to lose men like John, who had such independence, brain-power, and keenness". In his Colonel's opinion, "he stood out above all others whom I have ever met, as one who knew well what his duty was, and who did it, capably because he was clever, finely because he was a fine clean man, and cheerfully because he was endowed with a clear conscience and a merry wit". Also noted in his Obituary at the University of Birmingham is; "John Chamberlain was probably the most prominent British industrialist to be killed on the Western Front." John was awarded the 1914/15 Star, British War and Victory Medals, as well as his Military Cross, which were claimed by his widow, Mrs Gurney Dixon (remarried), of 'Ober House', Brockenhurst, Hants.

Collins, Arnold, Lieutenant. Arnold was commissioned Second Lieutenant into the 10th Welsh on 3 April 1915. He was later attached to the 15th Welsh, serving with them for the remainder of the war. For his service, Arnold was awarded the British War and Victory Medals, which were sent to him at 'Ffynon Bedw', Talycefn, North Wales.

Corser, Arthur Geoffrey, Captain. Arthur was commissioned Second Lieutenant from King William's Officer Training Corps to the 15th Welsh on 30 November 1914. After training with the battalion he was promoted full Lieutenant on 9 July 1915. He served with the 15th Welsh until being transferred to the Training Reserve on 1 September 1916. Returning to the Welsh in October 1917 he was promoted Captain, and served at a POW Camp. For his services during the war, Arthur was awarded the 1914/15 Star, British War and Victory Medals, which were sent to him at 'Lauriston', Shrewsbury.

Cowley, Daniel, Second Lieutenant. Daniel was from Swansea, and served as Guardsman, number 1667, with the Welsh Guards, before being commissioned Second Lieutenant into the 15th Welsh on 27 June 1917. He survived the war, and was awarded the British War and Victory Medals, which were sent to him at 'Hazeldene', Care Street, Cwmbwrla, Swansea.

Cox, John Ernest, Second Lieutenant. John was commissioned Second Lieutenant into the 20th Welsh on 13 September 1915. He embarked for France on 26 June 1916 and joined the 15th Welsh, serving with them for the duration of the war. John was awarded the British War and Victory Medals, and was also entitled to the Silver War Badge. His medals were sent to him at 'Springfield', Aberavon, Port Talbot.

Cox, William Stanley Ramsay, Major. William was originally commissioned Second Lieutenant into the 4th Battalion, King's Shropshire Light Infantry on 22 February, 1899. He then joined the Imperial Yeomanry, serving with them throughout the Boer War, where he gained the Queen's Medal with three Clasps. He was promoted Captain before returning to the 4th KSLI on 12 March 1902. At the outbreak of war William was gazetted as Major to the 15th Welsh, and served as Second in Command from June 1915. He embarked for France with the 15th Welsh on 2 December 1915 and remained as Second in Command of the battalion until being transferred to the Training Reserve on 1 September 1916. William survived the war but sadly died on 5 July 1921. For his services he was entitled to the 1914/15 Star, British War and Victory Medals, which were sent to his home at 'Ashe Lea', Ross, Herefordshire.

Cripps, William George, Second Lieutenant. William was commissioned Second Lieutenant into the 16th Welsh on 31 October 1917. He moved to France in January 1918, but the 16th Welsh was broken up to be used to reinforce other battalions, and William was then posted to the 19th Welsh. On 22 March 1918 he suffered wounds from a German gas bombardment on the 38th Division positions at Armentieres, and was admitted to the 131 Field Ambulance, who sent him to England for treatment. On his return in September 1918 he was posted to the 15th Welsh, and served with them during the final months of the war. For his war service, William was awarded the British War and Victory Medals, which were posted to him at 71, Egerton Street, New Brighton, Wallasey.

Dale, Francis Richard, DSO, MC & Bar, Captain. Francis was born 8 March 1883, the son of Mr J F Dale. He was educated at Oundle and Trinity College Cambridge, and had served as Classical Sixth Form Master, at Leeds Grammar School from 1906-1915. He was on the Territorial List, and was commissioned Second Lieutenant on 8 February 1916, and attached to the 21st Royal Welsh Fusiliers. Promotion to Captain rapidly followed, and Francis joined the 17th RWF, taking command of 'X' Company. He was awarded the Military Cross at Delville Wood in August 1918 while attached to the 15th Welsh [see Appendices; Awards to the Battalion], before taking command of 16th RWF, where he gained a second Military Cross and the award of the Distinguished Service Order. He left the Battalion for demobilisation on 21 February 1919, and went back into education as Headmaster, first at Plymouth College, then the City of London School. After retirement from university lecturing he was awarded The CBE in 1950. He passed away aged ninety-three on 15 May 1979. His DSO and MC are displayed in the RWF Regimental Museum, Caernarfon.

Daly, Oscar Bedford, Lieutenant. Oscar was commissioned Second Lieutenant into the South Wales Borderers. He joined the 15th Welsh on 25 September 1915. He was then transferred to the General List on 6 March 1917, and was Mentioned in Despatches and awarded the MBE (Military) for his services as a Staff Lieutenant. Oscar relinquished his Special Appointment on 5 January 1919 and moved into Diplomatic Service, which resulted in his being appointed Chief Justice of the Bahama Islands on 26 September 1938. He was later Knighted, becoming Sir Oscar Bedford Daly, MBE, of the Colonial Legal Service & Chief Justice of the Bahama Islands [His Majesty's approval of the Knighthood was signified in the Birthday Honours on 11 June, 1942.] For his wartime service, along with his MBE, Oscar was awarded the British War and Victory Medals, and an MID emblem, which were sent to him at PO Box 34, Nairobi, Kenya.

Daniel, James Alfred, DSO, MC, Captain. James was born in 1893, the son of the Reverend Alfred Daniel of Loughall, County Armagh. He was educated at the Portora Royal School and at the

RMC Sandhurst, and Gazetted to the Welsh regiment on 4 September 1912, joining the 2nd Battalion at Bordon. On the outbreak of war he was posted to the 1st Division Cyclist Company, with whom he went to France where he served until wounded in the Defence of Ypres in November 1914. He continued with the Army Cyclist Corps, serving at home and in France and Macedonia. In September 1916 he joined the 15th Welsh and served with them until being wounded on the Somme in August 1918. For his services he was awarded the DSO and the MC and was Mentioned in Despatches [see Appendices; Awards to the Battalion]. After the War he served with the 2nd Welch at Pembroke Dock and in Dublin and then became Adjutant of the 1st Welch in India. There followed a tour of duty with the Sudan Defence Force, further service with the 1st Welch and, later a tour at the Army Technical School at Chepstow. He commanded the 2nd Welch in India from July 1939 until August 1941 when he was appointed to command Lucknow Brigade Area with the rank of Brigadier. For his services he was appointed CIE. He finally retired in 1946 after attaining the rank of Brigadier-General. James died on 6 July 1959, at the Queen Alexandra's Military Hospital, Millbank, London, after a long illness. For his services during the war, in addition to his DSO and MC, James was awarded the 1914 Star and Clasp, the British War and Victory Medals, and the MID emblem, which were sent to him at Messrs Cox & Co., 16, Charing Cross, London, SW1.

David, Frederick John Louis, Second Lieutenant. Frederick was born in Swansea, the son of Edmund Joseph and Louise Elisabeth Josephine David. The family emigrated at the turn of the century, and took possession of Waldville Post Office, Saskatchewan, Canada. At the outbreak of war Frederick returned to Britain and enlisted into the Argyll and Sutherland Highlanders, as Private No S/8952. He was commissioned Second Lieutenant into the 15th Welsh on 30 April 1918 and served with them until his death at the Batte of Epehy on 18 September 1918. He is buried at Gouzeaucourt New British Cemetery. His medal entitlement was the British War and Victory Medals, which were sent to his mother at above address in Canada.

David, Thomas William, Captain. Thomas was commissioned Second Lieutenant into the 5th (TF) Battalion, Welsh regiment on 1 December 1914. By December 1915 he had been promoted Captain and in January 1917 went to France where he joined the 17th Welsh. Thomas was then attached to the 15th Welsh at Boesinghe, where he was killed in action on 27 July 1917. He is buried at Bard Cottage Cemetery. His medals, the British War and Victory Medals, were sent to his next of kin at 4, Oakfield Street, Cardiff.

Davies, D. Glan, Second Lieutenant. Glan was mentioned in the 15th Welsh War Diary in July 1916 as being among the list of Officers served at Mametz Wood. The only matching Officer was posted to the 9th Welsh as Lieutenant on 1 July 1917 from the 19th Welsh. He trained as a Machine Gun Officer in October 1917 before moving back to France, where he was attached for a short while to the Honorable Artillery Company. Glan was taken ill in France and sent back to Britain, after when he was seconded to the V Corps Staff at the end of the war. He was then sent for demobilisation at Prees Heath, Shropshire. His medals, the British War and Victory Medals, were posted to him at 95, College Street, Ammanford.

Davies, David Sydney, Second Lieutenant. David was commissioned Second Lieutenant into the 15th Welsh on 3 April 1915, moving to France with the battalion on 4 December 1915. He was later promoted Captain and attached to the 38th Divisional Train for the remainder of the war. David's medal entitlement was the 1914/15 Star, British War and Victory Medals.

Davies, Herbert Claude, Second Lieutenant. Herbert originally served with the Artists Rifles, 28th Battalion, London Regiment, which was a Territorial Battalion used as an Officer Training Corps. He was commissioned from there into the 15th Welsh on 30 May 1917, serving with the battalion for the remainder of the war. Herbert was awarded the British War and Victory Medals for his services, which were sent to him at Sandville, Mary's Street, Porthcawl. His Medal Index Card also notes an application for a Portuguese Medal. No further information on this is currently known, but the 15th

Welsh served alongside the Portuguese Expeditionary Force in Flanders, and so Herbert possibly gained an award for this period.

Davies, Percy Hier, Captain. Percy was the Son of Joseph and Hannah Davies, of Primrose Villa, Abercarn. He was commissioned Second Lieutenant 19 June 1915 into the 17th Welsh. He was then posted to the 15th Welsh, being promoted Captain with them after the fighting at Mametz Wood. Percy was killed in action at Boesinghe on 16 August 1917. His body was lost and he is commemorated on the Tyne Cot Memorial. For his services in the war, Percy was awarded the British War and Victory Medals, which were sent to his Mother, Mrs. Davies, at 'Mount Pleasant House', Kendal, Westmoreland.

Davies, Thomas John McLeod, Second Lieutenant. Thomas originally enlisted into the Artists Rifles, the 28th Battalion, London Regiment. He was commissioned Second Lieutenant into the 3rd Welsh on 27 June 1917, and was attached to the 15th Welsh. Thomas was promoted full Lieutenant on 27 December 1918.

Davies, William Brinley, Lieutenant. William was commissioned Second Lieutenant into the 5th Welsh (TF) on 2 December 1915. He didn't move to France until after the Armistice, when he became attached to the 15th Welsh. William remained with the battalion until its disbandment, and then transferred to the 6th Welsh (TF), resigning his commission on 27 October 1920, when he retained the rank of Lieutenant.

Demay, G A, MC, Lieutenant. Little is known of G A Demay, but the Welshman newspaper listed him as being among the Officers of the 15th Welsh to have gained the award of the Military Cross.

Dukes, A J, Lieutenant. Lieutenant Dukes was commissioned Second Lieutenant on 20 July 1915 into the 6th Welsh (TF). He was posted to the 15th Welsh in France after being promoted full Lieutenant, serving with them at Aveluy Wood where he was wounded during the abortive Trench Raid of 10 May. In November 1918 Lieutenant Dukes became employed at the Ministry of Munitions, and resigned his commission from the 6th Welsh on 30 May 1919, retaining the rank of Lieutenant.

Edwards, Arthur Evan, Captain. Arthur was commissioned Second Lieutenant on 20 February 1915, joining the 15th Welsh at Rhyl. He landed in France on 4 December 1915, and served with the battalion until being promoted Captain, and attended a Trench Mortar class at Locon soon after. Arthur was posted to special duties on 17 March 1917. He was awarded the 1914/15 Star, British War and Victory Medals for his time at war, which were sent to him at 'Ravendale', Cross Hands, near Llanelli.

Evans, Frederick William, Second Lieutenant. Frederick was commissioned Second Lieutenant on 11 August 1915 into the 21st Welsh. He was then posted to the 13th Welsh in France before being attached to the 15th Welsh on 5 September 1916. Frederick was not long with the battalion though, being wounded at Boesinghe the following month. He was moved to the Casualty Clearing Station at Remy Sidings where he died of his wounds on 28 October 1916. Frederick is buried at Lijssenthoek Military Cemetery. He is commemorated at Swansea Grammar School. His medals, the British War and Victory Medals, were claimed by his father, E W Evans Esq., 20 Bryn y Mor Crescent, Swansea.

Evans, George, Captain. George was commissioned Second Lieutenant into the 15th Welsh on 14 July 1915. He was promoted Lieutenant on 1 July 1917, then Captain on 19 August 1917. George served with the battalion until the end of the war, and was awarded the British War and Victory Medals.

Evans, John, Captain. John was commissioned Second Lieutenant into the 15th Welsh on 3 April 1915. He served with them throughout the entire war, being awarded the Military Cross for his gallantry at Mametz Wood [see Appendices; Awards to the Battalion]. After the Armistice John transferred to the 6th Welsh as part of the Army of Occupation in Germany, and on 21 July 1920 transferred to the 4th Welsh (TF).

Evans, Robert Charles, Second Lieutenant. Robert was born at Bangor-Isycoed near Wrexham, the son of Mr W.R. Evans, (Clerk of the Peace, for Denbighshire) and Mary Evans, and trained as a Solicitor at London. He married Edith Williams prior to the war, and the couple had a son, also named Robert Charles, who was later to become a Surgeon and one of the team who made the first successful ascent of Mount Everest. Robert had served as Serjeant, number 40798, with the Royal Welsh Fusiliers, before being commissioned Second Lieutenant into the 57th training Reserve Battalion on 28 March 1917. He transferred to the 15th Welsh, and joined them on the Somme, where he was killed during the Battle of Albert on 24 August 1918 when a German prisoner shot him. He is buried at Pozieres British Cemetery. His medals, the British War and Victory Medals, were sent to his widow at 'Plasyward', Ruthin, Denbighshire.

Eynon, Herbert, Lieutenant. Herbert had served as a Sapper in the Royal Engineers prior to being commissioned Second Lieutenant on 18 April 1915 into the 22nd Welsh. He was posted to the 18th Welsh from July 1915, and promoted Lieutenant and moved to the 16th Welsh on 1 July 1917. He was then transferred to the 13th Welsh on 2 August 1918, joining the Reinforcement Camp at Rouen. From here his posting was changed to the 15th Welsh, and he joined them during their drive from Albert on 28 August 1918, serving with the battalion until after the Armistice. Herbert was awarded the British War and Victory Medals for his war service, which were sent to him at 'Glamorgan House', Mary Street, Porthcawl.

Felton, Oliver (Gentleman), Captain. Oliver was commissioned Second Lieutenant in the 2nd Volunteer Battalion, the Welsh Regiment on 20 June 1900. At the outbreak of the Great War he was appointed Captain and Adjutant to the 13th Welsh, and remained in Britain when the battalion moved to France, becoming Adjutant of the 20th Welsh. On 11 July 1917 Oliver was posted to the 15th Welsh in France, serving with the battalion until the end of the war. Oliver was awarded the British War and Victory Medals for his wartime service, which were sent to him at 'Twyn y Deri', Aberavon, Port Talbot. Oliver was the father of Ronald Oliver Felton who was also an officer in the Welch Regiment in the Second War. Ronald Oliver Felton (1909 – 1982) was a prolific author of children's books, and wrote under the name of Ronald Welch, taking his pseudonym from the name of the Regiment. He won the Carnegie medal for the outstanding children's book of the year in 1954, and was for many years Headmaster of Okehampton Grammar School in Devon, where his pupils never learnt of his prowess of an Author.

Firbank, Godfrey Benjamin Joseph, Second Lieutenant. Godfrey had served in German South West Africa with the South African Infantry before being commissioned Second Lieutenant into the 15th Welsh. Obviously a man with a thirst for adventure, he joined the Royal Flying Corps, and trained as a Pilot, joining 23 Squadron RFC which flew the FE2b. Godfrey was killed in action, along with his Observer Lieutenant L G H Vernon, while flying FE2b, Serial 4851 on an Observation Patrol over Peronne on 11 September 1916. Like many airmen of the Great War Godfrey has no known grave, and is commemorated on the Arras Flying Services Memorial. His medals, the 1914/15 Star, British War and Victory Medals, were claimed by his mother, of Aldwich Court, Wrington, near Bristol. Godfrey is commemorated on the Arras Flying Services Memorial, and on a brass plaque inside Butcombe Church, Somerset, which states 'Pray for the soul of Godfrey Joseph Firbank, Lieut. RFC. Eldest son of Godfrey and Cecil Firbank, of Aldwick Court. Who fell in aerial battle near Peronne, France on Sept. 11th, 1916 during the battle of the Somme. The Cross in the Churchyard was restored in his memory. Eternal rest give unto him. O Lord and let perpetual light shine on him.'

Foster, William John, MC, Major. William was born in the parish of St Johns Cardiff on 5 April 1885, giving his address as 51, the Parade Cardiff. He attended St. Marys Hall School, Cardiff. William enlisted in the Glamorgan Yeomanry on 9 March 1909, at the age of twenty-nine and attended camp in that year at Llandovery, then in 1910 at Porthcawl. In 1911 William was promoted to Lance Corporal, and attended camp at Builth Wells. He was promoted Corporal in 1913 and attended camp at Llandeilo, he then attended camp at Porthcawl in May 1914, and was embodied for overseas service on 5 August 1915 in the machine gun section Glamorgan Yeomanry after having attended a machine gun course at Bisley in May 1915. On 30 May 1915 while a Lance Sergeant in the Glamorgan Yeomanry at Aylsham in Norfolk, he applied for a commission in the 16th Welsh, expressing a preference to join the machine gun section, his next of kin being given as Mr William Foster, 42, Park Place Cardiff. His application for a commission was accompanied by a certificate of moral character by Charles E Dovey JP, Cardiff in which he states 'an exemplary young man'. William was subsequently commissioned Second Lieutenant into the 16th Welsh on 9 June 1915, and moved to France with them in December that year. He was wounded several times; on 14 May 1916, 14 September 1916, 31 July 1917 and 5 September 1918. His worst injury appears to have been a deep gun shot wound shell fragment injury to the right thigh which became septic, at Ypres on 14 September 1916. William had been promoted to Captain whilst commanding a Company on 7 August 1916, and joined the 15th Welsh as Acting Major early in 1917 when the 16th Welsh was broken up. William had been awarded the Military Cross for the Pilckem Ridge [see Appendices; Awards to the Battalion]. As well as his Military Cross, William was awarded the 1914/15 Star, British War and Victory Medals, which were sent to him at 'Maindy House', North Road, Cardiff. He served in the Second War with the Home Guard, after having worked for some years as a valued member of the Regimental Benevolent Fund Committee. William died on 4 Dec. 1965 at Cardiff.

Fox, Benjamin George MC, Lieutenant. George had served at the outbreak of war as Lieutenant with the Nigeria Regiment. He transferred to the Welsh Regiment as Second Lieutenant on 7 September 1917, joining the 13th Welsh in France on 2 August 1918. Benjamin was posted instead to the 15th Welsh from the Reinforcement Camp at Rouen on 30 August 1918, joining the battalion in their drive towards the Hindenburg Line. He quickly made himself known in the 15th Welsh, being awarded the Military Cross for the Battle of the Selle [see Appendices; Awards to the Battalion]. He relinquished his commission on account of ill-health caused by wounds, on 4 May 1919, and retained the rank of Lieutenant. For his services during the war, as well as his Military Cross, Benjamin was awarded the 1914/15 Star, British War and Victory Medals, and the Silver War Badge, which were sent to him at 118, Durham Road, Maindee, Newport, Mon.

Gallop, Alfred Ernest, MID, Second Lieutenant. Alfred was serving as a Company Serjeant Major, number 9160, with the 1st Welsh at the outbreak of war, and entered France on 19 January 1915. He was commissioned Second Lieutenant into the 2nd Welsh, and then became attached to the 15th Welsh in 1917. on 26 July 1917 Alfred was attached from the 15th Welsh to the 3rd Nigeria Regiment for a while, before becoming a Lieutenant, and being posted back to the 15th Welsh in 1918, ending the war with the battalion. He had been Mentioned in Despatches on 1 January 1916, probably for Second Ypres, and was wounded twice during the course of the war. For his war service, Alfred was awarded the 1914/15 Star, British War and Victory Medals, as well as the MID emblem, which were sent to him at 'Ackland House', Victoria Place, Stow Hill, Newport, Mon. He served during the Second War as a Lieutenant, and retired on 16 April 1945, being granted the rank of Captain

Gardiner, Harry, DSO, Lieutenant-Colonel. Harry was listed in the 1915 Army Lists as Temporary Quartermaster and Honorary Captain in the 15th Welsh on 20 November 1914. He served with the battalion throughout their time at Rhyl up to July 1915 when he was appointed Captain with the 2nd Battalion Duke of Wellington's (West Riding) Regiment, and embarked for Gallipoli attached to their 8th Battalion. Harry gained the Distinguished Service Order at Suvla Bay [see Appendices; Awards to the Battalion], and was promoted Major on 1 September 1915. On 15 January 1917 Harry was gazetted Temporary Lieutenant-Colonel with the Herefordshire Regiment. For his war service he was awarded the 1914/15 Star, British War and Victory Medals, as well as his Distinguished Service Order.

Garsia, Clare James, Captain. Clare had served as Second Lieutenant and then Captain with the King's Shropshire Light Infantry during the Boer War of 1900-1901, gaining the Queens Medal with five clasps. He retired on 6 May 1908, and stayed on the Reserve List of Officers. In 1915 he was recalled to duty and served with the 15th Welsh at Winchester, probably on the Staff. Clare had retired from the Army by 1917 without having embarked for France. Clare lived at 'Holcomton Lodge', Bathhampton, Bath, Somerset, and was still alive in 1951.

George, Elmore Wright, Second Lieutenant. Elmore was the son of Lieutenant William W George, RASC, and Mary M George, of 'Laburnum Villa', Pembroke, and served in the Pembroke Yeomanry at the outbreak of war. He is recorded as having served as a Serjeant, number 46717, in the Welsh Regiment when he embarked for the Mediterranean with the Expeditionary Force, arriving on 19 September 1916. Elmore was then posted to the Connaught Rangers, number 20331, and the South Wales Borderers, number 45062, before being commissioned Second Lieutenant with the 15th Welsh on 30 October 1917. He served with the battalion at Armentieres, and moved with it to the Somme, where he was killed during the abortive raid on Aveluy Wood on 10 May 1918. He was 23 years old and is buried at Martinsart Military Cemetery. His medals, the British War and Victory Medals and the Territorial Force War Medal, were sent to his father at 'Laburnum Villa'.

Gibson, Reginald John Campbell, Second Lieutenant. Reginald originally served as Private, number 5653, with the Artists Rifles, 28th London Regiment, and was commissioned Second Lieutenant on 23 November 1916 into the 4th Welsh. He was posted to the 15th Welsh at Ypres, where he became wounded on 1 September 1917. Reginald was then posted to the 73rd Training Reserve Battalion and survived the war. He was awarded the British War and Victory Medals for his wartime service, and was entitled to the Silver War Badge. His medals were sent to him at Denton House, York Street, Norwich.

Gimblette, Clifford Donald, MC, Second Lieutenant. Clifford originally served as Private, number 1548, with the Royal Welsh Fusiliers, and embarked for France with the BEF in July 1916. He also served with the King's Liverpool Regiment, number 39759 before being commissioned Second Lieutenant into the 15th Welsh on 31 October 1917, serving with the battalion for the remainder of the war. Clifford was awarded the Military Cross for gallantry at Chateau D'Angles, [see Appendices; Awards to the Battalion], as well as being awarded the British War and Victory Medals and the Silver War Badge. The medals were sent to him at 32, Lisvane Street, Cathays, Cardiff. After the war Clifford resigned his commission due to ill health caused on active service, and became Landlord of the Barry Dock Hotel. He served again during the Second War, as Captain in the Royal Army Service Corps.

Griffiths, Gwyn Arthur, Lieutenant. Gwyn was the Son of John and Elizabeth Jane Griffiths of Ty Pica, Golden Grove, Carmarthenshire. He was commissioned Second Lieutenant into the 15th Welsh on 31 March 1915 and embarked with the battalion to France on 4 December 1915. In the summer of 1916 Gwyn transferred to the Royal Flying Corps, where he trained as an Observer, and was posted to 35 Squadron, RFC. On 2 June 1917 Gwyn, along with his Pilot Lieutenant E R Bottomley, where flying an artillery observation mission over Vermand in their Armstrong Whitworth FK8, Serial A2718, when they were hit by Anti Aircraft fire and forced down behind German lines. Both men were taken prisoner, but Gwyn had been badly wounded, dying that same day. He is buried at Mons en Chaussée Communal Cemetery. His medals, the 1914/15 Star, British War and Victory Medal were sent to his father at 'Ty Pica'.

Griffiths, Robert Albert, MC, Second Lieutenant. Robert served as Lance Corporal, number 17046, with the Royal Welsh Fusiliers, landing in France on 1 December 1915. He was commissioned Second Lieutenant into the 3rd Welsh on 30 October 1917 and posted to the 15th Welsh, serving with them throughout the rest of the war. At the opening of the battalions assault on the Thiepval Ridge on 24 August 1918 he distinguished himself in a gallant act which led to his award of the Military Cross [see Appendices; Awards to the Battalion], collapsing from loss of blood due to wounds. He survived the war, and was also awarded the 1914/15 Star, British War and Victory Medals, which were sent to him at

'Vicarage Lodge', Chester Road, Wrexham.

Hall, John Reginald, Second Lieutenant. John was the youngest son of Captain and Mrs Edward Hall of 17, Richmond Road, Cardiff. He was educated at The Cathedral School Llandaff, and at Felsted, and was subsequently in the employ of Messrs T.P. Thomas & Co., Cardiff Docks. John enlisted in the Monmouthshire Regiment in September 1914, rising to the rank of Serjeant before obtaining his commission in the 20th Welsh in August 1915. He was posted to the 15th Welsh on 7 June 1916, joining the battalion at Heilly in the Somme Valley. John was killed during the terrible fighting within Mametz Wood on 10 July 1916 aged just nineteen and, as happened with so many of his fellow Welshmen that day, John has no known grave. He is commemorated on the Thiepval Memorial. His medals, the British War and Victory Medals were claimed by his father at the above address. John Reginald Hall is commemorated on the Llandaff Cathedral School Memorial, Llandaff, Cardiff.

Hayward, Harold John, MC, Lieutenant. Harold was born in Alcester, Warwickshire in 1897, and was educated at Colston's School and Merchant Venturers Tech. from 1909 until leaving school in July 1914. He enlisted in the 12th Battalion, Gloucester Regiment (Bristol's Own) on 15 September 1914 and moved to France with them on 21 November 1915. Harold was commissioned Second Lieutenant into the 15th Welsh on 20 October 1917, and served with the battalion for the duration of the war, being wounded twice; at Guillemont with the Gloucesters and at Thiepval with the Welsh. Harold survived the war, earning the Military Cross, probably for the Battle of Epehy [see Appendices; Awards to the Battalion]. He was also awarded the 1914/15 Star, British War and Victory Medals, which were sent to him at 31, Manor Road, Bishopston, Bristol.

Heath, Ernest Harold, Lieutenant. Ernest was commissioned Second Lieutenant into the 21st Welsh, and posted to the 15th Welsh on 15 July 1915. He trained with the battalion at Winchester, but was transferred to the 10th Welsh prior to embarking to France in December 1915. He survived the war, and was awarded the British War and Victory Medals for his service, which were sent to him at 'School House', Waltham, Melton Mowbray, Leicestershire.

Helme, Ernest, DSO and Bar, Lieutenant-Colonel. Ernest was the son of Richard Mashiter, of Gower and Prince's Gate, London. He was commissioned Second Lieutenant with the Glamorgan Yeomanry in 1904, serving as Lieutenant at the outbreak of the Great War, and on 30 April 1915 was promoted to Captain, embarking for Egypt with them in April 1916. Ernest became attached to the 2nd Anzac Corps in Egypt, before returning to France to take up a posting as Second in Command of the 15th Welsh on 8 May 1917. He survived a direct hit on his bunker during the Battle of Pilckem in August 1917, and went on to share the command of the battalion with Lieutenant-Colonel Parkinson until the end of the war, earning himself two Mentions in Despatches and the Distinguished Service Order twice [see Appendices; Awards to the Battalion]. For his services during the war, Ernest was also awarded the British War and Victory Medals, and the Territorial Force War Medal, which were sent to him at 'Llanganydd', Reynoldston, Glamorgan.

Howell, Vernon, Captain. Vernon was commissioned Second Lieutenant into the 15th Welsh on 30 November 1914, and promoted Captain in July 1915. When the battalion moved to France Vernon remained in Britain, posted to the 20th Welsh, and he didn't get to France until August 1916, serving with the 2nd Welsh. On 30 August 1918 Vernon was posted as Lieutenant to the 87th Punjabi's (Indian Army), and he remained with them after the Armistice, earning the General Service Medal with Kurdistan Clasp, in addition to his Great War award of the British War and Victory Medals. His medals were sent to 'Glen', Burry Port, Carmarthenshire.

Hughes, D. J, Lieutenant. Second Lieutenant Hughes was commissioned into the 3rd Welsh on 9 December 1915. He was promoted Lieutenant on 1 July 1917 and was posted to the 13th Welsh on 7 August 1918. On arrival in France he was re-posted to the 15th Welsh, joining them from the Reinforcement Depot at Rouen on 1 September 1918.

Hughes, Thomas, Second Lieutenant. Thomas was the Son of William J and Elizabeth A Hughes, of 21, Evelyn Street, Barry, Glamorgan, and originally served as Private, number 524960, with the 14th Battalion, London Regiment. He was commissioned Second Lieutenant into the 4th Welsh before joining the 15th Welsh in France. Thomas was killed in action on 8 October 1918 and is buried at Moulin-de-Pierre British Cemetery. He was just nineteen years old. His medals, the British War and Victory Medals, were sent to his Father, Mr. Hughes, at the above address.

Humphreys, Hywel Llewellyn, Lieutenant. Hywel was the brother of Percy Lloyd Humphreys, who also served with the 15th Welsh, and was commissioned Second Lieutenant into the 21st Welsh on 27 July 1915. He was posted to the 19th Welsh on 28 September 1915 and embarked for France 6 September 1916 from Southampton. On arrival in France he was re-posted to the 15th Welsh, joining the battalion at Ypres. Hywel was admitted to 131 Field Ambulance on 2 December 1916 suffering a sprained ankle, and transferred to 46 Casualty Clearing Station, before being posted to No.7 Stationary Hospital for treatment. He rejoined the 15th Welsh late in January 1917, and was wounded in action on 5 June 1917, suffering a gunshot wound to his elbow, which required treatment at No1. British Red Cross Hospital, Etaples. Hywel then returned to England for further treatment, finally relinquishing his commission on completion of service, 1 September 1921. For his wartime service he was awarded the British War and Victory Medals, which were sent to him at 'Tylissa', Llangfaire, Welshpool, Montgomeryshire. Hywel remained in service with the 7th Welsh (TF) after the war, resulting in his award of the Territorial Force War Medal in 1955.

Humphreys, Percy Lloyd, Captain. Percy was the Son of Cadwallader and Sarah Humphreys of 'Tylissa', Llanfaircaereinion, Welshpool, and the elder brother of Hywel (above). He had worked at a Bank at Llandeilo prior to the war, and was commissioned Lieutenant into the 15th Welsh on 23 November 1914. He landed in France with part of the battalion on 3 December 1915 and fought at Mametz Wood in July 1916. At the opening of the Battle of Pilckem on 31 July 1917, Percy was killed by gunfire. He was thirty-five years old and is buried at Welsh Cemetery (Caesar's Nose), Boesinghe. His medals, the 1914/15 Star, British War and Victory Medals, were sent to his father at Welshpool after an application by his brother Hywel on his behalf.

James, Charles Llewellyn, Second Lieutenant. Charles was a Policeman at Bridgend prior to the war, and enlisted into the Dragoon Guards, entering war with them on 18 May 1915. He was commissioned Second Lieutenant into the 18th Welsh on 26 June 1917 and had been attached to the 15th Welsh by 1918. Charles was killed in action during the raid on Aveluy Wood on 10 May 1918. He is buried at Martinsart British Cemetery. His medals, the 1914/15 Star, British War and Victory Medals, were sent to his father Mr W. James, 'Llwyn yr Eos', Pontnewydd, Newport.

James, Evan, Second Lieutenant. Evan was commissioned Second Lieutenant into the Welsh regiment on 19 December 1916 and posted to the 15th Welsh, joining them at Ypres. He was killed in action at Boesinghe on 27 July 1917, and is buried at Bard Cottage British Cemetery. He was entitled to the British War and Victory Medals.

Jellings, Henry Ralph, Captain. Henry was originally commissioned Second Lieutenant into the Army Service Corps, and was later posted to the 15th Welsh, probably on 1 February 1916. He rose to Acting Captain with the battalion before rejoining the Army Service Corps, and saw out the war attached to the Labour Corps from 12 March 1918 onwards. Henry was awarded the 1914/15 Star, British War and Victory Medals for his service, which were sent to him at 52, Connaught Road, Cardiff.

Jenkins, G., Lieutenant. Lieutenant Jenkins was commissioned Second Lieutenant into the 4th Welsh (TF) on 29 May 1918. He was posted to France to join the 19th Welsh on 17 September 1918, but after just a month he was re-posted to the 15th Welsh during their final drive towards Mormal. He was admitted to 19 Casualty Clearing Station on 9 November 1918 suffering from bronchitis, and after being hospitalised for a while at No. 8 General Hospital, he relinquished his commission on 30 September 1921. He was entitled to the British War and Victory Medals.

248

Johns, Thomas Hywel, Lieutenant. Thomas was commissioned Second Lieutenant into the 15th Welsh on 3 April 1915. When the battalion moved to France in December 1915 Hywel transferred to the 21st Welsh. He then joined the 16th Welsh as a Lieutenant on 1 July 1917, but was subsequently posted to the 6th South Wales Borderers, with whom he was Mentioned in Despatches [see Appendices; Awards to the Battalion]. He was back on the Army List with the 15th Welsh after this, but was in fact posted to the 19th Welsh from 6 February 1918 onwards until he was admitted to 131 Field Ambulance suffering from Influenza. Upon his recovery Thomas was posted to the 9th Welsh, remaining with them until after the Armistice. Thomas was awarded the British War and Victory Medals, as well as an MID emblem for his wartime services, which were sent to him at 30, Essex Terrace, Plasmarl, Swansea, Glam.

Jones, Abel, Lieutenant. Abel was gazetted Second Lieutenant into the 15th Welsh on 31 October 1917/ The 15th Welsh War Diary mentions him on 20 September 1918 as being Battalion Signals Officer. He was Mentioned in Despatches during the war.

Jones, Arthur Douglas, Second Lieutenant. Arthur was commissioned from the University of Aberystwyth OTC as Second Lieutenant into the 15th Welsh on 1 April 1915. On 28 September 1915 he was posted to the 21st Welsh, and by July 1916 is listed in the Army Lists as attending the 16th Welsh. Arthur is listed in the University College of Wales Aberystwyth Roll of Service with the Colours in 1915.

Jones, Cecil Norman, Second Lieutenant. Cecil was the Son of Mr. and Mrs Charles Jones, of 158, Algernon Road, Lewisham, and the husband of Constance Jones, of 119, Embleton Road, Lewisham, London. He had enlisted as a Private, number 8005, with the 24th Battalion, London Regiment before being commissioned Second Lieutenant into the 3rd Welsh on 26 June 1917. Cecil embarked for France on 3 August 1916 where he joined the 15th Welsh at Boesinghe. He fought with the battalion at Pilckem Ridge and Langemarck, but died, possibly of self inflicted wounds, at Sailly Sur La Lys on 9 November 1917. Cecil is buried at ANZAC Cemetery, Sailly Sur La Lys. His medals, the British War and Victory Medals, were sent to his widow at the above address.

Jones, David, Second Lieutenant. David was from the Hamlet of Coedmorefach, in the Parish of Pencarreg, Carmarthenshire. He was commissioned Second Lieutenant into the 15th Welsh on 19 December 1916, and served with the battalion until after the Armistice. He was entitled to the British War and Victory Medals.

Jones, Evan, Second Lieutenant. Evan was commissioned from being a Cadet into the 15th Welsh on 27 April 1917. He served with the battalion for the remainder of the war, and was entitled to the British War and Victory Medals.

Jones, Francis Alun, Second Lieutenant. Francis was the son of Councillor Fred Jones of Newport, and had served as Private, number 39624, with the Royal Welsh Fusiliers, landing in France in July 1916, where he was wounded on the Somme. After recovering from his wounds, Francis was commissioned Second Lieutenant into the 15th Welsh on 26 April 1917, and joined the battalion at Boesinghe. He served with the battalion until after the Armistice, being awarded the British War and Victory Medals. The medals were sent to him at 'The Grammar School', Beaumaris, North Wales. He also had a residence at 'Minafon', Glyndyfrdwy, Llangollen.

Jones, Henry Myrddin, Second Lieutenant. Henry had enlisted into the 15th Welsh at Rhyl as a Private, number 21004. He landed in France with the battalion on 2 December 1915, but was commissioned Second Lieutenant and transferred to the 10th Royal Welsh Fusiliers. Henry was killed on the Somme on 13 November 1916, and is buried at Euston Road Cemetery, Colincamps. He had been Mentioned in Despatches during his time at war, and was awarded the 1914/15 Star, British War and Victory Medals, which were claimed by his father, Mr. H. Jones, 3, Gnoll Avenue, Neath, Glam.

Jones, John Humphrey, Second Lieutenant. John was the Son of Richard and Sarah Jones, of C. M. Chapel House, Meliden, Prestatyn, Flints. He was commissioned Second Lieutenant to the 5th Royal Welsh Fusiliers on 27 February 1918, then attached to the 5th South Wales Borderers. John was then re-posted to the 15th Welsh during the final months of the war, and was killed in action at Villers Outreaux on 8 October 1918 aged twenty-five. He is buried at Moulin de Pierre British Cemetery. John was awarded the British War and Victory Medals.

Jones, John Owen, Second Lieutenant. John was the Son of Thomas and Hannah Jones, of Twnan Uchaf, Dolwen, Abergele, Denbighshire. He was born 3 June 1895 at Cemaes, Anglesey, and educated at the Northern Institute Liverpool and University College Bangor, serving in the Bangor OTC. After his education John worked as a builder and contractor. He served in the 2/9th Kings Liverpool Regiment as Quarter Master Sergeant, but due to his education was employed as Superintending Clerk at the (TF) Record Office Preston. John was commissioned Second Lieutenant into the 15th Welsh on 26 July 1915, but within five months had been posted to the 16th Welsh. He survived the fighting at Mametz Wood, but was killed in action during a trench raid at Boesinghe while Acting Captain leading a Company, on 6 June 1917. John has no known grave, and is commemorated on the Ypres (Menin Gate) Memorial. He was twenty-two years old.

Jones, Thomas, Lieutenant. Thomas is listed in the Carmarthenshire Absent Voters List of 1919 as living at 'Hill House', Llangathen, in the Parish of Llanfihangel Aberythych, and serving as Lieutenant with the 15th Welsh. No further information is available.

Jones, Tom Watson, Lieutenant. Tom was the son of Charles and Emily Jones, of 5, John Street, Abercwmboi, Aberdare, Glam. He had been commissioned Second Lieutenant into the 14th Welsh on 27 June 1917, and spent some time attached to the South Wales Borderers before being posted to the 15th Welsh. Tom was killed in action at Villers Outreaux on 8 October 1918. He was twenty four years old and is buried at Moulin-De-Pierre British Cemetery. Tom was entitled to the British War and Victory Medals.

Jordan, Francis Henry, MC and Bar, Captain. Francis joined the Army in Belfast in 1915, aged 18 years, and was posted as a temporary Second Lieutenant initially to the 12th Reserve Battalion, Welsh Regiment on 14 August 1915. He was posted to the 15th Welsh on 1 July 1917, and was promoted Captain just two months later, after being awarded the Military Cross for his gallantry during a trench raid [see Appendices; Awards to the Battalion]. Francis gained a Bar to his Military cross during the final months of the war. For his services, in addition to his MC and Bar, Francis was awarded the British War and Victory Medals. He served during the wars with the York and Lancaster Regiment, and was awarded the Distinguished Service Order for his work during the failed Norway campaign in 1940. Francis retired from the Army with the rank of Colonel in 1948.

Kirk, Douglas Davies Croisdale, Captain. Douglas was born on 7 July 1890, the son of Mrs T. Croisdale Kirk, also of Llanishen. He was commissioned from the Royal Fusiliers as Second Lieutenant into the 12th Welsh on 22 May 1915. He was posted to the 21st Welsh before given a posting in France with the 16th Welsh on 26 August 1915. Douglas also served with the 15th Welsh after June 1916, before being posted as Acting Camp Commandant from 27 December 1916 to 11 March 1917. He then took up a posting as Traffic Officer and Acting Assistant Provost Marshal, to the 38th Welsh Division from 12 March 1917 to 14 January 1919, and became Acting Assistant Provost Marshal to the 28th Division. Douglas relinquished his commission in the Welsh Regiment on completion of service, 29 October 1919, retaining the rank of Lieutenant. He was granted the temporary rank of Captain in the Indian Army, with effect from 17 March 1920, and was appointed to the Indian Army Reserve of Officers, 7 August 1921. He remained in the Welch Regiment until retiring due to ill health in 1940, and was awarded the British War and Victory Medals for his service in the Great War.

Knowles-Williams, John, Lieutenant-Colonel. John had served in the South African War of 1900, with the Frontier Light Horse, gaining the Queens Medal with two Clasps. He was promoted to Major with the 15th Welsh on 8 December 1914, then transferred to the Royal Warwickshire Regiment, being promoted to Lieutenant-Colonel. John survived the war, being awarded the 1914/15 Star, British War and Victory Medals.

250

Lancaster, Arthur Claude, MID, Captain. Arthur was a member of Lancaster's Steam Coal Colliery Limited (Cardiff Docks) and originally joined the 7th Welsh Cyclists at Cardiff. He was commissioned Second Lieutenant on 20 October 1914. By the time he joined the 15th Welsh on 30 July 1916 he was a Captain, and served with the battalion for the at Ypres, gaining several Honours, the first of which was a Mention in Despatches for Pilckem Ridge, and two foreign decorations in 1918 [see Appendices; Awards to the Battalion]. Arthur transferred to the York and Lancashire Regiment, and then to the Scottish Rifles in 1918. At the end of the war he resigned his commission and moved to 2, Rock Terrace, Tenby, where he set up business trading as Delphi Garages Limited. For his services in the war, Arthur was awarded the British War and Victory Medals with MID emblem, the Chevalier of the Belgian Order of Leopold and the Belgian Croix de Guerre.

Lancaster, Gerald William, MC, Captain. Gerald was the son of Annie and the late William Henry Lancaster, of The Park, Nottingham. He was educated at Shrewsbury School, and commissioned Second Lieutenant in September 1914 into the Monmouthshire Regiment. Gerald and was dangerously wounded in March, 1915, during the mining of Hill 60. He went out again to the front in October 1917, attached to the 15th Welsh, and was wounded for the second time in April, 1918, and for the third time in August 1918 near Delville Wood. Gerald was awarded the Military Cross for his gallantry during the crossing of the River Ancre [see Appendices; Awards to the Battalion], just before receiving his third wound, which resulted in his being hospitalised at Wimille. Sadly he died as a result of this last wound on 14 September 1918, and is buried at Terlincthun British Cemetery, Wimille. He was twenty-nine years old. For his services during the war, Gerald was awarded (in addition to his Military Cross) the 1914/15 Star, British War and Victory Medals, which were sent to his sister Miss M E Lancaster, Care of Captain E Worledge, 'Woodthorpe', St Mary's Avenue, Wanstead, Essex.

Landman, Thomas, MC and Bar, Captain. Thomas was educated at the University of Wales College, Aberystwyth, and after attending the Officer Training Corps was commissioned Second Lieutenant into the 15th Welsh on 1 April 1915. Thomas remained with the battalion for most of the war, being Mentioned in Despatches for a trench raid at Boesinghe, and gaining the Military Cross and Bar for two outstanding episodes of bravery [see Appendices; Awards to the Battalion]. Thomas was on the books of the 14th Welsh for a short spell, but rejoined the 15th Welsh on 10 August 1918. He relinquished his commission on completion of service on 29 January 1919, and retained the rank of Lieutenant. At the outbreak of the Second War Thomas was appointed to a Regular Army Emergency Commission in the Royal Artillery. He relinquished his commission on account of ill health with effect from 21 September 1940. For his services during the Great War Thomas was awarded the MC and Bar, in addition to the 1914/15 Star, British War and Victory Medals and the MID emblem. They were sent to him at 83, The Oval, Guildford Park, Guildford.

Lauderdale, Thomas M., Lieutenant. Thomas was commissioned Second Lieutenant into the 15th Welsh on 19 December 1916. He served for less than twelve months in France, but became ill due to the strains of active service, and was forced to resign his commission on the grounds of his poor health, being granted the honorary rank of Second Lieutenant on 27 January 1918. His Medal Index Card just says 'T M Lauderdale, Hon. 2Lt. Welsh Regt. Address: 'Maitland House', Richmond Rd., Ilford, Essex.' Thomas was entitled to the Silver War Badge, No. 341170.

Lewis, Alexander, Captain. Alec was one of the nine sons of the noted Carmarthen Artist and Gas Engineer, Benjamin Archibald Lewis. He was commissioned Second Lieutenant into the 15th Welsh on 13 April 1915, joining his brother, Second Lieutenant Herbert Cecil Lewis, in the same battalion. Alec served throughout the war with the 15th Welsh, becoming a Captain by the end of the war. He relinquished his commission on completion of service on 15 October 1919 and was granted the rank of Captain. For his services during the war, Alec was awarded the 1914/15 Star, British War and Victory Medals, which were sent to him at Morfa House, Morfa Lane, Carmarthen. A third brother, Gwynne Lewis, joined the 38th Divisional Trench Mortar Battery and gained the Military Cross during the Battle of the Sambre.

Lewis, Bowen Arthur, Lieutenant. Bowen had trained at Blundells and Bristol OTC before gaining his commission as Second Lieutenant into the 15th Welsh on 28 November 1914. By June 1916 he was with the 20th Welsh, remaining with that Training Battalion until he was posted Lieutenant on 7 December 1917, joining another Battalion in France. He was awarded the British War and Victory Medals.

Lewis, Herbert Cecil, Captain. Bertie was born at Cape Town, South Africa in 1891, the fourth son [of a total of nine] of Carmarthen Gas Engineer and Artist Benjamin Archibald Lewis. He was educated at Queen Elizabeth Grammar School Carmarthen, University College of Wales, Aberystwyth, and at the London School of Economics and Political Science, and had served as Lance Serjeant with an OTC before briefly entering Bangor University. At the outbreak of war Bertie sought his commission into the 15th Welsh, joining them as Lieutenant on 23 November 1914 at Rhyl. His brother Alec joined him there soon after as a Second Lieutenant. Bertie took part in several recruitment drives while at Rhyl, which so successfully brought many of the Bolton and Farnworth men into the battalion. He embarked for France with the battalion, serving straight through the war with them, reaching the rank of Captain. On a period home on leave, after the Battle of Pilckem, on 1 November 1917, Bertie married his fiancée Olive Marsden at Llanllwch, just outside Carmarthen, where her father was Vicar. His brother Alec, also on leave, acted as best man and both he and Bertie were in uniform. Bertie and Olive travelled by train to the Lake District to spend their honeymoon at Bowness on Lake Windermere. When Bertie returned to his unit, his Commanding Officer told him that he should have been recalled earlier but his address had been lost. Bertie, as did all of his serving brothers, survived the war, returning for a while to the family house at Morfa Lane, Carmarthen. He was awarded the 1914/15 Star, British War and Victory Medals for his service. After the war he became very prominent in Welsh Society, becoming Assistant Commissioner, National Savings Committee; District Commissioner, Boy Scouts, Mumbles and District and a Welsh Hockey International, as well as playing Cricket, Badminton and Golf.

Lidgey, Frederick John, Captain. Frederick was commissioned Second Lieutenant into the 15th Welsh on 23 May 1915. He remained with the battalion for the duration of the war, being promoted Acting Captain in 1918. For his wartime services, Frederick was awarded the 1914/15 Star, British War and Victory Medals, which were sent to him at 'Ynys', New Road, Llanelli.

Lloyd, Hamilton Samuel John, Lieutenant. Hamilton was commissioned Second Lieutenant into the 15th Welsh on 4 April 1915. He subsequently transferred to the Machine Gun Corps in 1916, before being posted to the Indian Army, where he was attached to the 3rd/1st Ghurkhas from 16 September 1917. Hamilton survived the war, and was awarded the 1914/15 Star, British War and Victory Medals.

Lloyd, Thomas Glyn, Captain. Thomas was the Son of the Venerable Thomas Lloyd, Archdeacon of St. Asaph and Vicar of Rhyl, and Mrs Lloyd of the Vicarage, Rhyl. He was educated at Rossall and Clare College Cambridge (BA), and was a Schoolmaster in Rhyl before gaining a temporary commission into the 20th Welsh as a Second Lieutenant in August 1915. Thomas embarked to France on 26 June 1916 with the 15th Welsh, serving with the battalion until heath death during the disastrous attack on Aveluy Wood on 10 May 1918, by which time he was a Captain. Thomas was originally reported wounded and missing. His body was found and buried near Miraumont, but he was re-interred at Martinsart British Cemetery after the Armistice. Thomas was awarded the British War and Victory Medals for his services, which were sent to his father at Rhyl.

Lord, Arthur, Captain. Arthur was the Son of Robert E and Elizabeth M Lord, of 'Penlan', Wynnstay Road, Colwyn Bay, and was commissioned Second Lieutenant into the 3rd Welsh. He embarked for France with the 14th Welsh as Captain in December 1915, and served at Mametz Wood. Arthur must have been posted to the 15th Welsh at some time afterwards, as he is recorded in the Battalion War Diary as being wounded on 9 February 1917 when the battalion was in the trenches near Turco Farm. Arthur was brought to the Casualty Clearing Station at Proven, where he died of his wounds on 12 February 1917. He is buried at Mendinghem Military Cemetery, Proven. His medals, the 1914/15 Star, British War and Victory Medals were sent to his father at the above address.

Lort, R G, Lieutenant. Lieutenant Lort was educated at Oswestry School, and was a keen sportsman, having played Cricket for the 1st XI, and football for the School. He had originally been commissioned Second Lieutenant into the 15th Welsh on 19 December 1916. He was wounded at Ypres in June 1917, but remained with the battalion until after the Armistice. He relinquished his commission on completion of service, 27 September 1919, retaining the rank of Lieutenant. During the Second War he served in the ranks. For his service during the Great War, Lieutenant Lort was awarded the British War and Victory Medals.

Lowe, George Ernest, MC, Second Lieutenant. George was the Son of Elias and Grace Lowe of Halifax; and the husband of Florence Lowe of 2, Heath Hall, Halifax, Yorks. He was commissioned Second Lieutenant into the 15th Welsh on 31 October 1917. George was awarded the Military Cross the following year during the fighting near Gouzeaucourt [see Appendices; Awards to the Battalion], but was killed in action soon after, on 28 October 1918 at the Sambre. George is buried at Montay-Neuvilly Road Cemetery, Montay. He was awarded, in addition to his MC, the British War and Victory Medals, which were sent to his widow.

Lucas, Clifton Mallet, Second Lieutenant. Clifton was a man with a thirst for travel. He was born in Sydney, New South Wales on 13 October 1885, the son of Colonel H C E Lucas, before moving to Teignmouth in Devon. He had then served with the Punjabi Rifles before emigrating to Canada, working as a Land Surveyor. At the outbreak of war he enlisted at Valcartier, Canada, into the 7th Canadian Infantry Battalion, and embarked for Britain. Clifton was then commissioned Second Lieutenant into the 4th South Wales Borderers, and saw service at Gallipoli. On 1 April 1916 Clifton became a full Lieutenant, and was attached to the 15th Welsh in France. He was killed in action soon after, during the fighting at Mametz Wood on 10 July 1916. Clifton has no known grave and is commemorated on the Thiepval Memorial. His medals, the 1914/15 Star, British War and Victory Medals, were claimed by his father, Colonel H C E Lucas, at 'Eastcliff', Shaldon, Teignmouth.

Masterman, Walter Sidney, Major. Walter was a very interesting character. He had served as a Railway Staff Officer at Vryburg in the Boer War, with the rank of Captain. His brother, Captain H W Masterman died of enteric fever at Prieska on 29 November 1900, and another brother, the Right Honourable C F G Masterman MP, Chancellor of the Duchy of Lancaster, was a close friend of Lloyd George. Walter was a keen footballer and was a defender with the Weymouth Grammar School and then Weymouth College sides. He made an appearance for Weymouth Town FC in December 1896. At some time prior to the Great War, Walter was Assistant Grand Scoutmaster for the UK, in the British Boy Scouts. At the outbreak of the war he was gazetted Major with the 2nd Welsh, and embarked for France on 17 September 1914. Walter fought during First Ypres, and remained with the 2nd Welsh until he was posted to the 13th Welsh on 28 May 1917. He commanded the Battalion for a while, but was then posted to the 15th Welsh. Walter remained with the 15th Welsh for the remainder of the war. He was admitted to 131 Field Ambulance suffering from influenza on 21 June 1918, and rejoined the battalion on 7 July. In August he was given some well deserved leave and returned to Britain. There his leave was extended, and Walter was ordered to proceed to 80 POW Company for duty on 9 October. Walter was struck off the strength of the 13th Welsh on 9 February 1919 due to his health. For his wartime service he was awarded the 1914 Star, British War and Victory Medals, as well as being the holder of the Queens Medal, and the Order of St John, Knight of Grace. Walter then volunteered for service in Russia for four months in 1919, and returned to Britain to take up a post as Fisheries Officer. He was convicted of forgery and embezzlement in 1920; had his medals and orders forfeited and removed from the Army, after being given a three year jail sentence. Whilst in prison he started writing and subsequently wrote numerous crime thrillers which were popular in both the UK and the USA. He died in May 1946.

Matthews, Thomas M., Lieutenant. Thomas had served as Corporal, number 34003, with the South Lancashire Regiment, before being commissioned Second Lieutenant into the 15th Welsh on 27 June 1917. He remained with the battalion for the duration of the war, being Mentioned in Despatches by Sir Douglas Haig [see Appendices; Awards to the Battalion]. For his services during the war, Thomas was awarded the 1914/15 Star, British War and Victory Medals, and the MID emblem, which were sent to him at 38, Abbey Road, Port Talbot.

McCawley, Eugene, Captain. Eugene was originally commissioned into the 1st Welsh, on 15 August 1914 and embarked for France on 1 January 1915. He was promoted Lieutenant the following month, before being posted to the 15th Welsh after they had moved to Ypres. Eugene was mentioned in the Battalion War Diary as being wounded at duty at Ypres on 31 January 1917. Sometime after that he became attached to the King's African Rifles, and he served with them until the end of the war. After the Armistice he returned to service with the Welsh regiment, keeping the rank of Captain. For his services, Eugene was awarded the 1914/15 Star, British War and Victory Medals, which were sent to him at 'White Heather', Longton Avenue, Sydenham, London. Major Eugene McCawley died on 18 December 1959 in hospital in London.

McDonald, John Currie, MC, Major. John was born on 10 November 1892. He served in the ranks of the Territorial Force from August 1914 until 23 November 1914, when he was granted a commission as Second Lieutenant in the Essex regiment on 27 November 1914. John was then posted to the 15th Welsh, where he rose to Captain and was awarded the Military Cross at Pilckem, while Acting Major [see Appendices; Awards to the Battalion]. He transferred to the regular Army in 1918, and served with the 2nd Welsh, until joining the Royal Signals Corps in 1925, rising to the rank of Lieutenant-Colonel. For his wartime services, in addition to his MC, John was awarded the 1914/15 Star, British War and Victory Medals, which were sent to him at 12, Tokenhouse Yard, E C John died on 20 September 1962 in Wolverhampton. He was survived by his widow, Mrs Helen McDonald and son, Dr Alan McDonald.

McEwen, Richard Williams, Lieutenant. Richard was commissioned into the Welsh Regiment as Second Lieutenant on 28 August 1915. The Army Lists of 1916 shows him as being attached to 15th Welsh, but he was then posted to a Light Railway Company, then the 1st Canadian Railway Company. Richard took ill in France and was hospitalised for a while, before joining the 18th Welsh, and was employed as Adjutant with them in 1918, being granted the rank of Temporary Captain. Richard relinquished his commission on completion of service 1 September 1921, and was granted the rank of Captain. He was awarded the British War and Victory Medals, which were sent to him at 25, De Mayo, 179. Buenos Aires, Argentina. A second address on his Medal Card shows Cia Ferrocarrilera de Petroleo, Commodoro Rividaria, Chubut, Argentina, S. America. Richard was appointed Captain in the Pioneer Corps at the outbreak of the Second War, but relinquished his commission on account of ill-health on 31 January 1943.

Meggitt, Arthur Barry Prozer, CBE, Captain. Arthur had served with the Artists Rifles, 28th London Regiment prior to the war, and was commissioned Second Lieutenant into the 16th Welsh on 9 December 1914. He served with the 16th Welsh until it was disbanded in 1918 and joined the 15th Welsh, by which time he had been promoted Captain. Arthur survived the war, being awarded the 1914/15 Star, British War and Victory Medals. He served with the Cardiff Home Guard during the Second War, and died at Penarth on 29 December 1964 aged sixty-nine. Arthur was made CBE in 1958 for his long record of public service.

Minshull, George Henry, MC, Second Lieutenant. George served with the Liverpool Regiment as a Lance Corporal, number 15279, before being commissioned Second Lieutenant, and posted to the 15th Welsh on 31 October 1917. He fought with the battalion until he was killed in action at the Selle on 28 October 1918, after he had been awarded a Military Cross for the Canal du Nord [see Appendices; Awards to the Battalion]. George is buried at Montay-Neuvilly Road Cemetery, Montay. His medals, the MC, 1914/14 Star, British War and Victory Medals, were sent to his father, Mr J Minshull, of 170, Walton Village, Walton Liverpool.

Moorsom, Frederick William, Captain. Frederick was commissioned Second Lieutenant into the 16th Welsh on 20 November 1915. He joined the battalion in France on 18 October 1916 and remained with them until the battalion was disbanded in January 1918, joining the 15th Welsh as Acting Captain. Frederick remained with the battalion until after the Armistice, relinquishing his commission on completion of service, 25 November 1919, and retained the rank of Lieutenant. He was awarded the British War and Victory Medals, which were sent to him at 29, Claude Street, Cardiff.

Morgan, George Elton, Second Lieutenant. George had served as Private, number 39073, in the Royal Welsh Fusiliers prior to his commission as Second Lieutenant. He was posted to the 15th Welsh, and was Mentioned in Despatches by Sir Douglas Haig while with C Company. George was wounded at Langemarck in August 1917 and moved to the Casualty Clearing Station at Dozinghem, where he died of his wounds on 19 August 1917. His medals, the British War and Victory Medals, as well as the MID emblem, were sent to his Mother, Rebecca Morgan of 35, Park Street, Rhosddu, Wrexham.

Morgan, Hopkin Trevor, MC, Captain. Hopkin was commissioned Second Lieutenant into the 5th Welsh from the Honorable Artillery Company on 6 August 1915. He was a Lieutenant by the end of the year, and on 1 July 1917 was attached to the 15th Welsh at Boesinghe. Just two weeks later Hopkin was promoted Captain, and posted to command a Company of the South Staffordshire Regiment. Hopkin was Mentioned in Despatches late in 1917 and awarded the Military Cross while re-attached to the 1st Wiltshire Regiment [see Appendices; Awards to the Battalion]. He survived the war, gaining the 1914/15 Star, British War and Victory Medals with MID emblem, to go with his MC.

Morgan, Isaac Stanley, MC, Lieutenant. Isaac was commissioned Second Lieutenant into the 12 Welsh on 15 May 1915 and was posted to the 1st Welsh. He was then attached to the 15th Welsh from 1 April 1917, serving at Mametz Wood. He was awarded the Military Cross for his gallantry during a Trench raid at Ypres on 29 April 1917 [see Appendices; Awards to the Battalion], and subsequently promoted Captain. He remained with the battalion until being seconded to the Ministry of Labour in 1918, and relinquished his commission on completion of service, 1 September 1921, retaining the rank of Lieutenant. In addition to his MC, Isaac was awarded the 1914/15 Star, British War and Victory Medals, which were sent to him at 'Cefn Llys', Cambridge.

Morgan, Jenkin Rees Gwynn, MC, Major. Jenkin was commissioned Second Lieutenant into the 7th Welsh Cyclists on 17 December 1915. He was then posted to the 15th Welsh as Quartermaster and Lieutenant on 11 December 1915, remaining with the battalion until after the Armistice. Jenkin was awarded the Military Cross during the final months of the war [see Appendices; Awards to the Battalion], and promoted to Major with the Royal Engineers. He had also been Mentioned in Despatches in 1917. His medals, the 1914/15 Star, British War and Victory Medals, with MID emblem, were sent to 'Officer Commanding', Royal Engineers, 53rd Division TA, Drill Hall, Swansea.

Morgan, Mark Swinfen, Captain. Mark joined the Inns of Court OTC as Private, number 5797, on 23 August 1915, and was commissioned Second Lieutenant into the 3rd Welsh on 18 December 1915. He embarked for France on 15 December 1916, becoming attached to the 15th Welsh, rising to the rank of Captain. Mark was wounded at Langemarck on 8 August 1917, but returned to the battalion for the remainder of the war. He relinquished the rank of Captain on 4 December 1919, and was awarded the British War and Victory Medals for his services, which were sent to 168, Haverstock Hill, N.W.3.

Morgan, Thomas Lleurwg, Captain. Thomas was commissioned Second Lieutenant with the 15th Welsh on 3 April 1917. He was then transferred to the 301st Road Construction Company, Royal Engineers, and granted the rank of Captain, serving with them in France from 1 December 1915. He was awarded the 1914/15 Star, British War and Victory Medals for his wartime services, which were sent to 69, Springfield Road, Cotham, Bristol.

Morgan, William Ewart, Second Lieutenant. William was commissioned Second Lieutenant into the 4th Welsh on 1 May 1918. He was posted to the 9th Welsh and embarked for France on 9 August 1918, but was re-posted to the 15th Welsh. William relinquished his commission on 30 September 1921, and was awarded the British War and Victory Medals for his short time at war, which were sent to him at 4, Grongaer Terrace, Pontypridd, Glamorgan.

Morris, Cyril Bradley, Second Lieutenant. Cyril enlisted as Private, number PS/6121, with the 19th Battalion, Royal Fusiliers, and served in France with them from 14 November 1915. He was commissioned Second Lieutenant into the 3rd Welsh on 26 September 1916, and posted to the 15th Welsh, serving with the battalion until after the Armistice. Cyril was initially awarded the 1914/15 Star, British War and Victory Medals for his services, which were sent to 97, Christchurch Road, Newport, Mon., but his Star was later scrapped after it had been determined that he was ineligible for it.

Morris, Harold Spencer, Captain. Harold was commissioned Second Lieutenant into the 15th Welsh on 30 November 1914. He landed in France with units of the battalion on 4 December 1915, and was promoted Captain on 26 June 1916. He was invalided home at some time, being awarded the Silver War Badge, and was also awarded the 1914/15 Star, British War and Victory Medals for his services. The address given on his Medal Card shows him to have been resident at Llwynbedw, Boncath, Pembrokeshire.

Norvell, Herbert S., Second Lieutenant. Herbert had served as Private, number G/20159, in the East Kent Regiment prior to his commission in to the 3rd Welsh. The Army List of 1917 shows that he was attached to 15th Welsh. His Medal Card shows that he was entitled to the Silver War Badge, as well as the British War and Victory Medals, and that his address was 42, King Edward Road, Swansea.

Okell, George, Lieutenant. George was born on 27 July 1874, the elder son of George Okell, of Barrow, Cheshire. He was educated at Rugby School; at Balliol College from 1893-1896, and gained his BA, qualifying as a Solicitor in 1899. He practised at Ross on Wye since 1909. George joined the Inns of Court OTC on 1 February 1915, and from there was commissioned Second Lieutenant in the 15th Welsh in February 1915. He joined the battalion in France on 26 June 1916, and fought with the battalion for the duration of the war. George relinquished his commission on 1 September 1921, retaining the rank of Lieutenant. He was awarded the British War and Victory Medals for his services, which were sent to him at Fern Bank, Ross, Herefordshire.

Owen, Andrew Geraint Joseph, MC, Captain. Andrew was commissioned into the 4th Welsh, but was posted to the 15th Welsh. He rose to be Captain, commanding 'B' Company, and won the Military Cross for Pilckem Ridge [see Appendices; Awards to the Battalion]. He remained with the battalion until after the Armistice, and was awarded the British War and Victory Medals to go with his MC. His address on discharge was The Bishops Palace, Abergwili, Carmarthenshire. [This is now the Carmarthenshire County Museum, and has some interesting Military Artefacts and medals to men of the 4th Welsh within its collection.]

Owen, William David, Second Lieutenant. William joined the Inns of Court OTC, and was commissioned Second Lieutenant into the 1st Welsh on 26 September 1917. He was attached to the 3rd Welsh, but was then posted to the 4th Welsh, then the 5th Welsh before finally joining the 15th Welsh in France on 20 December 1917. William was killed in action at the Selle on 11 October 1918 and is buried at St. Germain-au-Mont D'Or Communal Cemetery Extension. He was awarded the British War and Victory Medals for his services, which were sent to his widow, Mrs W.D. Owen, at 6, Taswell Road,

Southsea, Hants. William is commemorated on the Cowbridge Town Hall War Memorial, Glamorgan.

Owen, William Seth, Second Lieutenant. William was commissioned Second Lieutenant on 26 July 1915, and posted to the 15th Welsh. He joined the battalion in France on 27 March 1916, and eleven months later transferred to the Royal Garrison Artillery. William was awarded the British War and Victory Medals for his services, which were sent to Tanydderwen, Talysarn, Carnarvonshire. He possibly served with the Royal Air Force during the Second War.

Packer, Richard, Second Lieutenant. Richard was commissioned Second Lieutenant into the 20th welsh on 20 September 1915. He embarked for France on 26 June 1916 and joined the 15th Welsh, serving with them until the Armistice. Richard was posted for service with the Chinese Labour Corps at the end of the war, probably working on battlefield clearances and the concentration of the many scattered war graves on the Western front. For his wartime services he was awarded the British War and Victory Medals, which were sent to him at Trefechan, 19, Aldegrove Road, Porth, Rhondda.

Palmer, Frank Cyril, MC, Captain. Frank was commissioned Second Lieutenant into the 15th Welsh on 25 October 1916. He joined the battalion at Ypres on 8 December 1916, and remained with it until after the Armistice, winning the Military Cross on 4 November 1918 [see Appendices; Awards to the Battalion]. Frank relinquished his commission on completion of service on 28 October 1919, and retained the rank of Captain. He was awarded the British War and Victory medals to go with his MC, which were sent to him at Northwood, Eaton Crescent, Swansea.

Parkinson, Thomas William, DSO, Lieutenant-Colonel. Thomas was born on 8 July 1880, and had served during the Boer War with the York and Lancaster regiment, rising to the rank of Captain by 1903, and gaining the Queens Medal with five Clasps and the Kings Medal with Two Clasps. He embarked for France with the 5th Yorks and Lancs on 13 April 1915, and later that year won the Distinguished Service Order [see Appendices; Awards to the Battalion]. In November 1915 Thomas was promoted Lieutenant-Colonel and given command of the 15th Welsh. He remained in command (although sharing it with Ernest Helme on a monthly basis during 1918) throughout the rest of the war. Thomas was Mentioned in Despatches twice, and proved a great leader of the battalion. Thomas relinquished the temporary rank of Lieutenant-Colonel on ceasing to command the 15th Welsh on 30 May 1919, and rejoined the Yorks and Lancs. For his wartime services he was awarded the 1914/15 Star, British War and Victory Medals, and two MID emblems to go with his DSO. The medals are now on display at the Yorks and Lancaster Regimental Museum.

Parry, Robert, Lieutenant. Cadet Robert Parry was commissioned Second Lieutenant on 31 October 1917 into the 15th Welsh. Little else is known of him as his Medal Card shows no details of medals awarded. His address on discharge was 89, Esmond Road, Cheetham Hill, Manchester.

Patterson, E L, MC, Lieutenant. Lieutenant Patterson was attached to the 15th Welsh from the United States Army Medical Corps in 1918. He won the Military Cross that year, but no more is known of him. The address on his Medal Card shows enquiries to the Army Headquarters at Washington.

Peers, C, Second Lieutenant. Private C. Peers was commissioned from the Army Service Corps into the 15th welsh on 31 October 1917. Formerly M2/076961, Army Service Corps. He is mentioned in the Battalion War Diary as wounded at Aveluy Wood during the raid of 10 May 1918, and remained with the battalion until after the Armistice. Peers was awarded the 1914/15 Star, British War and Victory Medals.

Perrott, Thomas Simon, Lieutenant. Thomas served as Private, number 16840, with the Royal Welsh Fusiliers, before being commissioned Second Lieutenant into the 21st Welsh. He joined the 15th Welsh for a short while before being posted to the 14th Welsh on 26 February 1915. Thomas remained with the 14th Welsh for the duration of the war, relinquishing his commission on account of ill health contracted on active service on 5 April 1919, and retaining the rank of Lieutenant. The relinquishment of his commission was subsequently cancelled, and Lieutenant the Reverend Thomas Simon Perrott, late

14th Welsh became a Chaplain, with the Royal Army Chaplains Department. He received the British War and Victory Medals for his services, and his medal card shows three addresses; Addison Villa, the Grove, Rhyl, North Wales; 'Rhyl', New Street, Lampeter, Cardiganshire and 95, Camp Street, Broughton, Manchester.

Phillips, Christian Gibson, Major. Christian was the Son of the late R. E. Phillips, MD, of Burlington House, Bromley, Kent. He was serving as Captain with the Royal Lancaster Regiment when he was attached to the 15th Welsh. He was then promoted Major, and fought with the battalion at Mametz Wood, where he was killed in action on 10 July 1916. Christian is buried at Caterpillar Valley Cemetery, Longueval. His medals, the 1914/15 Star, British War and Victory Medals, were sent to 'West House', Shepperley, Ampthill, Bedfordshire.

Phillips, Thomas Beddoe, Captain. Thomas was born around 1875, at Dafen, Llanelly, Carmarthenshire. He was aged twenty-four when he enlisted at Swansea on 24 January 1900, into the 3rd Glamorgan Volunteer Rifle Corps and served in 'H' Company, based at Gorseinon, and served with them in the Boer War, gaining the Queens Medal with five Clasps. Thomas Transferred into the 6th (Glamorgan) Battalion, The Welsh Regiment on its formation on 1 April 1908, and was awarded the Territorial Force Efficiency Medal (Edward VII) as Serjeant, number 131, in April 1909. Thomas was commissioned Second Lieutenant into the 15th welsh on 15 December 1914 and was promoted Captain after arriving in France in December 1915. He relinquished the rank of Captain on 30 June 1917, returning to Lieutenant, and served until the Battle of Albert in August 1918, when he relinquished his commission on account of ill-health, due to wounds. Thomas was awarded the 1914/15 Star, British War and Victory Medals for his services during the Great War, which were sent to him at 'Cefn-Glas', Radyr, Cardiff. He was also awarded the Silver War Badge

Pilling, William, MC, Second Lieutenant. William was from Astley Bridge, Bolton, and was one of the Bolton recruits, joining the 15th Welsh as Private, number 19940, at Rhyl. He was commissioned Second Lieutenant into the 2nd Royal Welsh Fusiliers on 27 March 1917, and fought with them up until being wounded during the final advance, where he also gained the award of the Military Cross for his gallantry [see Appendices; Awards to the Battalion]. William was evacuated to the Base Hospital at Rouen for treatment, but sadly died of his wounds on 22 October 1918. He is buried at St. Sever Cemetery Extension, Rouen. William was awarded the 1914/15 Star, British War and Victory Medals for his wartime service, in addition to his MC, which were sent to his Father, Albert Pilling, of 23, Holly Street, Astley Bridge, Bolton.

Postlethwaite, William, Second Lieutenant. William served as Private, number 19198, with the Royal Welsh Fusiliers, landing in France on 2 December 1915. He was commissioned Second Lieutenant into the 15th Welsh on 31 October 1917, and served with the battalion at Armentieres, where he died of wounds on 14 March 1918 after being wounded by shelling. William is buried at Merville Communal Cemetery Extension. His medals, the 1914/15 Star, British War and Victory Medals, were sent to his father Mr. W. Postlethwaite, at 15, Albert Grove, Longsight, Manchester.

Powel, David, Captain. David was listed as Temporary Captain with the 15th Welsh on 18 November 1914. He is noted as serving as Captain with the 15th Welsh in the July 1915 Army Lists, but no more is known of him.

Protheroe, William Bertram, Lieutenant. William was commissioned Second Lieutenant into the 15th Welsh on 3 April 1915. He landed in France with elements of the battalion on 4 December 1915, and served with the battalion until after the fighting at Mametz Wood, when he volunteered for service with the Royal Flying Corps. William gained his Pilots wings, and was promoted to Lieutenant, joining 53 Squadron, RFC in France. At 02.20 on the morning of 12 June 1917, William and his Observer, Lieutenant W Turnbull, were flying a Photographic Reconnaissance mission over Oostaverne in their FE2b, Serial A4207, when they were spotted by the German Vzfw Wittekind of

Jasta 28, which was commanded by Ritter Max Von Muller. The FE2b was easily out-manoeuvred by the superior German Albatross fighter, and was shot down in flames, killing both men. The bodies of both William and his Observer were burnt in the wreckage, and they are commemorated on the Arras Flying Services Memorial. William was awarded the 1914/15 Star, British War and Victory Medals for his wartime services, which were sent to his father, Mr W. H. Protheroe, at 'Delfan', Gilbert Crescent, Llanelli.

Pryce, Herbert Swain, Second Lieutenant. Herbert originally served as Corporal, number 15469, in the Welsh Regiment. After landing in France on 18 December 1915 he became attached to the Cheshire Regiment and promoted Serjeant. On 1 March 1917 Herbert was commissioned Second Lieutenant into the 5th Welsh, and spent several months attached to the 15th Welsh at Ypres, where he became wounded on 27 July 1917. After recovery, Herbert was posted to the 24th Welsh, then in Palestine, and disembarked at Alexandria on 13 January 1918. After a brief spell in Palestine, the 24th welsh were sent to the Western Front, and Herbert arrived at Marseilles with them on 11 June 1918. He served until after the Armistice, gaining the 1914/15 Star, British War and Victory Medals, which were sent to him at 37, Milton Avenue, Wellsway, Bath.

Radford, Frederick John, MC, MM, Second Lieutenant. Frederick was employed at the Imperial Stores, Abercynon prior to the war, and first served as Corporal, number 56642, with the 1st Royal Welsh Fusiliers in France, before being commissioned Second Lieutenant into the 9th Welsh on 26 September 1917. Frederick was awarded the Military Medal while serving with the Royal Welsh Fusiliers, and gained further honours with the award of the Military Cross in 1918 [see Appendices; Awards to the Battalion]. Frederick was demobilised on 2 February 1919, and was awarded the British War and Victory Medals to go with his MC and MM. His medals were sent to him at Glanavon, Gwendoline Terrace, Abercynon. After the war Frederick served in the Special Constabulary of the Glamorgan Police with the rank of Inspector during WWII. He was a member of the Officers Association and at the laying up of Colours in the Regimental Chapel in 1959 he carried the Colour of the 9th Welsh. In addition to his decorations and war medals he had the Special Constabulary Long service Medal. He died on 12 February 1965 at Abercynon, leaving a widow and three sons. His obituary stated that he served with the 15th Welsh before joining the 9th Welsh.

Radmilovic, John, Lieutenant. John was the son of a Greek immigrant from Dalmatia, who was a naturalised British subject. Born at St. Mary's Cardiff on 3 April 1882, he was employed prior to the war as a licensed victualler, at the Globe Hotel, Weston Super Mare. John enlisted into the 12th Glosters (Bristol's Own) at Weston, number 14993, on 30 September 1914, and by April 1915 had been promoted Serjeant, going overseas with the battalion on 21 November 1915. By July 1916 John had become CSM of 'D' Company, and suffered a gunshot wound to his left leg at Guillemont on 3 September 1916. He was commissioned into the 15th Welsh on 25 April 1917, serving at Pilckem Ridge and Armentieres. He was wounded during the raid on Aveluy Wood on 10 May 1918 and returned to Britain for treatment. John died of influenza at Redcar on 3 November 1918, and was buried back in Cardiff. John was awarded the 1914/15 Star, British War and Victory Medals for his wartime services, which were sent to his widow, Mrs J Radmilovic, The Globe Hotel, St James Street, Weston Super Mare. John was brother of Paulo 'Raddy' Radmilovic, Wales' greatest Olympian, who represented Great Britain in five Olympic Games, and who had Captained the winning Water Polo Team in 1912 and 1920. Paulo Radmilovic won four Olympic water polo and swimming gold medals.

Rees, Daniel Ivor, Lieutenant. Daniel was Commissioned Second Lieutenant into the 4th Welsh (TF) on 1 March 1917. He was posted to the 15th Welsh at Ypres, and remained with the battalion, being mentioned in the Battalion War Diary as missing at Aveluy Wood on 10 May 1918 after the abortive raid. He was subsequently 'found', and remained with the battalion until after the Armistice, after being promoted Lieutenant on 1 September 1918. His medals, the British War and Victory Medals, were sent to him, then Reverend Daniel Ivor Rees, at 85, Westwood Road, Tilehurst, Reading.

Rees, James Herbert, Major. James was posted as Temporary Major into the 15th Welsh on 7 December 1914, joining the battalion at Rhyl. He remained on the roll of 15th Welsh Officers throughout the war, but remained in Britain, attached to the 21st Welsh throughout the war, spending some time in France 'On Duty'. James was discharged on 27 May 1922, and was entitled to the British War Medal only, which was forwarded to him at Lloyds Bank Ltd, Old Bank, Caernarvon, N. Wales.

Reese, William, Second Lieutenant. William was from Narberth, and was commissioned Second Lieutenant on 23 January 1915 with the 15th Welsh. He landed in France with the remainder of the battalion on 4 December 1915, and was promoted Lieutenant on 27 April 1916. William fought at Mametz, but became ill and hospitalised to Britain. He died of sickness on 2 February 1917 and is buried at Carmarthen Cemetery. He was awarded the 1914/15 Star, British War and Victory Medals for his services, which were sent to his widow, Mrs W. Rees, c/o Barclays Bank, Carmarthen. William is commemorated on the Narberth War Memorial.

Reeves, Harry Charles, Lieutenant. Harry was the only son of Mr H Reeves, Jeweller, of 54A, King Street, Carmarthen. He was educated at Carmarthen Grammar School, and trained as an Optician at Halifax, before enlisting in May 1915 into the Royal Naval Division. Harry then sought a commission into the Welsh Regiment, and joined the 15th Welsh as Second Lieutenant on 21 July 1915. He arrived in France on 25 May 1916, but was then posted to the 2nd Welsh. Harry was killed in action on the Somme on 25 August 1916 and was buried about one thousand three hundred yards South East of Martinpuich Church, with the grave marked by a 'durable wooden cross with an inscription bearing full particulars'. His father received a letter from Harry's CO soon after; 'Your son has been with me in my Company for some months, and through all the fighting we have taken part in since the middle of July, and he proved himself a most excellent Officer. He was always most cheerful and carried out well every duty he was called upon to undertake. He was very much liked and respected by all his men.' Sadly his grave was lost during further fighting in the area, and Harry is now commemorated on the Thiepval Memorial. He was awarded the British War and Victory Medals, which were sent to his father at 34, Neville Street, Cardiff. Harry's medals, plaque, portrait miniature, original Warrant and several photographs are in a private collection.

Relding, A. George F, Captain. George was born 1887 in Canada, and commissioned Second Lieutenant with the 15th Welsh. He embarked for France on 2 December 1915, and served with the battalion until joining the 5th Tank Carrier Corps, where he was promoted Captain. The only details on his Medal Card show that he was awarded the 1914/15 Star.

Rhydderch, Aneurin, Major. Aneurin was born in 1894, the son of the Reverend J Rhydderch of Pwllheli, but was brought up by his aunt Miss Davies, of the Lodge Abercwmboi. He was educated Aberdare County School, and then at the University of Wales, Aberystwyth from 1912-1915, and was then commissioned Lieutenant into the 15th Welsh on 23 November 1914. His administrative talents were obvious from the start, and by March 1915 Aneurin was Captain and Adjutant of the 15th Welsh. He embarked with the battalion for France, and served with the battalion for the duration of the war, becoming promoted Major after the fighting at Mametz Wood. Aneurin was wounded at Pilckem Ridge, and returned home to recover, taking the opportunity to marry his fiancée, Miss Pritchard, at Hawarden Castle. Aneurin was Mentioned in Despatches several times during the course of the war [see Appendices; Awards to the Battalion], and relinquished his commission on account of ill health on 22 May 1918.

Richards, William John, Lieutenant. William was commissioned Second Lieutenant into the 20th Welsh on 22 August 1915, and joined the 15th Welsh in France on 20 June 1916. He served with the battalion until being killed in action on 12 October 1918. William was buried at Rocquigny-Equancourt Road British Cemetery, Manancourt. His medals, the British War and Victory Medals, were issued to his brother, D W Richards, at 'Maes-y-Ffrwd', Tonypandy.

Roberts, Arthur Hosbury Starkey, Lieutenant. Arthur was the Son of William and Annie Roberts, of 6, Ash Grove, Chester. He had served in the Mercantile Marine, before serving as Serjeant, number 788, with the East African Mounted Rifles. Arthur was commissioned Second Lieutenant and transferred to the 15th Welsh, and was wounded at the Foret de Mormal. He died of his wounds on 4 November 1918 and is buried at Forest Communal Cemetery. His medals, the 1914/15 Star, British War and Victory Medals, were claimed by his widow (re-married), Mrs E H Walter, at Bethuen, Brackenfield, Cape Colony, South Africa.

Roberts, Frank, MC, Captain. Frank was educated at the University of Wales, Aberystwyth, and was commissioned Second Lieutenant into the 15th Welsh on 1 April 1915. He served throughout the rest of the war with the battalion, gaining the Military Cross for gallantry during the final battles of the war[see Appendices; Awards to the Battalion]. Frank was awarded the 1914/15 Star, British War and Victory Medals for his war service, which were sent to his address at the 'Nurseries', Swansea Road, Llanelli.

Roberts, John Thomas, Second Lieutenant. John was commissioned Second Lieutenant into the 3rd Welsh on 28 March 1917. He was posted to the 15th Welsh, landing in France on 28 May 1917, joining the battalion at Boesinghe. John was wounded at Langemarck on 19 August 1917, but fought with the battalion for the remainder of the war, after being promoted to Lieutenant. John was awarded the British War and Victory Medals for his war service, which were sent to him at 183, Whitchurch Road, Cardiff.

Roberts, Victor George, Second Lieutenant. Victor was the Son of Joseph and Annie Roberts, of 'Y Goedwig', Lakefield Road, Llanelli. He joined the Inns of Court OTC on 2 January 1916 and was commissioned Second Lieutenant into the 4th Welsh on 28 February 1917. Victor was posted to the 15th Welsh in France, but was killed at Ypres soon after, on 27 July 1917. Victor is buried alongside many of his comrades at Bard Cottage Cemetery, Boesinghe. His medals, the British War and Victory Medals, were sent to his father at the above address.

Roberts-Morgan, D, DCM, MM, Captain. Captain Roberts-Morgan served with the Royal Welsh Fusiliers as Corporal, number 9358, before being commissioned Second Lieutenant into the Royal Welsh Fusiliers on 27 June 1917. His time in the ranks had led to him being awarded both the Distinguished Conduct Medal and the Military Medal for bravery on the Somme, while leading a Machine-Gun team [see Appendices; Awards to the Battalion]. He was attached to the 15th Welsh during 1918, being mentioned in the War Diary once, and survived the war. Captain Morgan was awarded, as well as the DCM and MM, the 1914 Star with Clasp, British War and Victory Medals for his wartime services, which were sent to 52, Birchwood Road, Uplands, Swansea. A Captain D R Morgan, was captured at the fall of Crete in the Second War with the 1st Welch.

Sampson, John Delahaye, MC, Captain. John was commissioned Second Lieutenant into the 15th Welsh on 30 November 1914. He remained with the battalion for the duration of the war, winning the Military Cross at Aveluy Wood, and being promoted Captain. In addition to his MC, John was awarded the 1914/15 Star, British War and Victory Medals.

Sampson, Richard Harry, Lieutenant. Richard was the Son of R H and E L G H Sampson, of Pontardulais, Carmarthenshire. He was educated at Shrewsbury School before being commissioned Second Lieutenant into the Welsh Regiment. He was posted to the 15th Welsh on 23 July 1915, and served with the battalion for a while until being posted to the 16th Welsh. Richard was appointed to the Staff of 114 Brigade on 26 February 1918, and was taken ill with pneumonia in October 1918. Richard was sent to the Base Hospital at Etaples for treatment, but died there on 29 October 1918. Richard is buried within the huge Military Cemetery at Etaples, and was awarded the British War and Victory Medals for his service, which were issued to his father at Pontardulais. Richard is commemorated on the Llanedy War Memorial.

Scobie, Mackay John Graham, CB, VD, DL, Lieutenant-Colonel. Mackay was born on 27 March 1852, the son of Mackay John Scobie, FGS, (who died just two years later), and Helen Forbes, daughter of A R Suter, Tain, Rosshire, Scotland. Helen remarried after the death of her husband, to Reverend Charles Maybery, MA, of Penderyn, Breconshire, who brought Mackay up as his own son. Mackay was educated at Hereford Cathedral School, and afterwards trained as a Solicitor, before marrying Edith Helen Brown in 1885, daughter of Reverend James Brown, Vicar of Lyde, Herefordshire. Mackay was Mayor of Hereford from 1882-83, and served with the Herefordshire Volunteer Force from 1871-1908, becoming its Commanding Officer in 1899, and fighting in the Boer War. He commanded the 1st Herefordshire Regiment from 1908 to 1911, then Commanded the Welsh Division TF, before being given the command of the newly formed 15th Welsh on 12 November 1914. Mackay organised the recruitment and training of the battalion before handing over the reins to Thomas William Parkinson. He retained in interest in military matters after the war, being active in the local TF Association, and returned to his home at 'Armadale', Hereford.

Silk, Evan, Lieutenant. Evan was born on 22 February 1890, the son of William Silk and Naomi Powell of Blaina. He was educated at Carmarthen College, St. Peter's College, and at Cambridge and Grays Inn, becoming a Barrister at Law. He had served with the Artists Rifles prior to being commissioned Second Lieutenant into the 4th Welsh (TF) on 26 September 1916, and was posted to the 15th Welsh at Ypres. Evan remained with the battalion for the duration of the war, being Mentioned in Despatches, and promoted Captain. He relinquished the acting rank of Captain on ceasing to command a Company of the 15th Welsh on 6 June 1919, and relinquished his commission on 30 September1921, being granted the rank of Captain in the 5th Welsh (TF). Evan was awarded the British War and Victory Medals, and the MID emblem, for his wartime service, which were sent to him at 142, Abertillery Road, Blaina, Mon. In returning to civilian life Evan was Headmaster of Nantyglo Secondary School, and a member of the Nantyglo and Blaina Urban District Council.

Simmons, Horace Enfield, MC and Bar, Lieutenant. Horace was commissioned Second Lieutenant into the 12th Welsh on 30 October 1915, and was posted to the 15th Welsh. He was promoted Lieutenant on 1 July 1917 after having won the Military Cross at Ypres [see Appendices; Awards to the Battalion]. Horace transferred to the Royal Air Force as an Observer on 3 May 1918, and served after the Great War in Operation Archangel, the expedition to Russia, where he served with 47 Squadron, and won a Bar to his Military Cross, as well as the Distinguished Flying Cross, the Order of St. Vladimir, and the Cross of St George. In addition to this fine array of gallantry awards, Horace was awarded the British War and Victory Medals, which were sent to his address at 'Holly Bank', Buckley, near Chester.

Simpson, Robert Archibald, Lieutenant. Robert originally served as Serjeant, number 56710, with the 14th Welsh. He was commissioned Second Lieutenant into the 15th Welsh on 31 October 1917 and served with the battalion until after the Armistice, being wounded at Aveluy Wood on 10 May 1918. Robert is mentioned several times in the book *Swansea Pals*, by Bernard Lewis [Pen and Sword]. He was awarded the British War and Victory Medals.

Skelding, Amos John, Lieutenant. Amos was commissioned Second Lieutenant into the 15th Welsh on 1 April 1915. He moved to France with the battalion in December 1915, and was then promoted Lieutenant. After serving at Mametz Wood, Amos was transferred to the Machine Gun Corps. On 12 April1917 Amos was promoted Captain, and posted to the Tank Corps, and then to Armoured Cars Detachment. Amos relinquished his commission on completion of service on 9 August 1921. He was awarded the 1914/15 Star, British War and Victory Medals for his services.

Soden, Wilfred Newell, MC, Captain. Wilfred was attached to the 15th Welsh from the Royal Army Medical Corps at the formation of the battalion. He landed in France on 3 December 1915, and remained with the battalion for the duration of the war, being promoted Captain, and being awarded the Military Cross during his time at war [see Appendices; Awards to the Battalion]. Wilfred was also awarded the 1914/15 Star, British War and Victory Medals for his services, which were sent to him at the 'Pension Hospital', Sunderland.

Sprague, Anthony Grafton, Captain. Anthony had held a commission as Captain with the 1st Herefordshire Rifle Volunteer Corps from 1903 to 1905, and resigned his commission to become deputy manager at the Midland Bank, at Ludlow. Obviously a trusted acquaintance of Mackay Scobie, Anthony was posted Captain in the 15th Welsh on 18 November 1914. He was probably wounded on the Somme in 1916, as he was discharged from the Army and awarded the Silver War Badge on 26 September 1916. His address at the time was 'Prospect View', Julian Road, Ludlow, Salop.

Stephens, Gordon Ewart, Lieutenant. Gordon had served as Private, number 2213, with the Royal Army Medical Corps in France from 15 February 1915. He was commissioned Second Lieutenant into the 15th Welsh on 28 November 1917, joining the battalion near Armentieres. Gordon remained with the battalion after the Armistice, being promoted to Lieutenant, and was awarded the 1914/15 Star, British War and Victory Medals, which were sent to him at 'The Police Station', St Mellons, Cardiff.

Stewart, Theophile Lecompte, Captain. Theophile was commissioned Second Lieutenant into the 15th Welsh on 30 November 1914. He landed in France with the battalion on 3 December 1915, and remained with the battalion until being promoted Captain and posted to the Cheshire Regiment on 1 September 1916. He was awarded the 1914/15 Star, British War and Victory Medals for his services, and also the Silver War Badge, which were posted to him at 44, Stepney Street, Llanelli. In 1923 Theophile was partner in a business named T L Stewart & Moggach, Land Agents, Surveyors and Auctioneers, at Llanelli.

Thomas, Arthur Clement, Lieutenant. Arthur originally served as Private, number 23030, with the 15th Welsh, landing in France in December 1915. After seeing action at Mametz Wood with the battalion, Arthur was commissioned Second Lieutenant into the 10th Welsh on 18 February 1917. He served with the battalion until it was disbanded in January 1918, and was posted to the Grenadier Guards. Arthur survived the war, and was awarded the 1914/15 Star, British War and Victory Medals, which were sent to his father, Mr A B Thomas, at 'Probate Court', Llandaff.

Thomas, D J L, Lieutenant. Lieutenant Thomas was commissioned Second Lieutenant into the 21st Welsh on 26 February 1915. The 1916 Army List shows him as serving with the 15th Welsh, but he later served with the 14th Welsh, becoming a Lieutenant on 1 July 1917.

Thomas, David Hopkin, Captain. David was commissioned Lieutenant into the 15th Welsh on 30 December 1914. He was promoted Captain just days before the battalions move to France on 4 December 1915 and remained with the battalion for the duration of the war, after a spell with the 9th Welsh. David relinquished his commission on completion of service on 26 October 1920, and retained the rank of Captain. He was awarded the 1914/15 Star, British War and Victory Medals for his services, which were posted to 1, Church Street, Llanelli.

Thomas, David Robert, MC, Captain. David had served as Private, number 1746, with the Queen's Own Oxfordshire Hussars, before being commissioned Second Lieutenant with the 15th Welsh on 27 June 1917. He served with the battalion for the remainder of the war, gaining the Military Cross for his gallantry at the Selle [see Appendices; Awards to the Battalion]. David was discharged on 12 February 1921, and was awarded the 1914 Star and Clasp, British War and Victory Medals to go with his MC, which were sent to 63, Banbury Road, Oxford.

Thomas, F L, Second Lieutenant. The Army List of 1917 shows Second Lieutenant Thomas as serving with the 15th Welsh, but no more information can be traced.

Thomas, John Hugh, Second Lieutenant. John was commissioned Second Lieutenant into the 15th Welsh on 13 April 1917. He served with the battalion until after the Armistice, and was awarded the British War and Victory Medals, which were sent to 3, Bulkely Terrace, Beaumaris, Anglesey.

Thomas, Lewis John, MC, Second Lieutenant. Lewis served with the Artists Rifles before being commissioned Second Lieutenant into the 4th Welsh on 27 June 1917. He was posted to the 15th Welsh in France, and was wounded during the Battle of the Selle, when he won his Military Cross [see Appendices; Awards to the Battalion]. Lewis was awarded the British War and Victory Medals in addition to his MC, which were sent to him at 5, Bracken Avenue, London, SW12. L.G.

Thomas, Oliver Hugh, Lieutenant. Oliver was commissioned Second Lieutenant into the 3rd Welsh. The Army List of 1917 shows him as 3rd Welsh attached 15th Welsh. He joined the battalion in France during May 1917,and served until after the Armistice, being awarded the British War and Victory Medals. His address was given as 'Lorrimore', Kilston Road, Whitchurch, Glam.

Thomas, Thomas, Lieutenant. Cadet Thomas Thomas was commissioned Second Lieutenant into the 15th Welsh on 31 October 1917. He embarked for France on 7 January 1918, and was transferred to the Indian Army, joining the 26th Cavalry, Indian Army. Thomas was awarded the British War and Victory Medals for his services, which were sent to him at 45, Clissold Road, Stoke Newington, N16.

Thornton-Jones, Henry William, Second Lieutenant. Henry was the Son of W Thornton-Jones of 'Borthwen', Anglesey. He was educated at Clifton College, becoming a solicitor in Practice at Bangor, North Wales. He was commissioned Second Lieutenant on 19 December 1916 into the 15th Welsh, and joined the battalion in France on 6 February 1917. He remained with the battalion until being posted to the Ministry of Labour in November 1918, and was awarded the British War and Victory Medals for his services, which were sent to him at 'Borthwen', near Menai Bridge, Anglesey.

Thresh, Norman Wade, Second Lieutenant. Norman served as Corporal, number 13135, with the Welsh Regiment, serving in France from 19 July 1915, and was commissioned Second Lieutenant into the Welsh Regiment on 12 June 1917. [His brother Stuart Garford Boothroyd Thresh served as Private with the Brecknocks]. He was posted to the 16th Welsh in France, but was transferred to the 15th Welsh when the former battalion was disbanded in January 1918. Norman suffered gas poisoning at Armentieres, and upon recovering was posted to the 13th Welsh, joining them after the Armistice. He then spent some time as Railway Traffic Officer before relinquishing his commission on 23 February 1921. He was awarded the 1914/15 Star, British War and Victory Medals for his services, which were sent to his home at 16, Guildhall Square, Carmarthen.

Tutt, George, MID, Lieutenant. George attested for the Welsh Regiment at Bognor, Sussex on 1 October 1914, aged forty-six, his trade being given as Clerk and Drill Master, and his address as 2, Nightingale Terrace, Benhill Avenue, Sutton, Surrey. He had seen prior service as Colour Serjeant Instructor with the East Surrey Regiment and had served twenty-one years prior to being placed on pension. He was married to Naomi and had three daughters. George was posted Colour Sergeant to the 14th Welsh on 1 October 1914, promoted Regimental Quarter Master Serjeant on 13 February 1915, and was appointed Warrant Officer II on 13 February 1915. By the time that the 14th Welsh left Southampton for France on 2 December 1915 George was Battalion Quartermaster and Honorary Lieutenant. During 1917 George is listed on the Army List as serving with the 15th Welsh, and had been Mentioned in Despatches twice [see Appendices; Awards to the Battalion]. He was wounded on 15 September 1918 at Etricourt, when a large aerial bomb inflicted a large wound on his arm; he also suffered from conjunctivitis attributed to gas fumes, and was also affected by deafness attributed to the bomb explosion which caused his injury. On 15 May 1919 Captain and QM George Tutt was posted for duty at a POW camp at Lewes On his demobilisation form his occupation is noted as gymnastic instructor He was awarded the 1914/15 Star, British War and Victory Medals, along with the MID emblem, for his services, which were sent to the 'Felscombe Training College', Newhaven, Sussex.

Twomey, George W., Second Lieutenant. George had served with the Artists Rifles OTC before being commissioned Second Lieutenant into the 4th Welsh on 23 November 1916. He was posted to the

15th Welsh in France, and was promoted Lieutenant on 23 May 1918, becoming attached to the Machine Gun Corps. George relinquished his commission on 30 September 1921, after also having served for a short spell with the 2/5th South Staffs. He was awarded the British War and Victory Medals.

Walker, Eric, Captain. Eric was educated at the University of Wales College, Aberystwyth, and was commissioned from their OTC into the 15th Welsh on 23 November 1914. He was promoted Captain on 11 June 1915, and served with the battalion until after the Armistice, joining the Royal Engineers. Eric was awarded the 1914/15 Star, British War and Victory Medals for his services, which were sent to him at the 'Training College', Pembroke Road Hostels, Erith, Kent.

Wall, Eric Rees, Lieutenant. Eric originally served as Corporal, number PS/3390, Royal Fusiliers. He was commissioned Second Lieutenant into the Welsh Regiment on 5 August 1916, and posted to the 16th Welsh. He served with the 16th Welsh until their disbandment in January 1918, and was transferred to the 15th Welsh, serving with them until November, when he became attached to the 1st KSLI, until after the Armistice. Eric was awarded the 1914/15 Star, British War and Victory Medals for his services.

Wall, G A, Lieutenant. Lieutenant Wall had been commissioned into the 15th Welsh on 19 December 1916. He was promoted Lieutenant by 19 June 1918.

Watts, Albert Edward, Second Lieutenant. Albert served as Serjeant, number 24084, with the 16th Welsh, before being commissioned Second Lieutenant into the 15th Welsh on 25 June 1917. He served at Ypres and Armentieres, and was killed in action near Aveluy Wood soon after the battalions move to the Somme on 22 April 1918. He is buried at Contay British Cemetery, and his medals, the 1914/15 Star, British War and Victory Medals were sent to his son, Mr E T Watts, of 22, Woodland Place, Penarth, Glam.

Wilcoxon, Harold, MC and Two Bars, Captain. Harold was commissioned Second Lieutenant with the 15th Welsh on 26 July 1915. Once in France he became attached to the 13th Welsh, working his way to Captain and being awarded the Military Cross and Two Bars for gallantry [see Appendices; Awards to the Battalion]. Harold relinquished his commission on 1 September 1921 on completion of service, retaining the rank of Lieutenant.

Williams, Arthur Gregory, MID, Captain. Arthur was commissioned Second Lieutenant with the 15th Welsh on 28 March 1917. Towards the end of the war he had been attached to 114 Trench Mortar Battery, promoted Captain, and Mentioned in Despatches [see Appendices; Awards to the Battalion]. He was awarded the British War and Victory Medals, with MID emblem, for his services, which were sent to him at 31, Legge Street, West Bromwich, Staffs.

Williams, Claude Hamilton, Lieutenant. Claude served as Lance Serjeant, number 56747, with the Welsh Regiment, before being commissioned Second Lieutenant into the 15th Welsh on 31 October 1917. On arrival in France he was posted to the Machine Gun Corps, serving with them at the Armistice. He was awarded the British War and Victory Medals for his service, which were sent to him at 74, Roath Court Road, Cardiff.

Williams, Daniel Gethin, Lieutenant. Daniel was commissioned Second Lieutenant into the 15th Welsh on 30 November 1914. He was promoted Lieutenant on 8 March 1915, and embarked for France with the battalion in December 1915. Daniel then transferred to the Royal Welsh Fusiliers on 28 February 1916.

Williams, Edgar Wynne, Lieutenant. Edgar had originally enlisted as Private, number 20166, into the 15th Welsh. He landed in France with the battalion on 3 December 1915, and had made his way to Lance Serjeant before being commissioned Second Lieutenant on 6 July 1916 into the Royal Welsh Fusiliers. Edgar survived the war, being promoted Lieutenant, and was awarded the 1914/15 Star, British War and Victory Medals for his services, which were sent to him at 'The Bungalow', Havard Road, Llanelli.

Williams, Ivor Bernall, Lieutenant. Ivor was commissioned Second Lieutenant into the 20th Welsh on 10 December 1915. He was posted to the 15th Welsh, where he became promoted Lieutenant on 1 July 1917.

Williams, John D, MBE, MC and Bar, Major. John was commissioned Second Lieutenant into the 15th Welsh on 27 December 1916 John fought through the war attached to the 15th Welsh, working his way up to Major after the Armistice, and volunteering for service during Operation Archangel in North Russia. During his time at war, John was awarded the Military Cross and Bar, and the MBE (Military) and the Russian Order of St. Stanislas, 2nd Class, with swords for Russia [see Appendices; Awards to the Battalion]. He was also awarded the 1914/15 Star, British War and Victory Medals.

Williams, John Glyn, MC, Lieutenant. John had originally served as Private, number 35358, with the Welsh Regiment, before being commissioned Second Lieutenant into the 15th Welsh on 27 June 1917. He was promoted Lieutenant before gaining the Military Cross during the crossing of the Ancre in August 1918 [see Appendices; Awards to the Battalion]. John was badly affected by gas during the crossing, and received the British War and Victory Medals as well as his MC.

Williams, William George, Captain. William was commissioned Second Lieutenant into the 15th Welsh on 31 October 1917. He was promoted Captain and promoted to the Machine Gun Corps, ending the war with them.

Williams, William Glyn, Lieutenant. William was commissioned Second Lieutenant into the 15th Welsh on 31 March 1915. He was later promoted to Lieutenant and posted to the 14th Welsh, finishing the war with them. He was awarded the 1914/15 Star, British War and Victory Medals for his services.

Wiltshire, Eric, Lieutenant. Eric served as Private, number 2091, with the London Regiment, before being commissioned Second Lieutenant into the 15th Welsh on 14 January 1915. He was transferred to General List for duty with a Trench Mortar Battery on 11 May 1916, and served with them through the remainder of the war. Eric was promoted Temporary Captain while commanding a Company of the 51st Graduated Battalion, Liverpool Regiment, (which was formerly the 60th Training Reserve Battalion), which in turn was formed from 20th (Reserve) Battalion of the Welsh Regiment in October 1917. He relinquished his commission on completion of service on 18 November 1919 and retained the rank of Lieutenant. Eric was awarded the 1914/15 Star, British War and Victory Medals for his wartime service. While not confirmed as being the same man, an Eric Wiltshire, Esq., District Engineer, Zanzibar, received the Fourth Class Insignia of the Order of the Brilliant Star of Zanzibar, conferred by His Highness the Sultan of Zanzibar, in recognition of valuable services, the award being notified in the *London Gazette* of 20 April 1937.

Appendix V

Battle Honours

The list of Battle Honours earned by the 15th Welsh (as part of the 38th (Welsh) Division) during the Great War were:

> The Battle of Albert,
> The Battle of the Pilckem
> The Battle of Langemarck
> The Battle of Albert
> The Battle of Bapaume
> The Battle of Havrincourt
> The Battle of Epehy
> The Battle of Beaurevoir
> The Battle of Cambrai, 1918
> The Battle of the Selle
> The Battle of the Sambre

Appendix VI

Order Of Battle, 38th (Welsh) Division 1915-1919

"D" Squadron, Royal Wiltshire Yeomanry.
119 Brigade, Royal Field Artillery
120 Brigade, Royal Field Artillery
121 Brigade, Royal Field Artillery
122nd Brigade, Royal Field Artillery
38th Heavy Battery.

Divisional Ammunition Column.
(a) "V" Trench Mortar Battery (Heavy).
(b) "X" Trench Mortar Battery (Medium).
(c) "Y" Trench Mortar Battery (Medium).
(d) "Z" Trench Mortar Battery.
123rd Field Company, Royal Engineers.
124th Field Company, Royal Engineers.
151st Field Company, Royal Engineers.
Divisional Signal Company.

113 Infantry Brigade.
13th Battalion, Royal Welsh Fusiliers.
14th Battalion, Royal Welsh Fusiliers.
15th Battalion, Royal Welsh Fusiliers.
16th Battalion, Royal Welsh Fusiliers.
113th Machine Gun Company.
113th Light Trench Mortar Battery.

114 Infantry Brigade.
10th (1st Rhondda) Battalion, The Welsh Regiment.
13th (2nd Rhondda) Battalion, The Welsh Regiment.
14th (Swansea) Battalion, The Welsh Regiment.
15th (Carmarthenshire) Battalion, The Welsh Regiment.
114th Machine Gun Company.
114th Light Trench Mortar Battery.

115 Infantry Brigade.
2nd Battalion, Royal Welsh Fusiliers.
17th Battalion, Royal Welsh Fusiliers.
10th (1st Gwent) Battalion, South Wales Borderers.
11th (2nd Gwent) Battalion, South Wales Borderers.
16th (Cardiff City) Battalion, The Welsh Regiment.
115th Machine Gun Company.
115th Light Trench Mortar Battery.

Divisional Pioneers
19th (Glamorgan Pioneer) Battalion, The Welsh Regiment.

Ancillary Units
Divisional Cyclist Company.
Machine Gun Battalion.
176th Machine Gun Company.
Divisional Train (Nos. 330—333 Companies, A.S.C.)
129th Field Ambulance.
130th (St. John) Field Ambulance.
131st Field Ambulance.
No. 5 Mobile Bacteriological Section.
49th Mobile Veterinary Section.
235th Divisional Employment Company.
38th Divisional Mechanical Transport Company.

Appendix VII

Summary

The 15th Welsh had been beaten to large numbers of Carmarthenshire recruits by the Territorial Battalions of the 4th Welsh and the Pembroke Yeomanry during 1914, which required it to be made up to fighting strength by the Bolton contingent, and also men from other parts of Wales, and indeed Britain on the whole.

The numbers of Bolton and Farnworth men who served, died and gained awards for their bravery while in the service of the 15th Welsh paint a remarkable picture, with over eighty men from this area being killed throughout the war. At least seven of the Military Medal winners were Lancashire men, as were three holders of the Distinguished Conduct Medal also. These Lancashire lads could never get over what they thought was dour hymn singing among the Welsh members of the battalion as they marched into action, and must have found the prolific numbers of Welsh speakers in the battalion very hard to get used to. Nonetheless, this strange mixture of Lancashire and Welsh men served the 15th (Service) Battalion of the Welsh Regiment well during its time at war.

To give an idea of the competition faced by the 15th Welsh, out of the 860 Carmarthenshire men who lost their lives while serving with the Welsh Regiment during the course of the Great War, less than a hundred of those served in the 15th (Carmarthenshire) Battalion.

Out of the approximate 30,000 men of military age from Carmarthenshire who served during the Great War, around 2,000 died as a result of the war during those four years. As 3.5 per cent of these men died in the service of the 15th Welsh, we can safely relate this to presume that 3.5 per cent of the men of Carmarthenshire who enlisted into the services joined the 15th Welsh, making a total of around 1,050 men of the county who served in their ranks.

A full strength battalion was made up of between 800 and 1,000 men, and allowing for deaths and casualties through the three years of its time at war (using figures worked out by the author using war diaries and SDGW entries), we can reasonably say that about 1,500 to 2,000 men passed through the 15th Welsh. It can safely be said that even with the problems faced by the battalion in getting local recruits within its ranks, a fair proportion of local men actually served with the 15th Welsh, confirming its status as the true 'Carmarthen Pals'.

Sadly though, even after the commitment shown by the men of the County towards their local Service Battalion, there is no individual war memorial to the 15th Welsh, although their sister battalion, the 4th Welsh, have the distinction of having a grand granite Celtic cross to commemorate the memory of its numbers who fell during the course of the Great War.

This Memorial is located in the town of Llanelli, outside the Parish Church. There is also a book of remembrance within the Llanelli Public Library containing the names of the fallen, and there is a granite obelisk situated in Llanelli which commemorates the men of the 4th Welch who died during the epic advance from Normandy to the Baltic during the last two years of the Second World War. Yet sadly the 15th Welsh have nothing.

However, all of the associate units which made up the overall strength of the 38th (Welsh) Division during their four years at war on the Western Front are commemorated as an entirety on the different Memorials to the Division.

The most famous of these is the dragon overlooking Mametz Wood, but there is a simple marble plaque affixed above the entrance to the concrete bunker at Goumier Farm, on the Pilckem Ridge, and inside the rebuilt Church in the centre of Mametz Village is a beautifully carved and decorated marble Memorial to the Division.

The three panels have a memorial written in French, English and Welsh:

'DEDICATED TO THE GLORY OF GOD THIS TABLET IN MEMORY OF THE OFFICERS AND MEN OF THE 38th (WELSH) DIVISION OF THE BRITISH ARMY IS COMMITED TO THE PIOUS CARE OF THE SONS OF FRANCE IN WHOSE LAND THEY REPOSE IN EVERLASTING ALLIANCE'.

This history therefore is written as a memorial to these brave young men of the 15th (Service) Battalion, the Welsh Regiment, with the hope that their memory and brave sacrifice will not be forgotten.

Acknowledgements and Bibliography

A variety of sources have been used in compiling the information for this history of the 15th Welsh, and thanks are due to several people for their assistance and kind donation of photographs.

The main source of reference used was the war diary for the 15th Battalion, the Welsh Regiment, held by the National Archives at Kew, under Catalogue Reference WO/ 95/2559, and also the following sources:

> *The History of the 38th (Welsh) Division*, by Lieutenant-Colonel J E Munby.
>
> *The History of the Welsh Regiment, Part 2, 1914-1918*, by Major-General T O Marden, KBE, CB, CMG.
>
> *Up to Mametz*, by Captain Wyn Griffith.
>
> *Swansea Pals, the History of the 14th (Service) Battalion, the Welsh Regiment in the Great War*, by Bernard Lewis.
>
> *The Welshman, Carmarthen Journal* and *South Wales Echo* Newspaper Archives, held at the National Library of Wales at Aberystwyth.
>
> *Mametz Wood* by Michael Renshaw, published by Pen and Sword. [In fact several of the Pen and Sword Battleground Europe books].
>
> *A History of the 38th (Welsh) and 33rd Divisions in the last five weeks of the Great War*, by Major General H D Depree.
>
> *Mametz Wood*, by Colin Hughes.

Many thanks are also due, in no particular order, to the people who sent details and photographs for inclusion in the book; David Harries [Private Arnold Cecil Ewart Lewis]; David Rawsthorn [Private Tom Whittle]; Martin Southern [No. 3 Platoon Photographs]; Phillip Slade [Rifleman Jim John]; Vince Collins [Private Harry Williams]; Mary Curtis [Photographs related to Private Peter Boardman]; Mark 'Spiker' Collins [RSM Isaac Jones]; Gil Jones and Michael Freeman, Curator of Ceredigion Museum [Aberystwyth Casualties]; Simon Jervis [James Seed Group Photo]; Mrs. Elsbrooke [Details of Farnworth All Saints Football Team]; Sue Richardson [Permission to use material from her book *Fallen in the Fight*]; Rob Newberry [Private Le Seelleur]; Alice and Denise Lodwig [Bible of Private Harry Allen]; Ann Dorsett of Carmarthen Museum [114th Brigade Trophy]; Aurel Sercu (late of 'The Diggers') [Photographs of Welsh Badges excavated at Yorkshire Trench]; Celia Green, Curator of the Museum of the Royal Welsh Regiment, Brecon [Early Trench Photographs]; Mrs Barbara Lewis-Webb [Lewis Brothers of Carmarthen]; Brian Owen, Curator of the Royal Welsh Fusiliers Museum, Caernarvon [Photo of 2nd RWF and Yser Canal Crossing]; Laura Clouting and Yvonne Oliver of the Imperial War Museum [15th Welsh HQ Staff at Pozieres]; Karl Noble of the Yorks and Lancaster Regiment Museum [Lieutenant-Colonel Thomas William Parkinson]; Virginie Radola [Foret de Mormal Photographs]; Rob Adams [Private James Prytherch]; John Dart, Curator of the Welsh Regimental Museum [Various]; David Cooke of Carmarthen Archives. Also I must give thanks and many apologies to anyone who I have mistakenly omitted from this list.

My utmost gratitude goes to Mr Bernard Lewis, (*Swansea Pals*) for his much appreciated help, advice and patience, and for his comments on the draft document of the book; and also to David Warren for his assistance with the Battalion Honours, Awards and Officer Roll. Much gratitude is owed also to Mr. Elwyn Rice Davies, of Melbourne, Australia, for his permission to use transcripts from the memoirs written by his Grandfather William David Shanahan during the last years of his life. William Shanahan first served with the 9th Welsh, before being posted to the Carmarthen Pals, after recuperating from an illness which left him hospitalised for a short while. His personal reminiscences have helped to bring this history to life.

I am very grateful for the help given by Bruce Sinclair of the *Carmarthen Journal*, and to Frank Elson of the *Bolton Evening News* for placing articles about my search for information on the Battalion, and also to the 'Pals' of the Great War Forum, and thank the ones who have so willingly helped me with information, and pointed me in the right direction with my research on the awards to the Battalion.

All efforts have been made to trace the owners of photographs and other material used within the book, and permissions have been sought to use the said images. Apologies are due to anyone who I have not been able to contact, but much time has been spent on trying to do so, and any omission from these acknowledgements is purely un-intentional.

A special mention and sincere thanks to both Brigadier Henry Wilson and to Roni Wilkinson of Pen and Sword Books, for being brave enough to accept my work under their banner. The work of Pen and Sword in publishing books such as this ensures that the men of the Great War will not be forgotten, and after suffering the problems of self-publishing my only other book, [*A Township in Mourning*, the Laugharne War Memorial] I am eternally grateful for their help and faith.

Finally, my greatest appreciation is to my family; to my wife Annette for her support and patience, to my daughter Sophia for her two maps which I have used in this book, and for her help with the photographs. Also to my young son David for his assistance with photographing the many war graves of the West-Walians who lie in the many scattered commonwealth War Cemeteries around France and Belgium, and for his excellent map-reading skills. We will get to Euro Disney one day kids – I promise!